# Speed Your Evolution

## Become the *Star Being* You Are Meant to Be!

Also by Lianne Downey

*Cosmic Dancer: An Interdimensional Fantasy*

*The Liberator: A Psychic-Spiritual History of the Orion Empire*

# Speed Your Evolution

## Become the *Star Being* You Are Meant to Be!

by

*Lianne Downey*
*& her Cosmic CoAuthors*

COSMIC VISIONARY MUSIC & BOOKS

San Diego, California

*Speed Your Evolution*
Become the *Star Being* You Are Meant to Be!

Text and illustrations copyright © 2013 Lianne Downey
Cover painting "Dew Collectors" © 2012 Saher Imran

All rights reserved. No part of this book may be reproduced by any mechanical, photographic, or electronic process, transmitted, or otherwise be copied for public or private use—other than for "fair use" as brief quotations embodied in articles and reviews without written permission of the publisher.

The contents of this book are not intended as medical advice. Please rely on your own research, study, intuitional guidance, and competent health professionals for your medical needs.

## COSMIC VISIONARY MUSIC & BOOKS

P.O. Box 420668
San Diego, California 92142-0668
info@cosvismb.com
www.facebook.com/CosVisMB

Author's *Soul Pursuits* blog: www.liannedowney.com
Find artist Saher Imran at: http://www.behance.net/saher_imran

ISBNs: Paperback 978-0-9824691-7-0
 Ebook 978-0-9824691-8-7

Library of Congress Control Number: 2013907623


KEYWORDS & PHRASES: Body, Mind & Spirit; Self-help; Reincarnation; Afterlife; Spirituality; Mental & Spiritual Healing; Cosmic Consciousness; Evolution of Consciousness; Self-empowerment; Self-improvement; Past Lives; Past-life Therapy; Interdimensional Science of Life; Personal Growth; Soul Growth; Soul Mates; Twin Flames; Polarities; Frequency; Vibration; Relationships; Family Therapy

## ✸ Dedication ✸

To Joseph Downey,
who is my number one Cosmic CoAuthor,
and
To Alan McGowan, for his stellar example of patience,
determination, and commitment as I've watched him give
a large portion of his life and his fortune to
the future benefit of humanity.

## ✸ Gratitude ✸

To Janna S. Sipes, J.D., Gary Kainz, Dondi Dahlin, and Neal D.
Bogosian for going beyond the call to read a digital draft;
to Joseph Downey for supporting this book in all ways possible;
to Lauren-Miranda Gilbert and Paul J. Downey for asking
the right questions at the right time;
to the many students who've helped me learn about
the diversity of past-life healing experiences;
to you—my readers;
and, always,
to my Cosmic CoAuthors:
Thank you!

*About*
COSMIC VISIONARY MUSIC & BOOKS'
*Survival Skills for the 21st Century™ Series*

*We believe that,* although our culture has entered into elements of decline, at the same time other factors have freed our ability to access knowledge; therefore, it is essential to arm ourselves with tools for the twenty-first century—tools of the body, mind, and spirit.

We think that to thrive, we must begin to access our interdimensional skill set, and work to develop a more highly evolved form of life on Earth, beginning with ourselves.

Our *Survival Skills for the 21st Century*™ series is designed to help you further that self-education.

# Contents

**Part I
Learn the
Basics**

### 1- From the Top Down   13

### 2- Your Future as a Star Being   15
A Brotherhood That Includes Sisters
Star Beings in Training
Making Contact
*Rekindle Your Memory  23*

### 3- Principles Not Laws   25
*Activate Your Receptivity  28*

### 4- We Are Cosmic Energy Beings   29
You're Unique—Just Like Everyone Else
*Save Your Treasures  34*

### 5- You're More Than You Think   37
Sine Waves, Circles, and Vortexes
*It's All Around You  44*

### 6- Meet Your Psychic Anatomy   45
Your Truly Personal Computer
What's a Higher Self, Really?
*Shore Up Your Superconscious  52*

### 7- How We Connect   53
Polarity
Frequency, Resonance, and Harmonics
*Make It Yours  65*

**Part II
Raise Your Frequency**

### 8- Choosing   69
Your True Power

*Fire Up Your Nano-Power* 73

## 9–Tuning Your Inner Crystal  75
"Change the channel."
Your Personal Broadcast System
Who Are Your Astral Companions?
Embrace Your Emotions—But Don't Marry Them!
*Master Your Emotions* 90

## 10–What If Karma Has Other Ideas?  95
Why Earth?
Your Interdimensional Biology
A Lost Traveler's Story
Try, Try Again
Cyclic Replays
What a Past-Life Energy Healing Feels Like
*Chart Your Cycles* 112

## 11–Building Polarity Relationships  115
A Polarity Demonstration
Your Many Polarities
Fill Your Treasure Chest
*Realize Your Best Relationships* 125

## 12–Who Was I?  127
Sometimes It Sneaks Up on You
Revisiting the Past
Tch, You Opened the Door!
Level 1: Immediate Measures
Level 2: Mental Analysis
Level 3: Back-tracking
Level 4: Confronting My Karma
Level 5: Higher Help (First Pass)
Second Pass
Third Pass
*Explore Your Resonance* 147

## 13–Accessing the Truth  149

## 14–Prove It  157
No Such Thing as Coincidence
*Sharpen Your Back-Tracking Skills* 168

*Part III*
*Speed Your Evolution*

## 15 – The Quest for Healing   171
How Slow Transformation Works
A Faster Way
You're Not Listening…
The Help Is Always There
So Why Aren't You Making Progress?
You're in Charge!
*Dig for Deeper Motivations* 184

## 16 – Breaking Free   185
Prepare Your Body-Mind for Progressive Change
Psych Yourself Up
Revisit Your Hidden Resistance
Family, Friends, and Former Associates
*Soothe Your Stress Reactions* 199

## 17 – Higher-Dimensional Learning   201
Night School
Beautiful Destinations
Infinite Landing Sites
*Where Will You Go?* 213

## 18 – Psychic Readings Good and Bad   215
What to Do When You Need Crutches
Reading the Akashic Record
A Cautionary Tale
A Happier Experience
Develop Your Energy Intuition
*Test the Spirits* 233

## 19 – Future-Life Therapy   235
An Interdimensional View of Hypnosis
My Noble Experiment with Hypnotic Regression
Not Likely!
A Common Mistake
Life Before Life
Trust Yourself
*The Truth Is Right Here* 253

## 20- Unmasking Your Creativity   255
Why You've Set the Treadmill on 10
Positive Projects
Experiments in Group Psychodrama
Intention. Motivation. Purpose. Goal.
The Unmasking
*Make Your Mask* 272

## 21- Powerful Family Healing   275
Soul to Soul Communication
The Never-ending Conversation
Unexpected Assistance
Karmic Resolution Defies Death
Old Hunting Grounds
Test Your New Analytical Powers
Letting Go
Finding Your Own Peace
*Heal Your Family* 297

## 22- Surfing the Cosmic Cycles   299
Cyclic Learning
Planetary Cycles
Group Cycles
Cosmic Cycles
*Calm Your Panic* 311

## 23- The Power in You   313
An Experiment
*Survival Skills for the 21st Century* 319

## Epilogue   323

## A- How This Book Was Written   328
Q&A: Psychic Transceiving

## B- Resources   332

# Part I

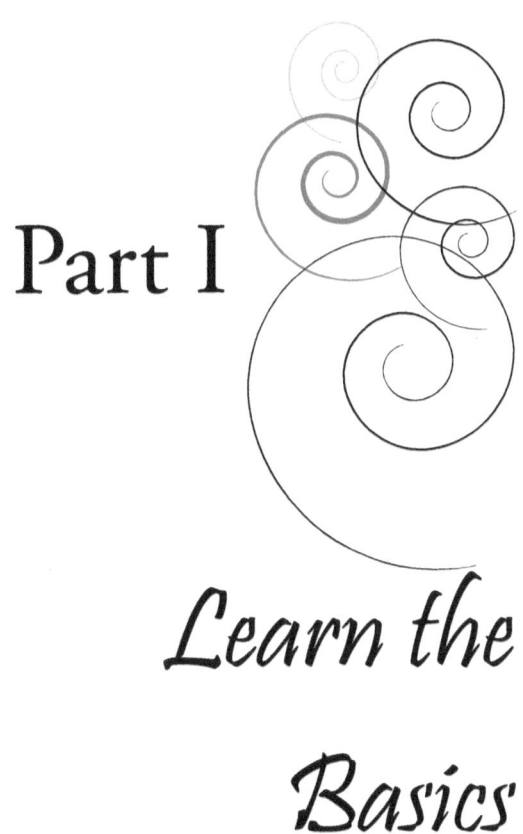

# Learn the Basics

*In rivers, the water that you touch is the last of what has passed and the first of that which comes; so with present time.*

— Leonardo da Vinci

# 1

## From the Top Down

*The science in this book* has been brought to you from the top down, through the use of visionary mediums.

It has been nearly sixty years since the visionary scientist Ernest L. Norman first began publishing a "universal, articulate, interdimensional understanding of science," i.e., his visionary cosmology. Since then, dozens or perhaps hundreds or maybe thousands of visionary individuals have followed in his footsteps, methodically proving—from the bottom up in their Earth-based situation—the principles of this universal energy science.

In all fields—astronomy, biology, physics, medicine—new "discoveries" are daily pushing the envelope of human understanding. The news of these Earth-changing developments may be slow to reach the public, due to political or ego-based or financial vested interests, but the tsunami of change cannot be held back much longer. Upheavals are underway, even in the field of Earth history!

You are fortunate to be leaping ahead of this new era of awakening. You are now holding the first tools for applying this advanced, new-era science in your personal life. But that's no accident.

You, too, have chosen this time to appear on Earth and reap the benefits of this opportunity. Your own evolutionary development will depend on how well you are able to conceive and use the new science erupting in all fields, even as old systems and beliefs are decaying and deteriorating visibly all around you.

Be brave. Be bold. Do not hesitate to step ahead of the crowd and use what you know. You will not be alone, even if you feel yourself to be. Supporting you from higher dimensions will be millions of advanced Minds who have gone before you, who now "reach down" in thought to supply valuable insight and information through as many open channels as they can find.

The time for Earth's rebirth has come and the new science is pouring into receptive minds as rapidly as it can be accommodated.

We welcome you into our Brotherhood of Light with open arms, and pledge ourselves to your personal, creative, evolutionary development with our minds, with our hearts, and with our words.

So be it.

*Your Cosmic CoAuthors*
June, 2013

*Note:* Because of the high-frequency nature of the information contained in this book, you might feel sleepy or drowsy while reading, falling "asleep" to continue your learning in a higher-dimensional classroom (as explained in later chapters). Like life, the book is arranged in ascending spirals, coming back around to revisit the earlier topics with greater detail and real-life anecdotes, winding up with the most advanced applications of interdimensional knowledge. Combined with your sleep teaching, these vital principles will soon become a part of your eternal Self. If you then re-read from the beginning, you might be surprised to discover elements you missed the first time around. The exercises at the end of each chapter will also help you apply this new, interdimensional perspective to your own life. You'll find endless ways to prove these principles to your own satisfaction.

# 2

## Your Future as a Star Being

A scene from the novel, *Cosmic Dancer:*

...the Teacher, a slender woman with silvery hair, began the lecture. She wore Earth clothes: a white lab coat over a dark blue suit. Only her shoes, shooting out sparks of red and blue light, gave a hint of the higher-frequency labs in which she normally conducted her work. Marta got the impression she'd dressed to make them feel at home. And at first she spoke without using telepathy, then gradually shifted into it as the students in the room grew more comfortable.

"Welcome to this remedial class in reincarnation science, which has been designed for Earth dwellers only, since your world is so backwards in this subject. You'll be well ahead of most people on your planet if you do well in this course."

She explained that she was a past-life scientist, "a breed soon to be born on your world, though perhaps not during your next lifetimes. You will have psychics, and readers, and hypnotists, and theorists, but as far as I understand, only a handful of scientists who fully comprehend and teach the science you are going to learn in this class."

Then she launched into a much-simplified explanation of the interdimensional physics governing the expression of life...

*Several people who read my* novel, *Cosmic Dancer,* asked if I had written down my perspective on reincarnation—the facts, details, and explanations I'd mentioned in personal conversations with them. I hadn't.

That's how I knew it was time to unveil that portion of the higher-dimensional class, "Remedial Reincarnation 101," that my heroine Amelia Longwood sleeps through in Chapter 15 of *Cosmic Dancer.* It was a between-lives class designed specifically for Earth residents and future Earth residents.

Until now, our collective cultural knowledge hasn't included a clear explanation of how Infinite Intelligence, in the form of energy, travels from dimension to dimension, supporting life continuously, and how we shape our lives and future lives from this raw material.

But that's beginning to change. Many resources for study are beginning to appear, reinstating the advanced interdimensional science the Atlanteans and prior civilizations lived by. I am given to understand that this information was lost somewhere between the fall of Atlantis and the rise of various religious and political leaders over the course of thousands of years. Now is the time to reinstate it, and many souls, like my novel's heroine, are incarnating with this knowledge implanted somewhere in their unconscious knowing. It only takes a slight spark to reignite that hidden knowledge.

It's likely that you've studied this course in the higher worlds prior to your present incarnation; in other words, between your physical lifetimes. My CoAuthors and I are here to trigger your memories of what you learned there, which is where all new learning begins.

Much of my novel *Cosmic Dancer* takes place in a higher-dimensional world; that is, a world that is not limited by third-dimensional elements of time and space. It's a non-physical world, an astral world, a luminous place where thoughts create every necessity of life, from buildings to clothing.

In this higher-dimensional world, food and drink are unnecessary, as are vacuum cleaners and dust rags. To our (inner or psychic) vision, all appears crystalline, transparent, see-through—a product of the higher-dimensional energy that flows into and through every living element of life in such a place.

But wait—energy does that here, too! On good ol' Earth.

*Then why don't we view our world as a pure energy world?*

Because we've been bamboozled by the illusion of solidity. Nevertheless:

✷ **We are energy beings.**

This is key to understanding the scientific basis for reincarnation.

Einstein first proved this mathematically ($E=MC^2$), which set off such a commotion among scientists, I was not taught Einstein's physics in high school. I suppose that's because Newtonian physics, although already outdated, was simply easier to teach even if it was wrong. Not sure what kind of thinking led to that decision, but I've heard that students still learn the wrong science. I'm hoping for big changes in the near future.

Fortunately for me, my education never began in nor ceased after high school and college. My true education began to emerge from the bludgeoning it had gotten in formal schoolrooms *after I left them.*

The real education of a soul happens between lifetimes, which is why my main character, Amy, spends so much time there in my novel. And her teachers in that higher-dimensional "school" are my very own Cosmic CoAuthors, as I've decided to call them.

Perhaps they are yours as well? See if you recognize them. They are, after all, members of a universal, humanitarian organization linked by a harmonious, oscillating frequency.

### A Brotherhood That Includes Sisters

When I first studied the principles of interdimensional energy physics that are the basis for my understanding of reincarnation, I called these individuals "Brothers of the Light," or Brothers for short, echoing my number one source, Ernest L. Norman. He also called them Advanced Intellects, Advanced Minds, and many other things.

Think of the greatest minds who've lived on this planet, those whom our current history has recorded, at least. Where did these magnificent individuals come from? And where did they go after death, assuming as we are that:

✻ **There is no death.**

So what happened to ones we knew (in random order) as Shakespeare, Mozart, Spinoza, Queen Elizabeth I, Einstein, Tesla, Akhenaton, Buddha, Gandhi, Pasteur, Yogananda, Hatshepsut, Leonardo da Vinci, Asoka, Voltaire, Beethoven, Faraday, Goethe, Clemens/Twain, Joan of Arc, Socrates, Lincoln/Kennedy—to name a very few among millions; an eclectic collection of Great Souls who've scattered their influence around our planet during their Earth lives. Did all their wisdom turn to ashes?

What happened to the Lemurian Master Scientists?
The spiritually advanced Atlantean priests and priestesses?
Where's Mohammed? Zoroaster? Atahualpa? Jesus?
Have they simply vanished? Have they reincarnated?

Here's where the concept of a Brotherhood of Light comes in. Don't be thrown by the language; the understanding of "brotherhood" was common for centuries, until late twentieth-century sensitivities caused an uproar over the term itself, accusing it of sexist exclusivity.

Of course, the humanitarian notion of brotherhood has nothing to do with gender, but try telling that to a class full of students who've been suddenly alerted to the fact that women have been mistreated for centuries on this planet. In past-life therapy classes we taught in the eighties and nineties, and even into the twenty-first century, my husband and I may have spent more time defending the terminology than explaining why this interdimensional collective of Advanced Minds is so vitally important to our personal growth.

Continuing their work for humanity after their so-called death, this fellowship of individuals is united by common concerns. They serve us as mentors, guides, and teachers, both in this world and beyond it, because they have already tread the paths we find so challenging in our personal evolution.

Many of them are no longer required to live on a physical, third-dimensional or "earth" planet as we currently must do for our educational development. They've graduated to live and express full-time in magnificent, higher-dimensional worlds of Light-energy.

However, many also choose to come back to this planet from time to time to bring knowledge with them, for the improvement of conditions and the enlightenment of their brother beings. Others work through other available methods to communicate their wisdom and guidance *interdimensionally*.

At their level of spiritual and mental development, they naturally work together in harmonious intent, thus accomplishing much more than a single being ever could. Hence the appellation "Brotherhood," despite the fact that they've lived on Earth in both genders, exactly as we do.

But of course, such advanced Beings are not limited to working with the people on this planet. Nor are *our* incarnations restricted to this planet. Still, let's stick with Earth for now, so as not to confuse the issue further.

Our recent fuss over gender designations in our language must to them seem beyond ridiculous, except for that compassion for which they are known—along with their earned wisdom, patience, and understanding.

So here's a primary principle of reincarnation, one to put the whole issue to rest:

✳ **All souls experience both genders.**

At first, we have little choice. We'll incarnate as either male or female. As we mature spiritually, we can exert some choice in the matter, but striving always for a balance between male and female experience. You can see around you that this is not always a smooth transition, accounting for some of the confusion that can be experienced.

By the way, you'll find that nearly everything you read in this introductory book will have a longer story and endless variations because we are talking about human beings, after all! And our subject is infinite in diversity and scope, as infinite as *we* are, and as the Infinite, Creative Intelligence from which we've sprung. (That's the term I'll be using for the ultimate Source, or as some have called it, the one God, Allah, etc.)

Since we're talking about Infinity, in this book I'll only be able to *introduce* you to the science of reincarnation or, to use the better term, creative evolution. But after you've learned some of the basics, I'll teach you how to raise your frequency, and I'll also share stories and anecdotes, exercises for you to try, and later on, I'll show you how to validate past lives for yourself and speed your personal evolution thousands of lifetimes ahead, on your way to becoming one of the Star Beings we've been talking about.

As the Teacher in *Cosmic Dancer* promises, by the time you finish this book, "You'll be well ahead of most people on your planet if you do well in this course."

## Star Beings in Training

Members of this Brotherhood of Star Beings I've just described have been my teachers—and perhaps yours, too—for countless lifetimes. That includes during our sojourns in their crystal palaces of learning between lifetimes, while in a higher-dimensional state of existence.

This is what souls on a progressive path typically do between lives.

This is certainly where my character Amy in *Cosmic Dancer* returns between her incarnations. She gives us a very satisfying and nostalgic visit over the course of her story. Many readers have written to tell me of the psychic awakenings they experienced when reading about these higher worlds! I didn't realize when I wrote it that it would have that effect on my audience, but I'm happy they could see what I've remembered about these places of study. Perhaps that's because they've been there, too, or to similar spiritual "worlds" compatible with their own understanding.

I should add that one of our brightest students complained once that he didn't necessarily want to go to a place where the blades of grass were "made of crystal," even if it was only energy that felt like velvet; he thought Earth grass was beautiful. He was right, of course—it is beautiful—and you'll go wherever your mind takes you after death! More correctly, *wherever your energy body's oscillating frequencies direct you.* The possibilities are limitless, i.e., Infinite. I've only narrowed it down to my own experience for the sake of discussion. But let's not get ahead of ourselves—this entire book will explain and elaborate about the importance of making that frequency exactly what you want it to be.

I believe that this not-quite-clear recollection of higher-dimensional experiences had by an older soul may be what motivates us in our quest for self-improvement. We vaguely remember, and we want to go back there! Many of us desire to return to progressively more advanced, more beautiful worlds of learning—eventually to reside there full-time and learn how to help our younger brothers and sisters coming up behind us on the evolutionary pathway. In other words, to become members of the Universal Brotherhood, to become Starlight Beings ourselves.

We all carry this potential. It's part of our Infinite Design. But not everyone's going to choose this path, or perhaps they're not ready.

Do you share this aspiration or memory with me?

**Making Contact**

Our Cosmic CoAuthors are no farther than a thought away. They earned their way to an advanced state of being—and so can we. They're available to help us do it, each in our own unique way and in our own time. All we have to do is ask inwardly.

Because I've chosen writing as my occupation, I began to call these Advanced Intellects, Great Souls, or Star Beings my "Cosmic CoAuthors," a much more comfortable term for the age in which I live and the work I do. Right now, writing is my most important creative expression, so it's as a writer that I most often attain a frequency high enough to experience their influence. (I describe our collaboration in more detail in Appendix A, if you're curious.)

Other people might make their contact with these higher resources while doing anything that raises their particular frequency to a creative, constructive level, or while "giving of self" in any humanitarian endeavor.

Because you're reading this book, I think it's safe to say that your own life has often been touched by these higher influences. Can you pinpoint a few of these experiences?

A most important principle of creative evolution is this:

✳ **Our purpose for living many lives sequentially is to develop the Infinite potential inherent in our design.**

Our Cosmic CoAuthors humbly insist that the horizon of spiritual/mental development stretching before them is limitless, but in turn, they are reaching back to help us along the evolutionary pathway. They are not "better than us," nor are they non-human beings who've never faced the struggles we do in our physical lives. They are graduates of the program we've enrolled in, and while they would not dream of interfering in our lives, they have countless ways of offering aid.

As you work your way through this book, clearing up the blocks and shocks that have caused your natural psychic sensitivities to shut down, you'll be encouraged to seek out your own mentors among these Lighted Ones. But reach high! As Jesus is reported to have said, "By their fruits ye shall know them." I've found this to be excellent advice.

Now let's get down to basics!

## Rekindle Your Memory

Throughout this book, you'll find exercises to help you test and apply what you're learning. They're optional, of course, but they present an opportunity to further speed your creative evolution.

1. As an accompaniment to your reading, my Cosmic CoAuthors and I hope you will use your personal journal as a primary tool for connecting with your inner self, and hence, to all the spiritual forces available to assist you. Decide now what forms you wish to use: pen and paper, pretty notebook, electronic notebook or tablet, desktop computer file, drawing pad, audio recorder, or sketchbook. Personally, I use pretty notebooks and a large, blank-paper sketchbook.

2. Experiment with both forms: writing and sketching. You'll be going for speed, so avoid more sophisticated forms of expression like composing or sculpting. You want to be fast enough to capture insights as they flow into your mind. Since I'm more writer than artist, I have many storage boxes full of

colorful and quirky notebooks I've used over the years, but only one giant sketchbook. Occasionally, however, what I need to communicate to myself, usually something inspired by my CoAuthors, can only be captured by sketching. Give yourself the opportunity to try both.

3. Make a commitment to record something every day, even if it feels like nonsense at first.

4. Be free with what you write or sketch. Don't self-censor. We'll do specific exercises later on. But make sure you maintain your goal of self-knowledge; don't get sidetracked by the kind of journaling that has you blaming others for your problems.

As you'll soon learn, your Infinite design precludes any such interference by others. Your sole responsibility for your own predicaments means that *you alone hold the key to making your life what you will it to be!* Not even your Cosmic CoAuthors will interfere in your soulic right to live as you choose. This is the most important principle of all:

✹ **You alone hold the Power over your personal evolution!**

# 3

## Principles Not Laws

*We've already mentioned three important* principles in the interdimensional energy science of reincarnation:

1. You are an energy being.

2. You experience both genders in your various incarnations.

3. The purpose of your many sequential lives is to develop your Infinite Potential. As you live, learn, and grow, you can choose to evolve into higher and higher worlds of existence, living a more progressive, integrated, and purposeful life with your fellow Beings of Light!

Here are three more:

4. Everything you think, say, and do is recorded in a permanent energy record that is not destroyed when your body dies.

5. This energy record, your *psychic anatomy*, contains information of your past lives and your present life. Not selected information, but ALL of it.

6. The contents of that psychic anatomy will determine your future life experiences, and the speed at which you personally evolve.

It sounds so simple, so cut-and-dried. But there's another element to consider:

7. While all of this play and replay is going on, you may be recording certain philosophical conclusions, higher principles, altruistic notions, humanitarian impulses, awakenings, epiphanies, sudden sensations of God-force or Infinite Intelligence, and every other good thing you distill from your life experiences in a very-high-frequency element of Self that we'll now term the *Superconscious*.

It's this Superconscious Self that separates human from animal. Which leads to another principle some of you may be wondering about:

8. Humans do not reincarnate as animals. You can come back and haunt one, but not revert back to live as one.

And then there's this, the very beginning of it all:

9. Life force or energy begins in that centrifuge of Intelligence many people on this planet term God, Allah, or Eternal or Divine Source. For the sake of expanding our concept, we'll call it the Infinite Creative Intelligence. It is the Wellspring of Life for us.

Which means that:

10. All energy is intelligent. It carries information like the old broadcast systems carried TV shows (and still do). This life-force

energy begins in higher dimensions and travels down into lower dimensions such as our third-dimensional world, and into our third-dimensional bodies, and into everything we see around us. It also travels back up into higher dimensions in a closed-system kind of loop, shaped and formed and carrying information.

Speaking of loops, you'll notice that Principle 10 loops right back to Principle 1: You are an energy being.

Well, that's it. Ten basic principles that should explain everything. Hah!! I wish!! If only it were that simple to comprehend.

But if it were, we wouldn't be stuck in all the messes we're currently stuck in, either personally or globally, right?

This is where the "remedial" aspect of the whole subject comes into play in my novel *Cosmic Dancer*. Currently on this planet, we're missing quite a few bits and pieces of even the most basic understanding of the interdimensional interplay of intelligent life force. You're about to fill in the missing pieces!

Since the topic is infinite in nature, being derived from an Infinite Intelligence, you and I are never going to come to the end of learning about these phenomena called Life. We'll travel through countless lifetimes gathering experience. (To arrive at this point in your questing, you've already lived thousands of previous lifetimes!) We'll study diligently between lives to understand and broaden our knowing—and still we won't comprehend it all.

But we can learn how to live much more beautifully, in integrated, intelligent, and higher forms of existence while we continue our learning endeavors, as our Cosmic CoAuthors have done. They're standing by, ready to help us succeed.

So let's make a start, because it is our infinite mandate to grow and evolve, and take on a larger share of the creative impulse of life. Can't you feel it? The desire to learn and grow? That is your Infinite, indwelling

Pulse of Life, destined to expand and improve.

And by the way, these are principles, not laws. The basic energy principles we're discussing in this book are interdimensional. They will apply throughout your experience, in this world or any other.

## *Activate Your Receptivity*

1. Write down all the questions or dilemmas that arise in your mind when you consider the basic principles mentioned in this chapter. Add any questions you have about your life in general.

2. As you go through the book, keep these questions in mind and don't rest until you find answers, no matter how long it takes. You WILL find them.

3. As new questions arise, add them to your list. Nothing in this book requires you to simply accept or believe it! This energy science proves* itself continuously, but you have to pay attention. Question, probe, and watch for answers and proofs to appear in your life. You rarely receive help unless you ask, and you never receive help until you're ready to take responsibility.

*Note:* We're not necessarily talking about the kind of "proof" that one duplicates in a laboratory, although that can happen. But the laboratory of life, being infinite in design, very often defies human-defined preconceptions and theories!

# 4

## We Are Cosmic Energy Beings

*Energy flows from the highest* frequencies to the lowest. Life begins in Light. We are sparks of the Infinite Intelligence. We are outpourings of Love from an Infinite Source. We are birthed from the Father/Mother of all things. We are Godsparks, awaiting the full ignition of our inner Flame.

Say it any way you like, and the result is the same: We are energy beings.

Well, that's all nice to hear, but what does it mean, exactly? In practical, applicable terms? And if I'm an energy being, why don't I combust? Or melt into the flames in the fireplace if I get too close?

Oh, wait a minute. If I get too close to the fire, I *do* melt. And one day, I *will* combust, whether by flame or by the natural forces of degeneration in play on this planet. My body will be consumed one day. It is inevitable, an immutable principle of life that no one who lives here can argue with. And why does my body disappear? Because it is an energetic construct. As Einstein proclaimed: energy and mass are interconvertible.

But what Einstein hadn't yet explained by the time his own physical body disintegrated is that our bodies are only one component of our energy selves. We are much, much more than these third-dimensional atoms we lug around from morning 'til night.

Thoughts, dreams, opinions, feelings—what about those? Do they dissolve when the flesh vanishes?

You want to say no, don't you? It's instinctive. Somehow we know that the larger part of ourselves, our personality, our self-ness, simply cannot be the product of a single lifetime, born of mutating cellular parts. (And by the way, who told those parts *how* to change, eh? Where's the direction coming from, and how?)

Some people describe the Intelligence evident in all life forms, including our own, as the whim of a God or Gods. In this book, we are going to expand that notion and discard the limitations of an irascible, bribable Being who can be sacrificed to, or prayed to for favors, or who strikes out as a human might: subject to alternating fits of anger or sentiment. Let's regard it instead as an *Infinite Creative Intelligence,* a source of life-energy that is ever-functioning, impersonal, eternally flowing.

In *The Infinite Concept of Cosmic Creation,* Ernest Norman writes:

> ...*this Infinite Creative Intelligence is not some emotional white-robed Santa Claus who, in some mysterious way, seems to know what is going on in the hearts and minds of countless billions of people.*
>
> *In view of the uncounted billions of worlds and planetary systems and their uncounted billions of people, such assumptions are ridiculous and must be replaced with a more comprehensive knowledge of function of the great Creative Intelligence, which is the sum and total of all things visible and invisible and which, through well-organized and directed principles, manifests and re-creates itself infinitely.*
>
> *It must be also thoroughly understood that, as this Infinite is all things, you are then a small part of this Infinite and as such, you are directly related in thought and action to this Infinite Intelligence; that every thought and action has vast and intricate implications which always result from any of your thoughts or actions as part of the functioning of these principles.*
>
> *Needless to say, when any person understands the full implications*

*which are involved in this concept, this person would immediately—if he were wise—attempt to cease any destructive or coercive thought action. In the full meaning and understanding of the Creative Principle by which everyone functions, you will then see how it is that individually or collectively we are all making our own future by our thoughts and actions of today.*

He then goes on to educate his readers in the scientific ins and outs, ups, downs, and spiraling roundabouts of interdimensional physics, but in non-mathematical language so anyone can understand it.

As energy sparks born from an Infinite source, then, we each carry within us a connection to an infinite storehouse. But this raw material, designated for our personal development, has yet to be completely shaped. That is our birthright and purpose.

**You're Unique—Just Like Everyone Else**

I am always astounded when people preach that you have it all now, that you are a God-being already formed, etc., etc., because it is my understanding that we must each *develop* this raw potential in our own way.

That's what makes the Infinite infinite, if you know what I mean. No two of us are going to have exactly identical experiences, and since experience is what shapes our portion of the raw energy of the Infinite, we are going to come up with something unique. We will each become yet another infinitely designed element of an Infinite Intelligence. And so on, and so forth, never-endingly reshaping and redesigning the raw material of Infinite Intelligence.

But you can also see how this unites us, this common and equal *potential*. Yet we are NOT equal at any time in our personal *development* along this spiraling pathway in and out of our earth lives, no matter how popular it becomes to say so. Even identical twins are not identical; if you've ever known any, you know this to be true. There's more behind the "identical

DNA" of twins than has yet been discovered, something that belongs in the new biology of epigenetics.

**You'll Soon Be Smarter Than NASA**

Isn't it wonderful that biologists, astrophysicists, and surely other branches of science are now admitting that they have discovered how little our limited, third-dimensional science explains?

"More is unknown than is known. We know how much dark energy there is because we know how it affects the Universe's expansion. Other than that, it is a complete mystery," say the authors of an article on dark energy at NASA's astrophysics website. [http://science.nasa.gov/astrophysics/focus-areas/what-is-dark-energy/]

With this state of awe and openness from our most respected scientists, we can't help but heal our collective ignorance.

This new attitude developed relatively recently, in 1998, when images from the Hubble Space Telescope showed that "a long time ago, the Universe was actually expanding more slowly than it is today. So the expansion of the Universe has not been slowing due to gravity, as everyone thought, it has been accelerating. No one expected this, no one knew how to explain it. But something was causing it." So say the NASA writers in their Dark Energy article.

Interestingly, this phenomenon was detected almost simultaneously by teams of astrophysicists around the world, working separately. I don't know about you, but to me that doesn't seem accidental. It certainly got everyone to pay attention faster than if one single team had made the discovery.

So the terms *dark energy* and *dark matter* were coined to signify the invisible forces of matter and energy that none of our instruments can detect, that no theories (except Ernest Norman's) predicted, and which are now clearly evident to science because of the influence they're having on the measly 4% of the universe that our third-dimensional instruments *can* detect.

It is a very exciting time on our planet, indeed. Some things may be falling apart, but other things are beginning to come together! We'll soon restore that interdimensional science the Atlanteans understood.

Mr. Norman predicted this development, but his books are still many steps ahead of conventional science's slow, jerky progress. The few credentialed scientists willing to speak with him prior to his death in 1971 either could not comprehend his interdimensional cosmology (as one admitted to him), or they took his ideas and profited from them (such as the cathode ray tube that Philo Farnsworth "invented," making television possible, after a young Ernest explained it to him one rainy Utah day when they met while seeking shelter from a storm). Most would not acknowledge his work because he was self-educated.

This insular attitude is slowly changing. Vital discoveries have been made in all fields by self-taught "amateurs," polymaths, and multi-disciplinary researchers and theorists, and that's likely to continue, filling in the gaps left by too much specialization. And who's to say these "amateurs" and generalists are not the Advanced Minds we've been talking about, incarnating at this precise time to help the world move ahead?

Thankfully, the frontiers of science are now approaching a new perspective that will overturn our way of thinking about the life we lead here, reaching conclusions Mr. Norman wrote about decades ago. Quite a few of his explanations are now accepted scientific truth (albeit uncredited), but much more remains to be "discovered" from the work he left behind. For instance, today I watched a video from The Electric Universe project that echoed essays in *The Infinite Concept of Cosmic Creation*. I won't be surprised if a "universal, articulate, interdimensional understanding of life" becomes the schoolroom standard, but recreated by someone with the accepted credentials, thus solving dark matter, dark energy, and many other scientific enigmas of the modern age.

Meanwhile, you and I don't have to wait. We can understand now that the invisible forces conventional science is beginning to detect derive from higher dimensions, where our lives begin and return. We are intricately interconnected at all times with these higher-frequency forces that infuse and support our lives in this third-dimensional world.

Back to our personal creative evolution: We shouldn't ask, "Where does it all lead?" Because it doesn't end, being an Infinite proposition. But we can ask, "Why do we do it?" And that's the next chapter.

## Save Your Treasures

1. In your journal, start recording dreams, as well as thoughts that come to you right before sleep or just after you awaken, during the *hypnagogic state*—that fertile time when you're half here, in your physical body, and half there, out in the higher realms where you go to study at night. Not every dream is golden, but some are. More on this in Chapter 16.

2. Also take note of any songs you find lingering in your mind when you awaken. Do the lyrics have any meaning for you?

It happens to me very often that my Cosmic CoAuthors send me musical messages, especially love songs, which I hear just as I'm awakening. Or sometimes the lyrics contain advice I need to hear. Or perhaps they come from someone else I know?

Since, unlike Joseph who has perfect musical memory, I rarely pay attention to song lyrics, it becomes a puzzle for me to solve. I hear the music very distinctly in my head and it won't go away. It's saying, *Pay attention.* Then I'll try to hum the tune for Joseph. Within a few notes he can often identify the song and even sing the lyrics for me. They're always dead-on appropriate and timely! Sometimes embarrassingly so. But I'm always grateful for the LOVE that comes with them.

Here's an example: A few weeks after Joseph put an album of "symphonic metal" by a group called Within Temptation into our 250-disk stereo shuffle, I woke up with one of their songs in my head, "Jillian (I'd Give My Heart)." He recognized it, I googled it, and the lyrics seemed to be about reincarnation. So I read more and learned that they were about characters from a book series I'd never heard of, despite my constant search for good reincarnation stories. (They are all too rare!)

A web search and a summer's worth of reading revealed to me the *fifteen* books of the Deverry series by Katherine Kerr. They had been published between 1986 and 2009 and I'd somehow managed to miss them! Ms. Kerr had a clever and complex way of depicting the continuity and individual evolution of characters from life to life. You'll now find the song and books listed in my Resources. What an amazing way to get my attention! So if you hear music when you awaken, listen to the lyrics.

*"This is just the beginning," says James Gillies, a spokesman for CERN. Scientists will keep probing the new particle until they fully understand how it works. In doing so they hope to understand the 96 percent of the universe that remains hidden from view. This may result in the discovery of new particles and even hitherto unknown forces of nature.*

— From a Yahoo news story about scientists thinking they've seen a Higgs boson particle, July 2012.

# 5

## *You're More Than You Think*

*The CERN scientists are in* for many more surprises, I wager, with their massively expensive and slowwww machinery. Meanwhile, you and I are going to speed ahead and learn the energy science of higher and lower dimensions. Don't worry, we'll stick with simple terminology, and no mathematics!

In Chapters 1 and 3, we said that you experience life as both genders, and that your purpose for living many sequential, physical lifetimes is to develop your Infinite potential.

You may notice that sometimes I capitalize *Infinite* and sometimes I don't. I mean it two ways: (1) as the all-evident Source of Life (capitalized), or (2) as a "quantitative" adjective, meaning neverending (not capitalized). I put *quantitative* in quotes because even that denotes some kind of measurable ending and beginning and in this case, there isn't either. Nor are there solid particles.

This means that when I mention your Infinite potential, I mean your potential to become a functioning Godbeing who takes on a greater role in the orderly processes of the Cosmos.

But if you think about the people you know right now, how many of them would you trust with the running of the Universe, eh? Would you even trust yourself?

No, not yet. You love them, you care for them, they make you laugh, you enjoy their company, but maybe you'll agree that they're not quite ready to take on the challenges of running a Universe, even as part of a larger Whole that could conceivably compensate for any little mess-ups. Yikes. But one day, with a lot of trial and error and plenty of life-experience and education in the interdimensional connections transpiring all around us, maybe…

So this is why we say it is your birthright to *develop* this potential. Everyone shares this opportunity. Everyone is at their own unique position on the scale of spiritual development. No one can judge where another lies along that line of soulic attainment, even though we almost always think we can. Hard enough to judge where we ourselves are along this continuum of soulic education!

Sometimes, we think we're idiots when we might actually be doing the very best thing. Sometimes, as you well know, we think we've got it all figured out. And you know where that leads: big ego deflation coming right up, just around the next corner. *Bam!* And we're humbled into striving again on our continuous quest for self-betterment.

Up, down, up, down—that's how life seems to go, doesn't it?

**Sine Waves, Circles, and Vortexes**

Actually, if you get into the more scientific explanations of life on an earth planet (meaning a physical, third-dimensional or material world), you will encounter exactly that: a sine wave as the conduit and pattern for the flow of energy in a linear world. We have time and space here, so energy here flows from a positive polarity to a negative polarity, then reverses and goes back to the opposite pole. Science depicts this as a sine wave:

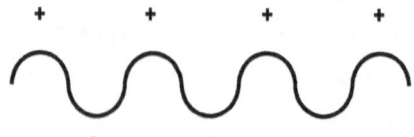

Whew, I swore I would not use diagrams in this book but I see my CoAuthors have induced me to reconsider. They're nothing fancy but they will help you discern an immediate difference between the flow of energy in our familiar, material world (sine wave), and the pattern and conduit for energy flowing in a non-third-dimensional world, what we commonly call a higher-dimensional or *astral* world (vortex):

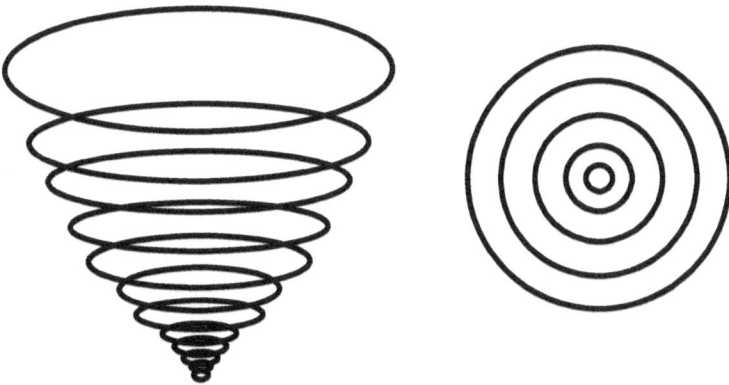

Familiar, isn't it? Because even though energy on Earth flows from a positive pole to a negative pole and back again in a sine wave pattern, giving our sense of the passage of time and distance, we can see all around us that nature is imprinted with the vortical design made up of complete circles or spirals, which indicate simultaneous "time." I like to think of these natural manifestations as imprints of the higher-dimensional energy that has infused the third-dimensional manifestation, such as the pattern of a snail shell. You can see this spiral influence in patterns everywhere.

And we humans mimic or celebrate this design in many ways. For instance, our very popular, fanciful heart symbol can be seen as a vortex when viewed from the side. Can you visualize it?

Or what about the concentric circle patterns and spirals favored by artists of many cultures, such as the Australian aborigines or the Maori or the Celts? Some say they're past-life memories, fragments of a science taught in Atlantis and Lemuria, which was depicted in simple graphic designs by the Master Scientists living during those epochs for the benefit of their indigenous students.

The point being made is that, in a fourth-dimensional or astral world, energy travels, not from point to point over time and distance like a sine wave, but continuously, in circling patterns, where every point on the circle connects to every other point with no separation of time or distance. Hence, the timeless, spaceless dimensions of pure energy that I sometimes, when I'm lazy, refer to as "Higher Worlds," meaning the places we reside between lifetimes. That's fairly imprecise. If I say "Higher Worlds," I'm usually talking about a *nice* place, a place you'd *like* to spend your time between lives. But technically, any place which does not have the limitations of time and space that our physical bodies require, in other words, a place where the sine wave is not the method by which energy travels, could be considered a "higher" dimension than our third-dimensional world. You could also call it an "astral" plane, world, or dimension. Yet the *quality* of that astral dimension can be anything from heavenly to hellish, depending on another factor we haven't yet discussed (frequency). It is still not a physical or sine-wave, time-and-space world. It is a world where energy travels in circular or cyclic patterns.

Why have we not drawn a simple circle, then? A "Circle of Life," as Elton John sings?

Because it's the concentric nature, the interconnections between circles, that matter to us most of all in our quest for expanded mental development, and a vortex or spiral form more accurately depicts that expansion of consciousness we're after. It also happens to portray the way energy travels interdimensionally, from the higher to the lower dimension, and back again. Remember, in this case when we say higher or lower, we're not implying a quality, but rather a level of dimension, such as third, fourth, fifth, sixth, and so on. The higher numbers are higher dimensions or rungs on the spiral.

What does this have to do with your Infinite potential? Everything.

First of all, you can think of yourself as the atom-dot at the end of this spiral:

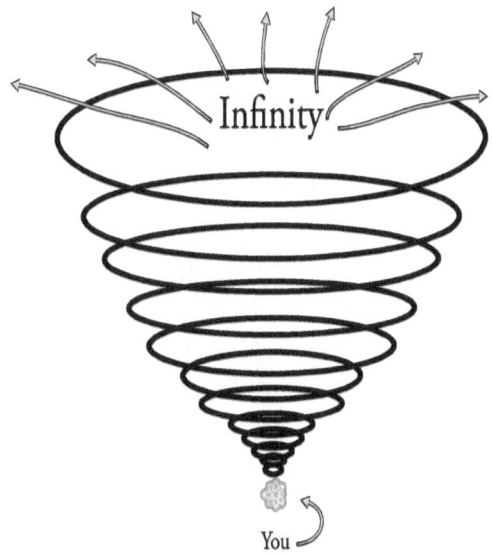

Above you (in frequency) spiral realms of Infinite Intelligence, knowledge not yet made a permanent part of you, since the tiny atom-dot is all you encompass presently. But this knowledge is clearly accessible via those interlinked, ever-expanding circles. It is not yet *you*, but you are linked to it. If only you could learn how to access or activate those links! (You can.)

Secondly, this design indicates that you are much, much more than your physical presence—the dot—would indicate. And since this "more" is attached to you, it is always there. No one can take it away, since it does not exist in the sine waves of Earth; i.e., it is not physical. You are the only one to have access to it, and consequently, any changes that take place in it are the product of your own doing.

(Unless you invite help, as you'll understand later.) That is a vital piece of information. So vital that I want you to think about the implication of these Infinite connections for a moment, while I go eat my lunch. My body may be only a small part of my true Being, but it's very demanding. Sometimes it seems like I am ruled by the vortex that overshadows my stomach chakra. (Yes, chakras are depicted as vortexes, and that's no accident).

...

Ah, that's better. Now, we were saying that this additional *you*, the expanding vortex that stretches up into higher-dimensional realms, *ad infinitum*, is strictly within your control. Well, it would be, if you knew about it and understood how to use it. And that's why we're here on Earth. We're at the beginning stages of this education.

Our diagram is merely an imitation of an abstract concept. You do not literally have lines of spirals attached to the top of your head, although for people who can intuitively sense the higher-frequency energy systems most closely attached to your body, those vortical or spiral patterns can become evident. Around the head it might be seen variously as a cone or flame or halo.

Also visible to those who can "see" non-physical energy are the many sine waves carrying energy-information throughout the body. These may appear in their complete form as figure-eights, a closed circuit, as positively charged energy flows to negative charge, then reversing as negatively charged energy flows back to positive.

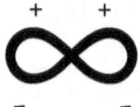

From my studies of Eden Energy Medicine, I've learned that both figure-eight and spiral patterns of energy exist all over and throughout the body, in small and large sizes. Practitioners learn to work with these energy patterns when stimulating the body's energies.

But from my interdimensional studies, I know that these figure-eight patterns, as well as the acupuncture meridians of Eastern medicine and the spirals of the chakras, are energies closer to our third-dimensional, material body forms. When I say "closer," I mean in frequency, like on a radio dial, but we'll expand on that concept as we come back to it in our spiral progression through this science.

Despite their importance and abundance, the body's energy patterns remain invisible to most people. Energy Medicine pioneer Donna Eden is one of the exceptions, clearly having trained herself in higher-dimensional sciences and healing arts between lifetimes; she was born seeing them. But she is not alone, and many ancient cultures have carried this knowledge forward for thousands of years.

Conventional, allopathic medical practitioners are beginning to access this ancient knowledge and use the body's electromagnetic properties in contemporary healing modalities, whether diagnostic or therapeutic. Recent scientific studies support this ancient/new awareness, and even the most reluctant enclaves of medical therapy have begun to embrace aspects of energy medicine and energy psychology which were only a few years ago considered "alternative." That's promising, but they're still far from the complete, interdimensional understanding you're learning here.

Chakras are visualized by intuitives and depicted in ancient drawings as energy moving in a vortical pattern, placed over key areas of the body. In addition to the seven well-known chakras, from crown to root, we have little chakra or vortical energy patterns in smaller or larger sizes associated with many other parts of the body; for instance, the palms of the hands or the bottoms of the feet. Ernest Norman calls this the body's "sprinkler system," distributing energy from the higher-dimensional, higher-frequency structures of the *psychic anatomy*—the real you; the complete package, including all the parts you cannot detect with your third-dimensional senses, and all the parts that remain undeveloped.

## 44  Speed Your Evolution

When Infinite Creative Intelligence, the fuel of your being, flows into you, it reaches you through this psychic anatomy. It's a vital concept in our pursuit of interdimensional knowledge, and yet I've only ever seen it described in one body of work. It is truly the missing link, the 96% of "undiscovered country" the boson scientists at CERN are all aflutter over, and you're going to learn about it in the next chapter.

## It's All Around You

1. Using your sketch journal, draw places you've seen these patterns in nature, both sine waves and vortexes or spirals. Let your designs be free; no worries about perfection.

2. In your text journal, write about the ways you can see your life mimicking these patterns, for instance in repeating events or feelings or experiences. Can you document sine waves and cycles?

3. For fun, build a chart with hours of the day across the bottom axis, and a range from High to Low down the side axis. Now at any given time of day, mark where you feel yourself to be on the high–low scale of emotion. Are you up? Or down? Or in the middle? This is your oscillating sine wave of life. Try it for a week! You can go further with this if you like: Indicate on the chart what caused the "up" or "down." (If you're flat-lined, you're either cheating or you're not living! We all have our ups and downs; it's how we learn and grow.)

# 6

## Meet Your Psychic Anatomy

*Because we are energy beings,* we communicate. Every moment of every hour, you are sending and receiving information. You are truly an interdimensional transceiver.

Information flows from your psychic anatomy, which exists in higher dimensions, down into your physical, third-dimensional body, and back again.

Energy radiates out from you carrying intelligent bits of information, much like the data flowing across the planet that now moves wirelessly to and from computers and phones and a myriad of electronic devices designed to pick up, codify, and replay this information.

We are constantly in communication *across dimensions.* When any element of that communication breaks down, so do we.

Mentally, physically, emotionally, we depend on this interdimensional communication for our life's breath. We communicate with each other, with nature, with all creatures great and small. We even connect with the rocks, flowers, water, and trees. If you search for it, you'll find science experiments that have proven each of these things. (Although I think it might be harder to find the rock communication studies, but I'll bet you could find some rock climbers who will swear by it, even if rocks do communicate more slowly than *ents.*)

Our world, even the small aspect we view through five *limited* senses, is not static. Life is a sea of energy, constantly moving, carrying information from one place to another, not limited by our dimensional constraints of time and space, but extending far beyond those five senses.

Our dreams, imagination, visions, intuitions, memories—they all hint of the extent of this magnificent centrifuge of energy in which we live. Intuitively, we know we are more than our five senses tell us. Even our newest branch of science, quantum physics, tells us so, for those few who speak its language. But in your own beating, electrically-timed heart of hearts, surely you sense this expanded You?

Full credit for the concept I am about to introduce goes, again, to our visionary scientist, Ernest L. Norman. The concept of the *psychic anatomy* is so essential to understanding the wider scope of human life, and yet I have not found any other explanation as lucid and complete as his. The psychic anatomy is but one small part of the interdimensional, cosmological science he depicted in his sixteen books, but it is a very vital part.

In conventional, traditional science, parts of this psychic or energy anatomy have been identified and lumped together in various ways; the concept of the subconscious, for instance. Forget your previous associations with these terms and clear your mind.

**Your Truly Personal Computer**

We'll start with what we'll term the *Conscious Mind*, that state of awareness that you're generally in when awake; the place you seem to be using to "think" and daydream and make decisions, the aspect of mind that, when we were children or before we embarked on our spiritual quests, we considered to encompass our entire mental function. We probably thought of it as "me." We were wrong, but it certainly feels as if everything happens there. It doesn't.

We also have our *Subconscious, Mental Conscious,* and, because we are no longer strictly animal, a rather undeveloped *Superconscious.* For the purpose of this book, we will refer to this entire configuration of your

## Meet Your Psychic Anatomy 47

human self as your *Consciousness* with a capital *C*.

Remember, these are merely arbitrary designations to facilitate our discussion of the flow and storage of energy-information in the expanded, interdimensional, human Consciousness.

In *The Infinite Concept of Cosmic Creation,* Ernest Norman used this diagram in the 1960s, before everyone had a computer device at their fingertips, to depict one aspect of the interaction of your mental energies, the construct we're calling your psychic anatomy, with the outside world.

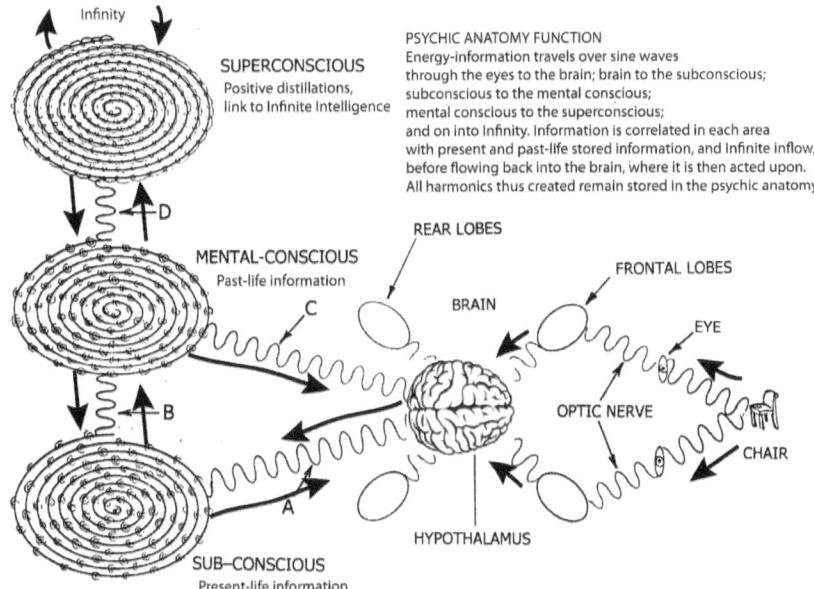

According to his text, information flows through this non-physical construct in various patterns, triggering responses and culminating in the life you're now living in the third dimension. [For a more detailed description of the diagram, see *The Infinite Concept of Cosmic Creation,* Advanced Lesson 5.]

We'll come back to this later but for now, I merely want you to observe that your psychic anatomy is your support system, storing and retrieving energy-information from all of your lifetimes, past and present, and correlating that information with what your five senses are retrieving from your physical life. In essence, it serves as your software for running the body you are inhabiting.

This is software first built as you evolved into a functioning human being. It knows about fuel and cells and electrical transmissions and blood and oxygen and so on. But you are also continually evolving and adding new information to your eternal Being as you encounter life experience. In fact, the higher structures of this psychic anatomy are not fully evident until you begin to revolve, from life to life, in human form.

Your basic design may have come from an Infinite Source—but your day-to-day programming of this psychic support computer? It's your own doing.

A little aside about health: Breakdowns in your system (for we all have them) involve various malfunctions or distorted information you've stored in your psychic anatomy. Such a breakdown can be repaired, but not always during a single lifetime. This kind of true healing (versus the suppression of symptoms) requires preparation between lifetimes, connection with higher-frequency Sources of healing energy-Intelligence, and intricate timing to bring all factors together in the right way, at the right junction of cyclic energy replays (what you might refer to as time).

But to our eyes, with our limited capacity for perception in this physical world, that healing might appear to be instantaneous, and credit is often given to the wrong resources. Most importantly, it requires participation by the individual who owns the psychic anatomy in question, although it might also involve catalysts such as healers, doctors, spiritual counselors, pills, foods, or almost anything that you believe in.

You can learn a great deal about your psychic anatomy from the book containing this diagram. Rather than repeat it here, I am going to focus instead on the psychic anatomy's role in reincarnation.

Because we are electronic beings we are, not only transmitting information via electrical signals in and out of our multi-dimensional Being (think of your neurotransmitters or your complex system of hormones), but we are also personalizing and storing that information. Where? In our psychic anatomy.

You've probably been told that you store information in your subconscious. Bruce Lipton, one of our newest visionary scientists and author of *The Biology of Belief*, explains how we draw more rapidly and easily from our subconscious storehouse than our relatively sluggish Conscious Minds. Anyone who has learned to play an instrument or drive a car can attest to this phenomenon. Without waiting for the slowness of thought, a musician's fingers hit the right keys or pluck the right strings.

So it is true: we store information from our present lives in our Subconscious cellars, ready to be retrieved at the slightest provocation. Rote memorization or schoolbook learning usually winds up here.

Additionally, when information pours in through one or all of our five senses, our Subconscious goes to work to match it with our previous experience—again, from our present lifetime—and we respond to the information according to everything we've stored about it, as well as the current input. Ordinary memories from your present lifetime will be found here.

Everyone is born with a "blank slate" *only in this Subconscious structure*. Moreover, the Subconscious unravels and dissipates at the end of our present physical lifetime.

However—and this is very important—*we are simultaneously storing every tiny aspect of our life in another energy compartment*, what Ernest Norman termed the Mental Conscious. This Mental Conscious energy structure oscillates at a higher frequency than our Subconscious. Hence, you might think of it as existing in a higher dimension than the Subconscious, but truly the two are linked and neither are physical, material constructs.

It is here in the Mental Conscious, as we've named it in our arbitrary divisions of mental function, that we'll say a person stores past-life information, every single detail. It is separated, for this discussion, as a way of visualizing the fact that these past-life bits of information are not readily accessible at all times to our Conscious Minds. It seems as if we've "forgotten" them, but they are just out of reach of our mental design. They can be sent to the Conscious Mind under certain conditions, however, kind of like forwarding an email message.

**What's a Higher Self, Really?**

By now, you may be squirming a bit because you realize that we've left out mention of some vital aspects of our humanity: feeling, analysis, emotion, judgment, selectivity, distillations of wisdom, *et al.* These are also stored in various compartments of the larger Consciousness, where our emotional reactions become very important elements of what we carry with us from life to life.

But stretching our little diagram and arbitrary divisions to the max, we'll say that the highest impulses, the most godlike qualities, the distilled Wisdom of our experience, our epiphanies and awakenings and sudden realizations of Infinite Intelligence—these travel that final journey to join with the rudimentary elements of our Superconscious.

It is in the highest frequencies of our Being that we meet the spiraling connections to Infinity, here in the Superconscious, as we've decided to call it. Infinite Intelligence flows into us through this portal, and we rise up to meet it with the positive elements we've extracted from our life experience.

We are actually building up this Superconscious Self by the fruits of our labors on earth worlds, by traveling into a lower dimension as we have done, life after life, to learn about the Infinite through hands-on encounters. Every time we achieve a positive goal, understand a new principle, overcome an obstacle of our own personalities, improve ourselves through personal effort, and so on, we are personalizing a small bit of Infinite Intelligence. When it's something positive or constructive, as with the instances I've listed, we are adding strength and wisdom to our Superconscious or higher self.

Needless to say, if it's something destructive we're regenerating, that will also remain a part of our psychic anatomy, there to live and reappear at future times in our lives. It will not contribute to the Superconscious, instead adding weight to what many people term the lower self. That is, until and unless you do something to change this energy-information.

The concepts of higher and lower selves are not new. But in the interdimensional schematic we're presenting in this book, we are not born in the Universe with the higher self or Superconscious part of ourselves completely developed. We earn our way, every step of the way. As Ernest Norman's wife Ruth often said to her students, "Luck has nothing to do with it." Every advancement we make in our understanding and mental development, we have earned through the hard toil of distilled experience. Even our healings, the ones that last, have been earned.

All that we know of Infinite Love comes to us through the elements we've stored in our Superconscious. Yes, you might consider Infinite Intelligence, the raw energy of the Universe, to be Love itself. But we can only sense it because of what we've learned and earned.

So you might say that the purpose of our entire journey from spark of the Infinite into full-fledged Infinite functionality is to develop that Superconscious into the multi-faceted Gem of our future Selves. A Gem that will serve the Infinite as a functioning, participating, intelligent facet of the Whole, but one that will never reach completion, for there is no such thing. We always have further to go, always a new horizon to seek.

Your drive for self-betterment? Look to the Superconscious as the source for it. We each possess the rudimentary ability to access the raw material of Infinity, linked to us through this energy construct of Consciousness, but it flows into our psychic anatomies in larger or smaller amounts, depending on how far along we are in our personal, evolutionary development. We start with training wheels before we learn how to ride a two-wheeled bicycle. Eventually, by our own desire and effort, we will learn to fly!

To speed toward that day of psychic liberation, you'll need to learn the interdimensional energy language of your own Cosmic Design; in other words, how you are constantly communicating with the Universe, whether you realize it or not. That's the subject of our next chapter.

∞✴∞

## Shore Up Your Superconscious

1. Gratitude is one of those positive emotions that fortifies the growing Superconscious Self. Make a gratitude list: What are you grateful for today, this week, or this lifetime?

2. Can you remember a time when you felt a sudden in-breath of realization of a Higher Source, an upwelling of spiritual feeling or knowing? A cosmic "aha!"? What triggered it? How did this feel? Did it have an effect on your subsequent life choices or ideas? Write about this incident in your journal. Writing about anything brings it more clearly to life in this third dimension, giving it more weight and influence in your life by reinforcing its impact in your psychic anatomy. Ernest Norman referred to this as "polarizing" the information, meaning you've taken Intelligence derived from a higher dimension (positive polarity/transmitting) and brought it firmly into the third dimension (negative polarity/receiving).

# 7

## How We Connect

> *"Einstein revealed that we do not live in a universe with discrete, physical objects separated by dead space. The Universe is one indivisible, dynamic whole in which energy and matter are so deeply entangled it is impossible to consider them as independent elements."*
> — Bruce Lipton, *The Biology of Belief*

*A large part of my* communication with you at this moment is taking place at higher frequencies than our Conscious Minds can access. Now that you've seen a truly inspiring and yet rather insufficient diagram ("The Psychic Anatomy") depicting the magnificence of your mental design—your Cosmic Being or Consciousness—you may have realized that a large percentage of the bigger You remains involved in transactions that *never reach your conscious awareness,* similar to the automatic functions such as breathing. Except your psychic anatomy is doing a lot more than that.

You no longer have to struggle with vague descriptions of Soul or Christ Self, Higher Self, Timeless Self, or whatever you've been calling the vast, unknown parts of yourself that we all somehow feel we surely must possess. Now you should be able to see that this is as complex and intricate, and yet as simple, as any piece of mechanical equipment. It's like your skeleton: the knee bone's connected to the thigh bone. Only it's:

>    Your Conscious Mind
>       connected to your Subconscious
>          connected to your Mental Conscious
>             connected to your Superconscious
>                connected to all of Infinity!

No limitations to the Who that you are! By your very design, you are linked to the Cosmos and everything that happens in it.
*So why are we folks on Earth so often lost and screwed up?*
Because we haven't fully activated the mechanism of Consciousness to *access* this Infinite potential.

First of all, we haven't generally got a clue how to do this. Lots of people have told us about this method or that one, but honestly, can you make it work? All the time?

We must begin by learning HOW we communicate—with one another, with our past, present, and future, with the natural world, with higher-dimensional Intelligences, with the Infinite. Communication is everything, remember?

We now understand that we are energy beings, that even the atoms of our bodies contain not a single detectable solid. (They've never found a solid particle at the root of an atom. Whenever they thought they had, they've always found something smaller. They never will find one, Higgs bosons notwithstanding, because the "particles" are actually energy parallaxes stemming out from higher dimensions into the third dimension. (See Norman, *The Infinite Concept of Cosmic Creation, Lesson 4.*)

So when we communicate, we are conducting an energy exchange as our form of connection with the universe.

Let's go back to the simple, Earth-bound sine wave. In our diagram, energy is traveling from a positive pole to a negative pole (or polarity) over time. Easy to see. And this is true no matter where you are in the

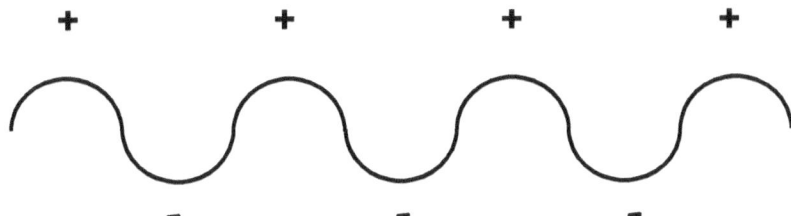

universe: *Surplus flows to deficiency.* We'll call this *polarity.* (And for you electrical engineers, let's not get caught up in Benjamin Franklin's confusions about electron flow.)

*Okay, that's fine, but doesn't that mean a lot of energy zinging around everywhere, resulting in total chaos?*

Some people think so. But truly, no.

Like attracts like. You've all heard that by now. And energy can also repel, as in the common magnetic-pole demonstrations you've seen in science classes, where the north pole repels a north pole, and south repels south. So we've got two more principles of energy: *attraction* and *repulsion.* We're starting to sort out a thing or two about how energy interacts with energy.

Another common science demo you might have seen involves *resonance.* Pluck a guitar or lute or harp string and it will *vibrate* at a particular speed or *frequency,* which determines the note or pitch that we hear. Meanwhile, similarly tuned strings around it will also begin to vibrate because they resonate at the same frequency. Now we're moving into a principle called *harmonics.*

So far, we've got:

**Polarity**
**Attraction**
**Repulsion**
**Speed of Vibration, aka Frequency**
**Resonance**
**Harmonics**

Six simple principles by which we communicate with the Infinite. This is how energy travels, carrying information on its back.

Can't be that easy, can it?

Let's elaborate.

## Polarity

I was once watering plants outside our house on the red-brick paved patio when an earthquake rumbled through. It was centered miles away, so in Southern California we didn't suffer damage. But it lasted a long time, in earthquake minutes.

Usually we get short jolts that throw books off the shelf—not long enough to consider much of anything. But standing there with my watering can, I had time to watch in amazement as the wall of the house rippled like a canvas tent and the red bricks lifted and fell beneath my feet as the quake rolled through, like a wave passing through a body of water.

And then it was over.

Nothing broke. Not a brick or board out of place. And at that moment, all my years of studying that "there's no such thing as solid" coalesced. I wasn't frightened because it was too exciting to see the truth of it with my own eyes!

Every "solid" thing around me had absorbed and discharged that energy wave as smoothly as could be, as if it had always known that it possessed this ability to ripple and sway but never let on to we mere humans how alive and pliable it actually is, lest we lose our false sense of security. I never viewed the strong, solid walls of the house the same way again.

Just like us, houses and bricks and concrete can bend and sway to accommodate any slight disruptions that pass through. That also means that these deceptively solid objects will take on energies presented to them, and pass them along again—as they did when the earthquake's energy wave rolled through.

Not taking *feng shui* seriously? Hm, perhaps the ancient Asian races, which originated from another part of the solar system (long story), knew a thing or two after all. All of your so-called material possessions—your house, the clothes you wear, the items you hold and use—take on your energy, and will discharge it when they're good and ready.

In other words, when *polarities* shift and such a discharge becomes scientifically mandated. (Surplus flows to deficiency.)

Think of pouring water into a glass from a pitcher. The water won't go in unless the glass is empty, right?

So, full pitcher = a positive polarity or surplus
Empty glass = a negative polarity or deficiency

To take it further, once you fill the glass and empty the pitcher, you can reverse the flow, pouring the glass of water back into the pitcher. In other words, they have reversed their polarities:

Full glass = a positive polarity or surplus
Empty pitcher = a negative polarity or deficiency

In electronics, this is what energy does: it flows from the positive polarity to the negative, then reverses itself and flows back again. You can see this in the sine wave diagram. (For techies: I'm speaking of conventional flow, not electron flow.) This back and forth reversal of polarities is called alternating current, as developed by Nikola Tesla, and because of his (under-appreciated) work, it now powers our world, carrying energy-information to and fro.

You'll notice that this exchange in the sine wave diagram takes place over a distance; it flows in a linear pattern, from top to bottom to top to bottom, etc. This also indicates a passage of *time*. But the principle holds true throughout the universe: positive energy-information flows to negative; polarities reverse and it flows back again. Yet in higher dimensions, we've already pointed out that without time and distance or space, energy flows in a cyclic pattern. All the information stored in your psychic anatomy is stored as spirals or vortexes of energy-information. *It is timeless.*

Where are the poles, positive and negative, in these cyclic patterns? This is a bit more difficult for us to draw, but imagine donuts sitting one inside the other, ever expanding in size. The rims where they touch are where the positive and negative charges exchange, thus linking these cycles of energy-information. This is how energy travels and connects in higher dimensions that are not linear, time-space dimensions. Time doesn't exist in such a configuration. Touch any point on the circle and you're linked to all the others.

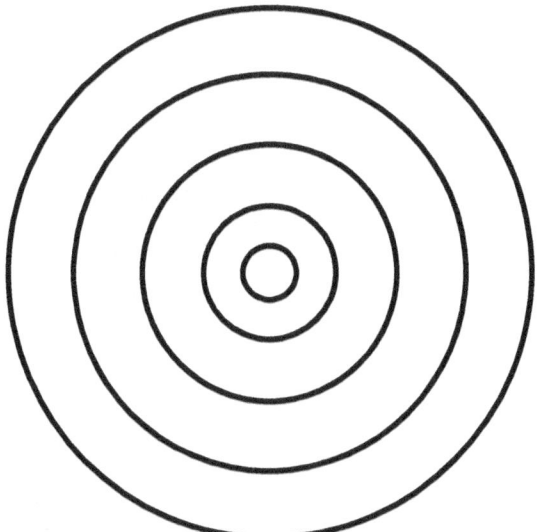

I happened to hear this described in an old movie we watched recently, *Peggy Sue Got Married,* a rather mediocre film that nevertheless involves time travel. The geeky character (who of course becomes the wealthiest) used the metaphor of a burrito, where the wrapped tortilla touches itself, thus eliminating the separations we have in our third-dimensional sense of "time." Well, it worked in the movie, anyway, helped along by a prodding little mention of Einstein's space-time continuum. The geeky character was referring to the same principle as our interlocking donuts, or rungs on a spiral.

To travel into our linear, third-dimensional world, then, the cyclic energy patterns of our psychic anatomy must "step down" into a sine wave pattern, although they still carry the Intelligence embedded in their design. Here's an imagined picture of the transfer point:

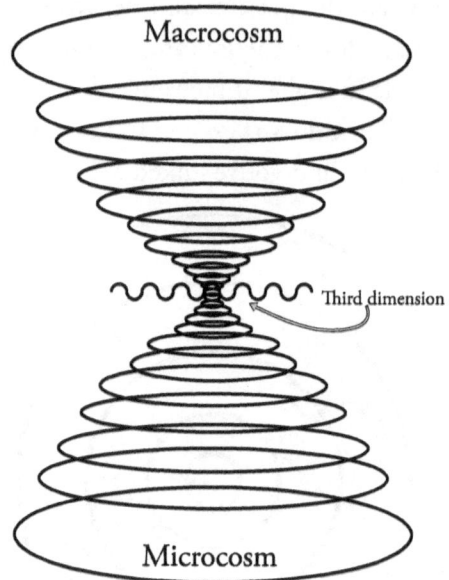

Once again, you'll have to make allowances for the fact that a two-dimensional diagram is only that (and mine aren't fancy!) but it's a starting place for our understanding. We've also vastly simplified everything so you can grasp the big picture. You can delve more deeply into these energy concepts later but for now, add one more element to the picture:

We, while on Earth, are like the empty glass and the higher-dimensional information flowing to us is similar to the pitcher. That is, we are the negative polarity or deficiency, and the information coming to us from cyclic dimensions is the positive polarity or surplus.

If you're ahead of me, you already know that means information will be flowing back when the polarities reverse.

*Voilà!* This is how the information of your life is stored in your psychic anatomy, and how the information contained in your psychic anatomy's storehouse flows into your life. There's a constant exchange of information, in and out of your psychic anatomy.

You've just solved a very big question: How does my past-life experience affect my present life? Or, some might put it this way: *Why should I care about past lives?*

Because your past-life experience, emotion, shocks, blocks, traumas, and all the good things too, are flowing straight into your present life directly from your psychic anatomy. These past-life bits of information know no time and space; they are as real and current as if they happened moments ago, or more precisely, they are immediate. And that's how they feel to you, as well. Which is why you don't instantly identify them as unusual or out of place.

They are energy constructs, right? And all of our life, even our bodies, are energy constructs. Therefore, they are as real as anything you know. In fact, they are the power source for your present moment.

**Frequency, Resonance, and Harmonics**

*So if everything's flying at me at once from within my own Being, it still sounds like chaos! How do I make sense of any of it?*

First of all, it's not all flying at you at once. Only the elements of your stored information that relate to your external life at this very moment will be conveyed to you.

*Why? Does someone—God or me—choose what to bring forth at any given time?*

Actually, you are choosing, even though you might not realize it. That's because energy has the characteristics of frequency, resonance, and harmonics that govern where and how and when it travels.

Go back to the diagram in Chapter 6 that depicts the psychic anatomy. See the chair? When the individual in question views a chair, it sends an impulse into the brain that seeks out all similar impulses, anything and everything related to *chair* in that individual's experience, past or present. *Chair* oscillates or resonates in that individual's consciousness at a particular compound *frequency*, a unique energy identification that is far more complex than our diagrams can indicate. Our real "vortexes and sine waves" are much more elaborate, compounded configurations, carrying a lot of information in their design.

Here's what your electronics course will show you about frequency. It's the speed at which energy oscillates from a positive pole to a negative pole; from the top of the sine wave to the valley.

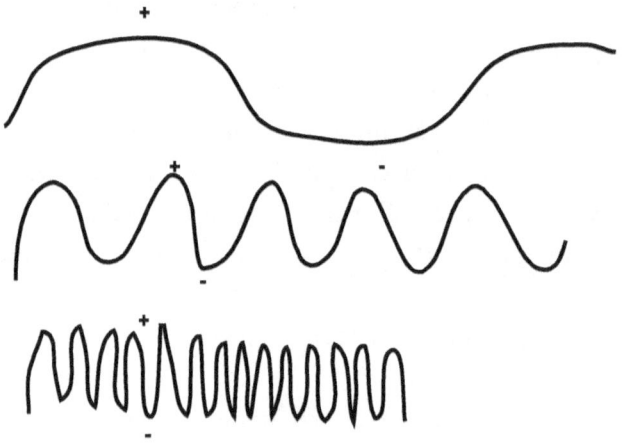

long waves = low frequency
short waves = high frequency

I drew these by hand to demonstrate something else: It's not likely anyone could duplicate my squiggles exactly. The irregularities are what make my sine waves distinctive. Imagine that those distinctions of frequency and pattern are how energy carries specific information.

In school you learned about the electromagnetic spectrum, the infrared, the ultraviolet, etc. The colors of our rainbow each oscillate

*How We Connect* 63

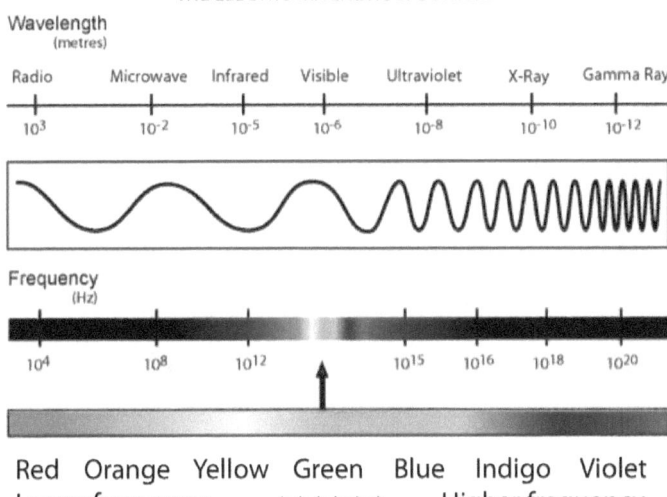

at a specific spectral frequency, giving them specific visual qualities. You can see from the diagram that frequency is one indicator of the characteristics of the energy pulse in question; i.e., orange differs from indigo; microwave differs from x-ray.

So the nature of the thought you're carrying in your mind—*chair* in this case—denotes its entire energy "signature," a compound of frequencies and patterns that determine the nature of the information that will pour out of your psychic anatomy in *harmonic* association or *sympathetic resonance* with those energetic details.

It's not that you've plucked the A string of your guitar and an A string resonates nearby; in this case, you've plucked *chair* and all harmonics of *chair* begin to play in your Conscious Mind, pouring out of your Subconscious and Mental Conscious. Even your Superconscious, if anything's been activated there in your personal experience, say a really transcending spiritual experience you associate with *chair,* will add its bit of higher input to the mix.

However, you won't necessarily differentiate separate bits of information as coming from past or present life or Superconscious. Even

Subconscious (an influence that doesn't rise into conscious awareness but still factors into our reactionary response) and Memory (a vivid recall of a past incident) won't necessarily be sorted out by your Conscious Mind as coming from a different part of your mind. It's all one big mixture.

Generally, we humans simply act and react based on all these unseen influences working together in a stew. Conscious thought is only one small factor in the energy mix influencing our lives.

Ernest Norman describes the Conscious Mind as nothing more than a switchboard where all the input from various aspects of your psychic structures connect. Reasoning, memory, emotion—these are centered in other areas of our mental design.

Now, of course, the process is a lot more detailed and complex than *chair*, or we wouldn't be able to make sense of a detailed and complex world. But remember the popular story of the South American natives who couldn't see the Spaniards' ships because they'd never seen one before? They had no stored information from past or present life of ocean-going vessels; they called them "floating islands."

Have you ever seen something, maybe even at a distance, that for a few moments you could not really "see" because your brain simply would not compute the image? You had no relevant, or resonant, harmonics with which to associate the thing before you. Not until you drew closer to it, or some lighting changed, or some other factor changed what you were seeing into something that you'd had some previous experience with and could identify by the information stored in your psychic anatomy. This is how we make our way in this world.

We are constantly flooded with information we've acquired in our many life-journeys. This energy-information flows into play in our present moment, stimulated by events, by all of our emotions, by the people around us, by Nature herself, by sound and touch and smell and sight and taste. We are little sensing computers, accessing information and spitting information back out. We are truly amazing beings. And far more than we ever considered ourselves to be! Because we've only begun, on Earth, to use this computer-self to its fullest capacity. Nope, we're not even close.

But now you're just a tiny bit closer.

## Make It Yours

1. To play with the concepts of polarity, resonance, vibration, frequency, and harmonics, see what you can find around the house that makes a sound when you strike or pluck it. (No, I don't mean the cat or canary or little sister!) A musical instrument, kitchen pot or pan lid, rubber band, wet glass rim, and so on.

2. Now see if you can feel the vibration, remembering that it's created by the transfer of energy traveling from positive pole to negative pole and back again, at a particular frequency. Try placing a ringing guitar against your stomach, for instance. How do you feel? Try another location. Does the sensation occur because you're resonating in harmony with the original source? Or because you are out of synchronization with it?

3. If you don't have two stringed instruments lying around, see if you can find two items that will begin to resonate together when you activate one or the other.

4. In your journal, write about an incident in your life where you feel that you were responding harmonically or resonantly with another individual, or they were responding to you.

5. Have you ever noticed how one individual in a group can set off a chain reaction of emotion among others, whether positive or negative emotion? Write about it.

6. Here's a little trick for couples—the ultimate, resonant polarity association. Joseph and I learned this during a weekend workshop with Donna Eden, pioneer of Eden Energy Medicine, when she discovered it was our wedding anniversary.

Stand facing your partner. Place your palm on the top of his or her head and your other palm on the back of his or her neck. Leave them in place and have your partner do the same to you. Donna swears that if you stand that way for a few moments, you'll sync up into blissful energetic harmony. She couldn't resist adding that it would cause the energies to "rise up" between you.

Well, it certainly caused laughter to rise up from the two hundred energy medicine practitioners in the audience! And it did make our faces turn red. That energy affected the others well into the next morning, too, when they all raised their eyebrows, winked, or giggled at us.

# Part II

# Raise Your Frequency

*"Only true knowledge of the Infinite gives the individual the power of selection, and in selection there is quite naturally a much higher state of evolution, a greater development of consciousness. As these developments of consciousness so transpire within the individual's mind, so do they encompass an ever-increasing number of interdimensional forms.*

*"The ramifications of this ever-expanding consciousness are infinite in themselves, and will, as has been previously presented, create within the individual the effigy of the true God, the true expressive personal potential of the Infinite Creator, which is contained in the individual nuclei [sic] of intelligence."*

— Ernest L. Norman, *Infinite Perspectus*

# 8

## Choosing

*"Your life is what you choose."*
Ah, don't you wish?
"I choose to be a princess."
"I want to be a fireman."
"I'm going to climb Mount Everest."
"I want to be a mother."
Those aren't choices. Those are goals.

A choice is that thing you did when you picked up this book to keep reading it. And you'll have a choice about stopping, and choosing to do something else.

You're also choosing your reaction to these words.

Is it to remain open-minded until you've finished reading?

Or is it to decide that this is surely nonsense, clearly written by a non-scientist, and it couldn't possibly be right. In other words, your mind might be closed by some prior prejudice you've chosen to maintain.

Actually, those are still mega-choices.

*The real power in your life lives at the level of nano-choices,* the almost imperceptible ones we are making constantly, with every nanosecond of breathing on this planet.

Are you smiling? You chose it. Are you frowning? Another choice.

Are you enjoying this nanosecond? No? You've chosen not to.

You've probably read this sort of self-management information before, given the plethora of books on the subject now readily available to us. In fact, it's a wonderful development on this planet that such books are being written! But we're going to go further.

WHY does it matter what you choose in the nanosecond, or even smaller increments of choice?

Because every such choice sets in motion the interdimensional mechanism of your Consciousness.

I can't help at this stage of the chapter to hear in my head a song my husband was playing on the stereo this morning. It's from a Disney film by a Disney-kid group called Lemonade Mouth. "Determinate, determinate," goes the electrified chorus. "Gotta turn the world into your dance floor! Determinate, determinate." Catchy tune. True principle. And in this important principle lies your true power as a human being.

So perhaps you can't choose to be a princess, and maybe you wouldn't really like it anyway, but you can choose your response to that roadblock. You could choose to do like the song says, "Push until you can't and then demand more" of yourself.

Or you could choose to do as I instinctively did when I typed that sentence: I chose to think I wouldn't really like being a princess in this lifetime. Maybe I chose that because at the word *princess,* my interdimensional Consciousness immediately fed me a bit of information from my own past lives about princesses. Terrible things have happened to them. I might have witnessed some of those things. Certainly I've by now read about them in history. And while we may have been talking about a Disney song, we are not discussing Disney princesses!

But as you can see, if the Disney concept is the one you associate with *princess,* you might indeed want to be one. Although I don't think their lives were so easy, either.

What is clear here is that whatever you place in your Conscious Mind, you will automatically trigger a landslide of information into your present life from your own past lives (Mental Conscious), from your Subconscious storage bin, and from your Superconscious, if you've stored anything good there.

Furthermore, if you've activated your links to higher resources via your Superconscious (such as my Cosmic CoAuthors represent), information from those higher levels may also filter into your present life. Useful, helpful stuff.

But at the same time, and by the same principles of *polarity, attraction, repulsion, resonance, frequency,* and *harmonics,* if you've fostered links with subastral influences, that, too will feed into your present life. Nasty, destructive stuff. (More on this important subject in the next chapter.)

When I say "place in your Conscious Mind," it sounds so clean and controlled. But most of us don't have that much self-mastery. We usually bounce from one thought to another, and most significantly, from one emotional reaction to another. We freely oscillate with whatever crosses our paths, without consideration for the vast, intricate interplay we're engaging in, and the number of dimensions through which our thoughts, deeds, and emotions will be resonating.

We also don't stop and say, "Now that's going to become a permanent part of me." Well, most people don't, anyway. Not until they've learned a little bit about this interdimensional science of reincarnation we're discussing.

Most people don't stop and say, "Wait a minute. If I oscillate with this anger for a few minutes longer, if I let it take me over and I don't do anything to cast it off, it's going to become a permanent part of me and I'm going to have to deal with it for all future lifetimes, whenever I hear the name Sally." (Apologies to any Sallys reading this; it was a random name choice.)

Oh! And since we are discussing random *choice,* this might be a good place to introduce the random number generator experiments conducted at Princeton University. To many people's satisfaction, they've proven that the human Consciousness functions in ways our science has barely begun to identify. In fact, they've demonstrated that there's no such thing as "random," since human thoughts and intentions can influence their mechanical number generator. [More at: http://en.wikipedia.org/wiki/Princeton_Engineering_Anomalies_Research_Lab]

But they haven't explained the "how," which is what you are now studying.

**Your True Power**

The power we have over the nature of the life we're leading is truly awe-inspiring. A shame so few people exercise that power. It's all in the nanoseconds of selecting what we'll oscillate with. Books and counselors now abound telling you this. But they wouldn't still be selling if it were such easy advice to follow.

*Why? Why do people choose misery, because if the principle is true, then that must be what they're doing.*

Ah, now we're getting into the subject of karma.

It's not as simple as, "I killed you, so now you come back and kill me." Or, "I hurt others, so now I will be hurt." Matter of fact, for millions of people, there's no decision-making involved because they haven't yet reached that point of self-defined incarnations. (And even if they have, the cause-and-effect principles of energy still apply and they cannot escape them.)

First, we as humans evolve through the natural, evolutionary, interdimensional forces of energy we've been discussing. We come and go, not freely, but guided by the principles guiding all energy interactions. It is not God who decides to punish or reward us. We are the Godsparks who've set our futures in motion, and we must play them out in accordance with energy principles that are universal, interdimensional, and inviolable.

What we've said, thought, felt, and done, to ourselves or to others, and what we feel about what we've done, or what has been done to us or for us, is what will determine the nature of our lives, present and future. Rich or poor, the quality of our life is what we've engraved into our psychic anatomies. The experiences we encounter in the present, we've drawn ourselves into based on past-life associations. We attract what we oscillate in harmony with; we repel what we do not oscillate with.

*And that oscillation is taking place throughout your entire psychic anatomy, much of which is far beyond your Conscious Mind's perception.*

This is the part a lot of people miss. We can chant and visualize all we want, but if we've got some unresolved bit of energy embedded within our psychic anatomy, it WILL express its universal Intelligence in our lives, until we do something to change that bit of energy-information at the source, in the higher rungs of oscillating frequencies in our psychic anatomy; i.e., the parts our Conscious Minds are not fully aware of in ordinary states of mind.

Inherently, it is only energy; we are the ones who place value judgments such as "good" or "evil" on that bit of energy-intelligence. But as energy, it will follow these principles, and no one is immune to them.

That does not mean that every foul thing that comes to you must be embraced! Quite the opposite!

Every element of these energy principles should indicate to you that YOU are in charge. You choose. You are the one who can "determinate" what happens next. But you can't stop that energy from flowing out of your psychic anatomy and into the shaping of your present life.

What you can do is reshape it when it appears. How? Read on.

## Fire Up Your Nano-Power

1. Write briefly about choices and consequences that you think made a difference in your life.

2. Now write briefly about incidents from your life that you suspect came at your "blind side" because they were pouring out from your psychic anatomy. In other words, times when you didn't feel like you'd "chosen" this circumstance that impacted your life so significantly.

3. Choose a nanosecond habit-breaking project for practice: Select a simple goal (to start). Then think about how your tiniest choices in life can support that goal. Keep it easy at first so you'll experience the effects of your choice immediately, not years from now.

For instance, let's say you want to get to bed earlier so you can sleep better during the dark hours of night. At each turn of the day and evening, make conscious choices that support that goal of an earlier bedtime. Make a brief note in your journal every time you do something differently than you ordinarily would (or write them down as soon as you can).

If you achieve this first goal, be sure to pat yourself on the back or reward your success! Habits are challenging to break.

4. Spend some journal time meditating on the fact that choices even that tiny are becoming permanent parts of you, affecting not only something as seemingly small as tonight's hour of repose, but perhaps creating a habit you'll be trying to break for lifetimes into the future!

# 9

## Tuning Your Inner Crystal

*In many ways, the science* of a creative evolution is the science of letting go. We must discard the old, unnecessary, outworn, retrogressive energy elements of ourselves in order to take up a new, radiant, purposeful position in life. It's a constant process of renewal.

At first, it's difficult. Much of what's shed involves your personal ego. But with practice, this becomes easier. And the rewards are multitudinous.

For the first time since Atlantis, you are learning for yourself, without interference, the principles of energy that govern your many lifetimes as you pass from physical, earth life to the higher spiritual worlds for a period of recuperation, study, and preparation, then back again to planet Earth to continue your schooling.

And what is the ultimate purpose of these back-and-forth journeys? Personal, evolutionary development. You are building your inner crystal into a jewel most magnificent! You are tuning up your consciousness to higher and higher levels of awareness, so that in your future, you, too, will serve humanity as a radiant life source, as many before you have done.

This is what we call *creative* evolution! And the Power to accomplish it is entirely in your hands.

Now most people take a long, slow path through their many lives.

They make mistakes and learn, same as you have done. They gradually work out their karmic entanglements with others. Over time—perhaps thousands or tens of thousands of lifetimes—they will evolve, if they consistently make progressive choices.

However, this book is helping you to take the quick road to personal, soulic, evolutionary development. Of course by quick, we don't mean the kind of hurry-up, breakneck course that so many promote—*2 Easy Steps to Enlightenment, 4-Hour This or That*. Still, by learning the science of reincarnation, you will carve thousands of years and lifetimes off your course and begin to experience a wonderful, rewarding, richly meaningful life right now.

No tricks. No magic. Simply an application of universal principles of energy that govern all life—in your third dimension and beyond.

Indeed, this shortcut is the method that the CoAuthors of this book have used in their own evolutionary development, rising up through multiple layers of understanding to reach a state of clarity and comprehension that you can also achieve, if you are so willing. It's all up to you.

But until now, you've not been given all the proper tools. We're about to fix that!

**"Change the channel."**

"Change the channel." When I first learned this important principle of mental maintenance, I was able to think back to the days of dial-shaped TV or radio channel selectors, where a single click could raise or lower the frequency of the channel you were receiving. You could hear the resounding click of your choice settling into harmonic resonance with your speakers so that you could enjoy whatever was being broadcast from the radio or TV station on that frequency at that moment. (Beatles, Rolling Stones, *Bonanza*, so you know how old I am. Ah, but I am ancient, as are you!)

Nowadays, we're more likely to "click" away from or toward an Internet site that represents a complicated amalgamation of frequencies. Think of your Facebook news feed, for instance (if Facebook still exists as you read this): You're scrolling through a steady stream of frequencies put out by friends, family, or strangers. If you click into one to pursue it further, who knows where you'll wind up—or how long you'll stay in resonance with that particular compound frequency. Ever click away feeling slightly nauseous or headachy?

The principle remains the same:

✳ **Wherever you tune your mental dial, that's the frequency you'll receive and resonate in harmony with, for better or for worse.**

Knowing how and when to change the channel is a skill you're going to need in order to raise your frequency every time it drops below your personal standards. Actually, there's not much skill required, simply a knowledge of the energy principles involved and a quick determination to "change the channel" to mitigate the damage.

I credit this single tactic of *selectivity*, which I learned from my interdimensional studies, with making my marriage happy and long-lasting! Fortunately for me, Joseph also studied this principle. If either of us loses our temper, we know the personal consequences and we will work individually to change that channel as soon as possible. Sometimes it takes a while; sometimes we can catch it before anything explodes and splatters both of us.

Shifts and changes in emotion are inevitable in our Earth lives; this is how we're learning. But lingering at a low frequency such as anger, envy, resentment, guilt, blame, and so on, is neither required nor wise! Have I said this already? Well, I'll probably say it many more times before this book is finished—it's that essential to your creative evolution.

**Your Personal Broadcast System**

It's not only your outer reception that you must be concerned with. Think of yourself as a television screen, reflecting into this world everything that is being broadcast to you from within.

That includes everything radiating from your Subconscious, your Mental Conscious, your Superconscious, and your Conscious Mind, plus any elements of Infinite Intelligence projecting through your Superconscious Self and out into the world.

How clear is your screen? What are you reflecting into your own life and the lives of others?

On the other hand, this is a two-way system. What are you taking into yourself, feeding back into your psychic anatomy, and broadcasting back into the Infinite? Whatever it is, it's going to remain a part of you for all time. Is it building your Superconscious Self with positive input?

Or is it going to attract things you'd rather not attract?

Both the inflow and outflow of your personal electronic system combined together create a frequency that resonates in harmony with others. It attracts and repels, electromagnetically.

Quite a few people in this world want you to pay them to tell you how to exploit some fragment of this process for selfish gain. We're going to talk about something entirely different. Something you probably don't want to know but—sorry—it's truly important and a key to your future health and well-being.

We can try to ignore the ebb and flow of energy in which we live, but sooner or later you'll become a victim of it if you don't educate yourself about all aspects and learn how to navigate safely through that sea of energy.

The following was taken from a *Soul Pursuits* blog post I wrote some time ago with my Cosmic CoAuthors. After reading the previous chapters, you'll recognize some of the principles discussed, but the more you think about these relatively new concepts, the more likely they'll be ready and waiting for you when you need them!

*Tuning Your Inner Crystal* 79

Most importantly, the post introduces the concept of astral obsession, which will underline why the "change the channel" or *selection* principle is so vital to your well-being. The post was originally titled:

## Who Are Your Astral Companions?

We spent a lovely Fourth-of-July weekend enjoying our own uncrowded fairy garden, Joseph's gourmet cooking, and seven consecutive episodes of the first season of *Downton Abbey*, courtesy of Netflix streaming into our TV. We love that series, those characters, both "good" and "evil"!

But as Joseph pointed out this morning, the last episode contained a brilliant illustration of an important—nay, a vital energy principle: that of *astral obsession*.

I do hope you'll seek out this series, now on DVD, and watch it for yourself. If nothing else, the costumes are glorious and Maggie Smith and others are fabulous at what British actors do best. Even Elizabeth McGovern (think *Ordinary People* if you're my age) is surprisingly well suited, once you realize she's playing the rich *American* heiress who saved the Grantham estate for the current generation. But will her eldest daughter, Mary, be able to do the same in these changing, brink-of-World-War-I times?

Let's go straight to this principle of astral obsession. What I mean by that is actual entity influence upon one's thoughts and actions in the present lifetime, entities who are not so positively-oriented, who have fallen into an astral state that is often termed "lower," although in actual fact, their frequency is "higher" than third-dimensional because they are oscillating in a fourth-dimensional state—i.e., a non-physical, invisible-to-the-Earth-eye state of being.

Scary, huh? Don't be scared; just become informed. How do

these entities, these lost astral souls, attach to us and influence our choices and our words? By frequency association.

When we think a thought, it's like a radio beacon, broadcasting a certain frequency out into the universe. If you learn a little about frequency and harmonic association, you'll realize that your thoughts not only radiate outward, but also bring energy back to you, oscillating along the carrier wave of energy that you've created by your thought. And the nature of that thought determines the nature of the energy you bring back to you.

Uh-oh! We've stumbled across some tiny element of that ol' Law of Attraction everyone's so excited to discover these days. But there are so many more implications of the actual energy principle behind that fragmented idea people have now. And it is a principle, not a law. Laws can be broken, Universal Energy principles cannot, to paraphrase my Cosmic CoAuthors in a book I haven't yet published. [Ed. note: Refers to this book, *Speed Your Evolution.*]

Perhaps our discussion of the obsession aspect of the principle of frequency and harmonic attraction will help clear up some of the confusion folks have about this attraction business—and some terrible mistakes they may be making.

\*\*\* Spoilers, Spoilers, Spoilers \*\*\*

Okay, you've been warned; I'll try not to, but I can't guarantee I won't give away something. One of the characters in *Downton Abbey* is so evil, so mean-spirited, cruel, selfish, grasping, and cold-hearted, that you want to shake her as the episodes unfold and it becomes clear that she's not like ordinary humans. Because ordinary humans are never fully evil. She's a literary character, created to make the plot nice and juicy, and she does a brilliant job of it—she and all the others.

Still, her actions in the seventh episode clearly demonstrate the principle of obsession that Joseph pointed out.

Ever since we first met her, she's spoken nothing but vile sentiments, nursed nothing but negative attitudes, fueled her jealousy, fed her anger, believed the worst of everyone and everything. Ugh! By the seventh episode, she's been caught up short a couple of times, but still persists in her foul and destructive state of mind.

Now, at last, she's become the victim of her own negative thinking. She fully believes that others are about to treat her as she's been treating them, and this only gives her more justification for, not only foul thoughts, but foul deeds! The most unthinkably foul deed! One that is life-threatening to another! A murderous act!

In the midst of it, she catches her reflection in a mirror and speaks to herself, musing that this is not like her real self. At last! A moment of self-reflection (quite literally). For a split second we think there's hope for this character and at last we'll see a turn in her attitude…until we hear the scream. Too late. The deed was done and no amount of guilt could undo it.

We still don't know what will become of her. Will she change? Or persist? Or be worse? Or succumb to the hell she's created for herself?

But right there, in that moment of choice to act as she did, the principle was clear as crystal: she'd allowed astral obsessions—destructive entities—to propel her actions. And she let them in by letting down her mental guard rails.

**We Are Not Powerless**

How did she lower the guard rails of her consciousness, evaporate her natural barriers of protection from the subastral worlds?

In the only way we connect to non-physical worlds of any frequency: via her thoughts, streamed out day and night, sending their beacons off into the universe.

The vile nature of this character's thoughts, reinforced by actions that gave them even more power, attracted the vilest of influences. They tilted her balance even further from her own personality, damaged as it was.

As I said before, a real human (versus a fictional character) always has at heart a positive spark of Infinity, always has the potential to do the right thing. Unless, of course, they're pushed over the edge into bad behavior by inner demons—literally—who've been unwittingly invited to stream their influence into one's consciousness, same as we streamed those Netflix videos into our living room!

But of course, such entities live in astral states of partial-being—often at a level that is no longer fit to establish a physical body for a sojourn of learning on an earth world like ours. Having lived degenerate lives of their own, lives that deteriorated their consciousness into this low level of non-existence and have kept them from ascending into higher-frequency worlds where they might find some corrective assistance, they're now stuck.

They've not learned a better way. They've chosen their path, and now must derive their sustenance from the energy-thoughts and lives of others, people who are living physical lives and might be persuaded to carry out what the astral entity no longer has the body to carry out. They become parasites, leeching onto the consciousness of the unsuspecting.

They might want to drink, or smoke, or take a drug, whether prescribed or black-market—addictions they still feel but can no longer satisfy without "help" from their unwitting victim.

Or they might simply want to continue committing the crimes they'd committed during their physical lives.

If they could, they'd seize a womb and find their way back into our world. But their damaged energy bodies no longer maintain enough cohesion to do that.

These entities we're describing are among the lowest of the low, and the most troublesome for Earth inhabitants.

Crimes of passion often have this hidden energy reality, the principle of harmonic association, at their root. How often do citizens, ignorant of this principle, unwittingly commit terrible deeds of murder and mayhem, and then "wake up" some time later as they regain their own sense of self to discover the horrible result? They plead an insanity defense, and in truth, their situation is indeed a form of mental lapse. But it is preventable, and we do not have to be victims of the general ignorance of this harmonic principle!

**Your Life Is a Constant Invitation**

*Shudders.* Yes, it can happen to any of us. And it does happen more sleekly than we realize, more often than we'd like to know. Of course, for most of us, the influence does not stay beyond that flash of temper, that cruel thought, that jealous surge when we say something we dearly regret and hopefully do not go further than that.

Most of us catch ourselves and realize that nursing such a state of mind is not fun. Some are sensitive enough to physically feel the plunge in consciousness, the sickness at the pit of the stomach, the choking in the back of the throat. These are two areas where astral entities attach to our energy bodies. Most of us change our thoughts almost immediately and go back to a more positive state of mind, a general tone of upbeat attitude. We set down our glass of wine and say, okay, I've had enough now, or we consider that maybe eating chocolate for breakfast, lunch, and dinner, or drinking six cups of coffee a day might have been a bad idea.

Indulging in addictive substances or habits or prescriptions is another way to wear down your natural protection. When you choose to partake, you invite in the astral beings who wish to indulge but cannot. They're happy to join in your fun. If your habit is long-lasting or strongly pursued, so much the worse. Your personality changes noticeably under this astral influence, as their own personalities begin to dominate, or they may come to the fore only now and then.

If truth could be known, and visibly seen, many would throw down the addiction in question and never touch it again!

I just read a paragraph [of this post] to Joseph and he says to cue the creepy music! I feel like I'm writing a ghost story. Actually, I am.

But wait—the difference is that not *all* astral beings are evil, but not all are happy spiritual guardians or deceased relatives come to offer their assistance, either. And not all are lost souls: some love what they're doing; they thrive on playing mischief. (Remember the character in *Ghost,* the guy in the subway?) Some are worse than others; some are wonderful.

It's up to us to learn who is who, what is what, and to practice discernment when we choose our companions from the astral worlds, as we do when we choose life partners in our physical lives.

How do we choose when it seems as if we have no choice about who visits us in the dark of night? First we must know that *we do have choice*—we always have this choice. But putting a veil of protection, Christ Light, or whatever you choose all around you won't work if your thoughts—your energy beacons—are sending out a different message!

I was called by a friend the other day, querying for another friend who was being troubled by nighttime visitations of unwanted dark forces. How could she get rid of them, send them packing?

The answer is always the same: *We attract such things by our thoughts, by what we carry around in our minds during the day.*

A few questions on my part revealed that the woman in question had suffered a recent trauma, an injury in her immediate family that was devastating, both financially and emotionally, requiring her loved one to undergo repeated surgeries and draining bank accounts. She'd also taken up a nighttime drinking habit.

So no, it wasn't the "angels sent to her house by participation in a chain letter" who turned out to be "evil." It was rather a chain of thoughts and worries and emotions, following a sudden breakdown of her natural protective forces (her daily positive approach to life), that produced, shall we say, a gap in her back fence through which unwanted entities were raiding her life's storehouse. And she was continuing in her negative attitudes, which only fueled their intrusions further.

So how can we break a vicious circle of negative thinking, followed by negative astral chiming-in, further strengthening the dark and dour thoughts? Or influencing our behavior, as with the *Downton Abbey* character who portrayed the worst-case scenario for us?

For each of us, it's a different method, but we must change the channel of our thinking to a higher frequency.

### Discover Your Natural Protection

Changing the channel for some of us means putting our minds on the kind of endeavor that makes time disappear for us—you know, the thing you love doing so much, the hours zip by unnoticed.

For others who are more mentally nimble, perhaps they might succeed in an effort to stop every negative thought in its track and replace it with another perspective on the issue at hand.

Not that we should ever suppress our emotions! That invariably leads to other problems. But that we should refrain from carrying our mental baggage around hour after hour, sending out that radio beacon of negativity that only the worst of the worst thrive upon.

Be your happy, cheerful self. It really does pay off. This is the source of our natural protection. If the general frequency of your daily thoughts is high, no lower frequency can resonate in harmony with you, invading the peacefulness of your calm life. If you greet problems with a positive attitude, you're strengthening that protection while attracting all the positive forces in the universe into your private world.

Meanwhile, until you've mastered that, learn as much as you can about the myriad levels of consciousness existing in this sea of Infinite Intelligence in which we all swim together, linked and relinked by harmonic association. Learn how to steer your ship in and out of troubled waters, without taking on the sea monsters at the edge of the whirlpool of destruction!

Some advice if you're exploring that "law of attraction" that's become a popular catch-phrase: Check your motivations carefully if you're doing affirmations, chanting, meditating, or visualizing. Be scrupulously honest with yourself, because these set up one of those "wave-trains" of thought, sending a strong beacon into the universe that will be discerned, *not by the words you may use to color it*, but by the basic energy frequency at its root—by your unconscious motivations, in other words.

For instance, are you really trying to "manifest" something constructive for the benefit of others?

Or something personal you think you deserve?

Is it possible that you're unknowingly sending a very powerful message of *self-centeredness, self-interest, greed, ignorance*, or *acquisitiveness?* Are you ready for the individuals who share those attributes to come and share your life with you, following up on the invitation you've sent?

And when you pray, are you praying for selfish motivations? Or for the good of others?

Prayer, too, is a powerful tool of energy, a proven healing aid which can be used by the highest forces for good in our universe to add to their healing projections. But it can also be used for destruction if that is the *actual frequency* this earnest thought-form carries into the universe. And if you are sending destruction or harm, *a la* the voodoo practices of old, you will inevitably become the victim of your own foul intentions—like our sorry character in the wonderful *Downton Abbey* series!

Whom did you invite into your astral home today?
What channel have you streamed in?

Clingers-on. That's what my teacher Ruth Norman called astral entities who attach themselves to unsuspecting earth people. Maybe that's why the bad guys in *Star Trek* were aptly named Klingons? The series' visionary originator Gene Roddenberry was a very interdimensionally savvy communicator.

**Embrace Your Emotions—But Don't Marry Them!**

You've learned that whatever you carry in your Conscious Mind constitutes the nature or frequency of the radio beacon you project. And what travels back to you reflects this frequency signal you've personally designed.

So the simple solution to avoiding destructive influences in your life—whether astral or physical—is to maintain a positive, constructive state of mind at all times. Thus, you will ring in a positive, harmonious, constructive influence and aid from the higher realms of Consciousness—your own Superconscious, and all Those among your Cosmic CoAuthors to whom it helps you connect.

Hah! Again, it sounds so easy! But we are emotional creatures. We, at our present stage of evolution, are easy victims of our own wild reactions! And that's good—because these emotions are a vital part of our learning phase of development. We're learning about things we term *love* or *hate, affection* or *anger, compassion, empathy, guilt,* and *fear.* We need these things. And we need to express them.

Let me stop right here and elaborate on that last sentence: *We need to express our emotions.*

Many people get into trouble when they begin a spiritual course of study by trying to suppress their natural reactions and emotions, in order to appear as if they are winning the battle against their lower selves. And it is a battle! But it's one we've prepared ourselves to fight, and fight it we must.

Taking a long vacation with a life of silent abstinence, or relegating oneself to the hinterlands and avoiding human interaction for a lifetime—yes, we've probably all tried this if we're older souls. I certainly have! But it's merely a delaying tactic. Sooner or later we have to face our own demons, the ones we've unwittingly created for ourselves. And they come in many forms and disguises.

So don't rush off and start trying to *eliminate* anger, guilt, fear, and so on from your expressions. It's a very close distinction we're making: Don't pretend or ignore your feelings. Recognize them. Understand and forgive them. And then if necessary, turn your mind upward to seek out a better frequency with which to oscillate. Don't suppress, but *change* your thoughts if they veer into some dicey area! Never dwell in the subastral, because that's what you'll be oscillating in harmony with if you allow negative, destructive states of mind to perpetuate within your being.

Again, that does not mean repress. It also does not mean indulge, wallow, or prolong. It means feel it, know it, accept it, and *let it go.*

If you understand the principles of interdimensional communication we've been laying out for you, then you'll quickly grasp why you can't afford to carry on with some negative emotional state that's taken you over. With absolutely no lapse of time, you can ring in some "friends" from the subastral realms, following our principles of attraction, harmonics, and frequency. We call this the principle of obsession. Some people call it spirit possession.

For now, remember that this frequently undetected, subastral influence is as common among we humans as the higher-realm influences of the Advanced Minds with whom you might communicate. If we could see how many beings we are in connection with at any given time, or if we could see the subastral hordes clustered about our planet at present—whew. Good thing we know what to do to keep ourselves afloat, right?

At all times, you choose the frequency at which you are associating! You're choosing the astral company you keep by the nature of the thoughts you carry. YOU are in charge. No one can influence you whom you have not invited into your consciousness. But you will always have these influences working with or against you, because you are constantly communicating, *interdimensionally*.

Frightening? Not really. Not when you know about your interdimensional self and learn how it functions. It's actually the simplest thing in the world to maintain a higher roster of associations.

The only holdups and difficulties have to do with your past-life affinities, proclivities, associations, and habits. To use the now-popular term: your *karma*.

**Note:** While I was putting this chapter together, one neighbor a few feet beyond my window was using a jackhammer to remove a pool. Another crew was using a similarly loud, bone-jarring piece of heavy equipment to build a new patio for another neighbor, also a few feet away from my office. It sounded like a giant dentist's drill. They'd start, vary the pitch as they ground or mashed whatever, then stop. *Ahhh. I can think!* Then they'd start again.

This went on all afternoon like slow torture, vibrating the wall on my left and the bones in my knees and skull. Fortunately, I'd honed my writing focus as a journalist working in a cacophonous news room. But as five o'clock finally neared, I was ready to scream. So I went on Facebook to vent instead. (Letting off steam, especially with humor, is actually a helpful energy tactic, as long as no one gets hurt physically or emotionally!)

As soon as I'd articulated my frustration, I found these posts by two my of consciousness-savvy friends blaring at the top of my news feed.

**If you always speak of your troubles,
you will always have troubles to speak of.**
and
**Be thankful and stop complaining.**

You never know how your Cosmic CoAuthors might help you laugh at yourself! Actually, gratitude is a wonderful antidote to many unhappy and unfriendly emotions. It's a quick way to change your perspective, and hence, your frequency. So I laughingly came up with this:

"I'm grateful I am able to live in a place where my neighbors have sufficient funds to make their homes more beautiful!"

And you know what? I feel better, because although I was being sarcastic at first, it struck me as quite true when I said it aloud. In fact, I remembered other places I've been and seen, and I really am quite fortunate!

You see? I changed the channel (my perspective) and my frequency followed. I'll try to remember this tomorrow when we all get back to work on our respective projects, me and the jackhammer crews!

## Master Your Emotions

Do you have a pet emotional reaction or reactions that you'd like to get rid of? Let's say, a critical response to a particular individual, or a lingering anger that's not doing you any good?

Greater minds than ours have, throughout history, brought forth many ways to conquer destructive thought-habits. I recently found a chart for this kind of self-mastery in Benjamin Franklin's autobiography. I also filled out many such charts in past-life therapy workshops. Here's a simple version for you to try.

1. Using either your sketch or text journal, make a list of the destructive emotional habit or habits you want to counteract across the top of a page. If you can think of a counter-emotion, list it next to the culprit you'd like to dispense with.

2. Now in the space below, allow yourself a line for every day. You don't need to mark them, just make sure you've got room for at least a month's worth of days.

3. At the end of each day, go across the chart and make a mark for every emotion you've expressed that day, good or bad. If it's been more than once, make that mark a number indicating how many times. (Use more pages if necessary!)

4. If you've managed to convert an emotion into its positive counterpart through conscious effort that day, give yourself a gold star. Any day with gold stars deserves celebration and congratulations! Whether stickers, glitter, or gold pen, make it stand out as the important achievement it is!
(P.S. If you're only pretending to convert your anger into understanding, you're only cheating yourself and tricking your gullible Conscious Mind. Your psychic anatomy still records the truth.)

|           | Grief/Gratitude | Fear/Trust | Panic/Joy | Criticism/Praise | Anger/Understanding |
|-----------|-----------------|------------|-----------|------------------|---------------------|
| Monday    |                 |            |           |                  |                     |
| Tuesday   |                 |            |           |                  |                     |
| Wednesday |                 |            |           |                  |                     |
| Thursday  |                 |            |           |                  |                     |
| Friday    |                 |            |           |                  |                     |
| Saturday  |                 |            |           |                  |                     |
| Sunday    |                 |            |           |                  |                     |

Of course you can alter the chart's design to suit your taste; be as simple or elaborate as you like. The most important elements are to list and consider these emotional reactions, and to learn to take control by noticing when they erupt and doing something to counter them. Thinking back over them at the end of the day is also a very fruitful "back-tracking" habit, one you'll cultivate further as you get into other applications for it later in the book.

5. Keep up this chart for as long as you need to, or until it no longer serves the purpose. Even the cleverest technique can wear out. I've returned to this one occasionally over the past thirty-eight years and each time, I've found new reflexive emotions that I need to work on, or new variations on an old theme. Sometimes self-betterment is like trying to squeeze gel into a too-small container: soon as you get one side neatly closed off, some new goo emerges from the other side.

Eventually, however, you won't need the chart at all. You'll have trained yourself mentally to take countermeasures automatically, throughout your day. I can't tell you what a huge, positive difference this is going to make in your life! You'll soon see for yourself.

6. To take this further, learn a simple self-help form of the new energy psychology, such as Emotional Freedom Technique or EFT. Then apply it to any stubborn emotional reflexes. It takes mere moments to implement. I've listed resources for learning how in Appendix B. You might also want to apply it to elements of your life that you'll be listing in the next chapter's exercise.

Energy psychology tapping techniques, such as EFT, may seem weird and impossibly simple at first—until you experience their astounding effectiveness. Why do they work? Tapping creates a pulse, and your system communicates in energy pulses. Tapping acupuncture points sends a message straight to your brain, new research indicates. In Resources, I've listed an article by psychologist David Feinstein that delves further into the "how it works and why" aspect of energy psychology. This is a new healing technique still in its infancy, but traditionally trained therapists are taking notice of its rapid effectiveness with post-traumatic stress (PTSD) victims, and they're signing up to learn how to incorporate it into their practices. Fortunately, you don't need a degree to learn the self-help version! I use EFT on myself, and recently helped a young woman overcome a crippling, long-enduring phobia in less than half an hour with the same EFT you can learn for free: http://www.emofree.com/eft/eft-tutorial.html

*To become a Light Being,
you must first clear the darkness
from your mind.*

# 10

## What If Karma Has Other Ideas?

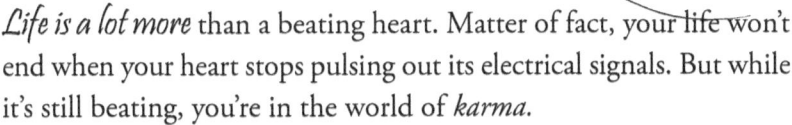

*Life is a lot more* than a beating heart. Matter of fact, your life won't end when your heart stops pulsing out its electrical signals. But while it's still beating, you're in the world of *karma*.

It's an old word, now made new and useful by the awakening consciousness of many people in both Western and Eastern cultures. They even made a TV show out of it. Joseph loved that show, *My Name Is Earl*. Every time poor Earl tried to do the right thing, or go back and make amends (like Step 9 in a 12-step program), things happened that he didn't expect to have happen. As Earl tries to explain later, "Karma had other ideas."

But Earl's concept of karma was a bit different than ours, somewhat limited. So let's define it clearly.

*Karma,* good or bad, is a word we'll be using to describe the energy impingements in your psychic anatomy, the ones that return to you again and again, in all future lifetimes, until and unless you do something to change them.

Okay, in truth every bit of energy in your psychic anatomy regenerates endlessly, carrying its little information imprint into all your future lives. Matter of fact, some of that energy is rebuilding your cells from scratch, right this minute. They don't mutate, they grow from scratch, following your DNA blueprint, which is powered by information from your psychic anatomy.

For instance, if you're average, you're building 46 billion new red blood cells alone every day! You even build new brain cells. You're 98% new at the end of the year, according to current science. So why do you age? It's a matter of spiritual progression: you need to die and discard that body, so its degeneration is all part of the plan being followed from your psychic anatomy when those cells start to rebuild in new ways that make you "age," gracefully or not. (Don't confuse age with illness, in other words.)

Often when we use this fancy word *karma,* you can pretty much guess we're talking about the bad stuff, the things you really don't want to reappear in this life or any future lifetime!

Energy is not destroyed, as Einstein proved. So unless you reshape it in some way, the design of that energy—the emotional content, the physical attributes, the events inscribed in your fourth-dimensional energy body (aka psychic anatomy) —will repeat its intelligence, flowing out into your present experience whenever it is triggered by some harmonic association with which you've oscillated.

## Why Earth?

If you're alive on the planet today, in addition to your personal agenda, and whether you are a pacifist or patriot, you are in the larger society gaining insight into the subjects of war, violence, poverty, wealth, politics, prejudice, disease, and religion. No matter where you stand on these subjects, you are storing up new information, making new determinations, adding to or subtracting from your karma.

You've come here specifically to learn everything you can about living a physical life. There are no right or wrong answers. But how you shape your ideas will determine how you live your future lives. You alone will make those choices, just as you alone can determine what experiences you need for your personal growth and development.

It's very popular right now to talk about the planet's vibration rising.

We don't have to wait for that presumed event, should it happen.

In our future, you and I are most likely to gravitate to a planet where we have a reason to be, one where we resonate in harmony with its existing frequency. That might be because we have karma to resolve in that environment! So even if Earth destroyed itself, or if it becomes a shimmeringly beautiful, higher astral world, we will still go to the place with which we've developed a relativity and will seek out opportunities to resolve our karmic issues with people, places, and things, wherever that might be. You can see the advantages of raising your personal frequency by resolving your karma with this planet and its people as soon as you can manage: you could graduate to lives in better places!

We can speculate about such things as, "But what if I have karma with planet Earth itself and someone blows it up?" Interesting thought—but one to take up with your spiritual mentors between lifetimes if you find yourself stuck in that situation. Truly, what we need to concern ourselves with right now is resolving what we've come here to resolve, this time around. It's usually the people, not the planet, that we're working out with, and we'll always find them. It's science!

**Your Interdimensional Biology**

In his ground-breaking book, *The Biology of Belief,* Bruce Lipton explains how quantum physics is radically changing our understanding of human biology at the atomic level, finally validating the vortical, interdimensional energy principles I first learned from Ernest Norman in the mid-1970s. Here's what Lipton wrote in 2005 about the new biology:

> *Quantum physicists discovered that the physical atoms are made up of vortices of energy that are constantly spinning and vibrating; each atom is like a wobbly spinning top that radiates energy. Because each atom has its own specific energy signature (wobble), assemblies of atoms (molecules) collectively radiate their own identifying patterns.*

*So every material structure in the universe, including you and me, radiates a unique energy signature."*

Sound familiar?

This was very exciting for me to read, because I've been living my life with this applied belief for the past four decades. That knowledge has transformed my life millions of times over into a profoundly richer, happier, and more satisfying state of being. It's wonderful to know that conventional biologists in the future will not regard Lipton's work as fringe science. He's got all the right credentials in genetic research, and he's a former Stanford medical school professor.

But it could be a slow process, as in the past, for this branch of science to turn itself upside down and rethink the entire theory of genetics, replacing its flaws with this new concept of the interdimensional exchange of energy-intelligence, into and out of our bodies. They'll also have to be willing to admit this to the public, and dismantle a lot of promises they made when promoting genetic theory, which is what Lipton calls biology's former "Central Dogma." You might also notice that a lot of medical procedures and drugs are still (literally) banking on out-dated genetic theory and your ignorance of the new biology. People making money from the old ways always slow down the adoption of new ways.

Thankfully, we don't have to wait for these individuals to catch up with us!

My greatest excitement right now is sharing with you the first practical applications of this new understanding. Or as Ernest Norman termed it, this universal, articulate, interdimensional understanding of science. The next few chapters will be all about how to use this information constructively in your own life. You will learn how informational vortices in your psychic anatomy that have been causing you trouble, perhaps for many thousands of lifetimes, can be rebuilt.

In the previous chapter, we talked about maintaining a positive attitude in order to determine (or "choose") to resonate with good things in your present circumstances. That's all well and good—until, like Earl, your personal karma "has other ideas!" Namely, the ideas you've imprinted in yourself.

Okay, time for an example. Don't try to get this all at once; we'll be going over it again in future chapters. Simply enjoy the tale for now.

**A Lost Traveler's Story**

Let's say you've climbed a mountain and lost your way and fallen victim to a sudden blizzard. You're cold, you're freezing, you're dying, you're dead. You're slipping out of your body into an astral world.

But all the time you were fading from life, while your body was slowly shutting down, you weren't going peacefully. On your mind for the entire mountain trip was a fight you'd had with someone you loved, perhaps a family member; perhaps a lover. You started out very angry. That's why you took off for the wilderness. And you brooded over the injustices that had been done to you. Perhaps your wife or girlfriend had cheated on you. Every step: brooding, angry, vengeful.

In this state of mind, as you now understand, you've lost what we refer to as your *attunement*. This is shorthand for "your mental frequency oscillating in a constructive harmony with a higher input—your own Superconscious and its higher affiliations." That's your positive attunement.

This is your inner GPS, frankly, and when you fall *out of tune* with it, you can become truly lost. Physically lost is only one part of the equation. You can become spiritually lost. You might spend an entire lifetime in this miserable state, or even lifetimes.

But for our example, let's say this individual has become temporarily lost, mentally, spiritually, and hence physically. He was no longer alert to the subtle warnings or directions stemming down into his inner knowing from his Superconscious. His spiritual guides and tutors were unable to reach him in that angry state of mind, because they don't oscillate at that low frequency. And they know this is how we learn: the hard way. They won't interfere.

At our stage of evolution, we are very stubborn creatures. It's best to let us go our way and find out, in most cases.

Of course, there are exceptions and circumstances when some kind of "rescue" seems to have been undertaken by spiritual agencies—and we've all heard those stories. You can bet the person involved had set up some kind of resonant consciousness that allowed that "rescue" to take place! Some overriding purpose or educational reasoning or self-developed situation lurks behind this apparent "miracle," probably something that's been in progress for lifetimes for that soul, because your Teachers from higher worlds won't otherwise interfere in your lessons. You would then have to come back and start all over again until you'd mastered them. And to these evolved Masters, life and death do not mean what they do to our current perspective.

From the non-physical perspective they see the big picture, much as we older souls can do while between lifetimes, when we can decide to set certain circumstances in motion if possible in order to bring about some kind of healing or completion of a soulic lesson. So any "miracle" or "rescue" is going to be a result of some joint agreement made long before between the individual and his spiritual mentors.

That's not to say we aren't constantly receiving input from our higher-world associates—if we pay attention, keep our consciousness clear and "attuned," listen to our inner guidance. Warnings, advice, insight—it all depends on the higher relationships you've developed.

But our lost traveler is right now doing the opposite.

He is dying all alone in a snowstorm, but even worse, he's dying angry, bitter, and vowing revenge. When his true Self awakens in a higher-frequency world—if he awakens at all; many don't become aware of higher-frequency surroundings, if they haven't developed at least some understanding about all this. But let's say he does awaken.

He may at first find himself in a dark and dismal, *subastral* state. It is a place of his own making, a frequency that resonates with what he's carried in his mind as he made his transition out of the physical dimension. Not pretty.

**Try, Try Again**

Now, depending on who this traveler is, in terms of spiritual development, he may or may not remain in that dark place during his sojourn between lives. From there, he might be drawn instantly back into any body he can resonate with comfortably enough to get born.

Since we don't want to go down that road with him, let's say instead that he's done a lot of work with himself over the sequence of many lives, and he has set up some course of spiritual development. He's lived many lifetimes with a plan for his steady growth and improvement. He's created a relationship with higher spiritual forces who can reach him now, in his time of need, as he flounders in the subastral worlds, and because of that, they can assist him.

(Remember, this is a soul who's done his homework; no one gets a free ride for long. However, his friends and family, if they know of his troubles, can assist by calling upon their own higher-astral connections in what many call "prayer" and their positive energies so directed might bring help to his side. But again, those are friends and family *he* has formed relationships with. See how the positive connections become vital at all levels?)

However they arrive, these knowledgeable, higher-dimensional helpers assist him in finding his way back, at the very least, to the astral "school" where he left off prior to his last physical incarnation. He goes back to his own level. If he's made a lot of progress toward his spiritual goals during that most recent incarnation, prior to getting lost in anger in the mountains, he might even find himself in a better situation to learn and grow faster, in one of the many spiritual universities designed to aid in this way. (See Resources for more about higher astral universities.)

But our traveler now has a self-created black hole of trouble in his energy storehouse that he needs to resolve. And he's the only one who can do it.

Eventually, after a lot of study and preparation, our traveler will reincarnate to clinch what he's learned about this situation during his time of reflection in the higher worlds. You can't count it as true growth until you've returned to a material dimension and tested and proven what you've learned between lives. (My novel *Cosmic Dancer* is all about this challenge.)

So our interdimensional traveler comes back to Earth, where his "karma" originated. Only in that place of origin can he resolve it, and until he does, he can't move on.

But he's got a plan. One part of that plan really isn't a choice: the interdimensional physics of energy will send him back into an encounter with his former life partner, the woman he was so angry at when he died. They'll be attracted like opposite magnetic poles. But what he can try to plan and prepare for is how he's going to deal with the situation when they meet again.

Now, technically, he might not meet her in his very next lifetime. Or he might. These are all variables that can occur with reincarnating souls. Things happen. Plan B becomes Plan C, D, E, and so on. There are all sorts of extenuating circumstances in the complicated relationships we form with one another. I didn't want you to think it's as cut-and-dried simple as my example needs to be. So bear with me on that.

Let's say they reincarnate in opposite genders again, only this time our traveler is the woman, and the former allegedly cheating wife is now the man. (We don't really know if she cheated, only that he thought she did. See? Extenuating circumstances.)

They meet, they feel an instant attraction to one another. It's a kind of electromagnetic attraction that has a lot to do with many past-life associations they carry within their psychic anatomies, but most of us call this "love at first sight."

This initial attraction can feel really good. Or it can feel, right from the beginning, fraught with some kind of undercurrent of emotional unease. Tense. Anxious. Fearful.

If it's the latter, this new "love" relationship doesn't bode well for a long-term involvement. If you've studied past lives for any length of time, you learn to recognize these signs. These two people have some kind of negative karma that might not be in play at the moment, but if the right trigger comes along—*bam!* They're going to find themselves flooded with all sorts of inexplicable, illogical, and unpleasant emotions.

For instance, our two love birds may decide to take a skiing vacation one sunny afternoon, fly off to some mountainous region, and as the snow falls and they should be snuggling by the fire—they fall instead into the worst argument of their lives together! Unfortunately for them, "karma had other ideas."

From that point on, their past-life emotions and experiences have been triggered. Without some form of recognition of the factors of the past that have entered into their lives, they are likely to keep fighting and arguing until they can no longer remain together. One or the other is going to "get off the teeter-totter" and walk away. Or they might stay and fight it out for years. Lifetimes. Or they might find some other slow and grinding way to "work it out" between them.

If they don't have access to the fastest, shortest way—direct knowledge of past lives—and they're really determined in their individual course of evolutionary growth, they're likely to seek out all sorts of counseling and/or self-help methods until they find something that helps, no matter how long that takes. (That is, if they're prepared for some improvement. We won't even talk about the folks who aren't. You can probably guess how their story would go.)

This is how most people "work out" their karma, by the way. The slow way. Trial and error. Willpower. Determination.

For instance, someone you've killed on a battlefield shows up in a future lifetime as your offspring, because you've forged a bond of energy-experience engraved in your psychic anatomies that will inevitably attract you to one another again. Only now, you learn how to love your (former) enemy simply by the nature of the parent-child relationship.

Going back to our story, to give our couple a happier ending, let's say they're privileged and fortunate to come across the kind of information contained in this book. With that insight, they're able to make quick work of discarding past-life, ego-based attitudes, and while they're at it, they resolve many other past-life traumas as they come around over the course of their relationship, as cycles of past experience shift in and out of phase with their present lives. It's a never-ending process, but a very fruitful one for these two. Everyone who meets them wonders what secret lies behind this glowing, happy couple's loving relationship.

Which reminds me again how fortunate I am to have such a relationship with a fellow student of life! But of course, I suffered through some very bad ones first in order to recognize the good one. As we all do! (See the next chapter for more on this subject.)

Meanwhile, let me elaborate on what I mean when I say, "as cycles of past experience shift in and out of phase with their present lives."

**Cyclic Replays**

There are infinite variations on the forms of karma we've incurred. There's also "good karma," but for healing purposes we don't focus on that. That's the stuff that makes us whole and loving and keeps us going in life! What we need to pay attention to is the "bad karma," the things that are interfering in our present life as they remanifest and take over our emotions, and even our physical circumstances.

Past-life energies come around cyclically to replay in our present lives. Not all at once, thankfully! But over time, what goes around, comes around. You can learn to identify the passing influences that reappear in your life.

I remember a past-life therapy student who was suddenly *in tune* with a life she'd lived as a very unhappy Chinese woman. The cycle had swung in. Eventually, she learned the details of the past lifetime and the trouble it carried into her present life, but until she'd done that homework and taken some measures to heal the old wound, she found herself suddenly wanting to paint the rooms in her house bright red—Chinese red. And her affinity with that culture was manifesting in other ways and choices she was making in her present life.

It might be that you suddenly want to eat a particular kind of food. Or dress a certain way. Or watch only British movies (me! guilty!). This can be evidence of your fondness for a particularly happy time in your evolutionary history, or it can be an indicator of a life that's coming to the forefront of your consciousness, albeit surreptitiously, because you've come to that time and cycle when you can "do something to work it out."

What do I mean by work it out? I mean resolve the old energy dilemma, dissolve and discharge the negative impact, shocks, traumas, and emotions of some past-life incident. I mean the application of your new knowledge of the principles of creative evolution.

But before we get into the healing of karmic impacts, let's go back to the last chapter for a moment.

We said that you can protect yourself from substral or destructive influences in your life by what you carry in your consciousness from hour to hour and day to day, i.e., by raising your frequency. But often what we're carrying are old energies from negative, past-life experiences. These energies live with us in the constant undercurrent of our lives. Some teachings refer to an aggregate of these destructive energies as the *lower self*. They oscillate at a lower-than-desirable frequency. Very often, they surface as roadblocks to progress. Or they might not surface, but remain hidden to your conscious awareness while they nevertheless send out their *beep beep* of energy-information into the universe and into your life.

Our lost traveler in the example above really only wanted to live a happy married life. But instead, he found himself involved in a big brouhaha with his mate—both times! When he was *he*, and when he came back as a *she*. His past-life experience, his own choices, were interfering in his evolutionary progress. That is, until he/she and she/he sat down and decided to free themselves from the old anger, jealousy, rage, and sorrow. Individually, they began the hard work of soulic, spiritual, mental, emotional growth and progress.

What did they give up in the process? Personal ego. To grow, you have to let go of something.

Matter of fact, our traveler wouldn't have needed his partner's acquiescence to free himself by changing his role in their conflict. He could have made great strides on his own initiative. This is one of the most important survival skills you can learn!

When a cycle of the past brings in some negative or destructive energy as it remanifests in your present lifetime, you can apply all that you know to counteract its influence. Simply understanding that this can occur, seemingly very suddenly, puts you way ahead of the individual who doesn't notice or sort this influence from the general miasma of daily consciousness. With your new knowledge, you can begin immediately to put it "out of phase" with the energies of your present life. How do you do that?

In each and every lifetime, we are presented with three things: past, present, and future.

We've already talked about the past swinging into phase with your present life. In that present, we are also a vessel for the Infinite Intelligence pouring into every moment through our Superconscious connections to it. Not only our past experience floods our present consciousness; so does this higher input. And in this present moment, we will determine our future by what we choose to align ourselves with and thereby, what we *regenerate* in the present moment.

Are you going to deepen the groove you dug in the past by repeating those thoughts, deeds, and feelings mindlessly, completely unaware that this is what you're doing?

Or are you going to select new choices and shape that old energy into something new and useful, drawing upon the Infinite Intelligence that is also available to you in your present moment?

You don't need to know about past lives to make small positive improvements in your present moment, of course. You do that every time you choose a constructive approach to your life. You are automatically turning aside the influx of old energies that are no longer valid in your life, and replacing them with new, fresh, meaningful elements of Infinite Intelligence, thus raising your frequency back up to a constructive level. Hopefully, this is how you always strive to live.

However, it's not always easy to turn aside a negative influx when "karma has other ideas." That is, unless you know what's actually occurring within your interdimensional self.

So let's look deeper, into a form of healing that is not superficial.

**What a Past-Life Energy Healing Feels Like**

Again, the three elements—past, present, and future—coincide at every second of your existence. That means that it's true what people say about living in the Now. That's the only place you have choice and control over your destiny. *Now* is when you decide.

And when you do, if you choose to change and improve—thereby initiating a very positive state of mind—you're going to ring in many healing harmonics from your highest resources, your Infinite Tutors, Advanced Beings, Higher Minds, Cosmic CoAuthors—whatever you want to call them. You might not be aware of this infinite connection. But if you are, so much the better because you'll be able to make the most of it.

If you've really extended an effort to grow and improve, then healing to the most advanced degree becomes possible. We're not talking about the alleviation of symptoms that often passes for "healing" on this planet. We mean the kind of healing that completely reconfigures the information in your psychic anatomy and serves you into all your future lifetimes. We're talking about full and lasting healing, such that you may no longer remember that a problem ever existed.

Here's how it works, in a rather simplified example:

The Minds with whom you've been working in the higher reaches of your Self can aid you in reconfiguring (healing) the past-life energy patterns impinged in your psychic anatomy. But it all depends on you: your acceptance of your role and responsibility for the past, and your willingness and ability to let this past go.

Past-life healing doesn't mean you will forget the important lessons involved in the past-life experience. That remains as part of your acquired Wisdom. But the damaging, destructive influence in your present and future lives is eliminated for all time. That is true, permanent healing.

Of course, you can always renege on your commitments to self-improvement. You can even reinstate the damage of past lives you thought you'd healed. Choice is always yours. But most of us are going to feel overwhelmed with gratitude, and use that new surge of positive energy to propel ourselves forward in our evolution—and quickly.

Let's use our lost traveler as an example of this form of healing.

Say he's chosen to let go of his anger, forgive past transgressions, and truly desires to replace his former small-minded prejudices and limitations with a more expanded, compassionate perspective. He's willing to give up the ego stance involved in these emotions. And he's formed a harmonic association with Advanced Mentalities who can help.

Now remember: He reincarnated as a woman, but we'll still call this soul *he* for clarity. He's been suffering the replay of this past during his present association with his former partner, only now the emotions are completely out of balance with the incidents they're presently living, meaning he's got anger way out of proportion to anything they've experienced in the present life. In addition, his blood pressure is high, he can't stand cold, etc. He's got inexplicable symptoms, in other words, that seem to bear no relationship to his present life. That's a major clue that the problem resides in a former incarnation(s).

So, knowing what he does about the energy science of reincarnation, he puts out a mental call for assistance. That's when the flashback appears.

His guides and teachers come to his aid. They project an image of his past-life experience into his mind, either during a dream state or, if he's really been studying and understands the entire principle of reincarnation, during his waking state.

Instantly, our now-stellar student of interdimensional science *recognizes* himself in the image, *accepts* it as a true past-life incident, and feels tremendous *remorse* for his actions.

Because of this change in his mind and attitude about the incident, *he's changed his frequency association to it,* and therefore his spiritual mentors are able to assist with their healing energy projections. This happens only because of his participation and acceptance, and because of their advanced development and skills in interdimensional healing. It's a mutual, previously agreed-upon endeavor.

Since our traveler's Superconscious Self is not yet developed sufficiently to create an equal and opposite energy configuration to reform the energies in his psychic anatomy by cancelling out certain waveforms of information residing there, these Advanced Beings project their Mind energies to perform this service for him. Again, this is all according to what his studies have earned for him in this very fruitful relationship with higher spiritual agencies, and according to preparation and agreements made before he reincarnated.

So the configuration of higher-dimensional energy-experience once encoded in his psychic anatomy is essentially reprogrammed with this assistance, and he is "healed" of the damaging effects this configuration had been creating in his present life.

The first impact of this higher-dimensional healing is often a sudden outburst of healing tears, which Ruth Norman referred to as a *releasement*. The negative energy compiled in the traveler's past is discharged through this reflexive crying—which, embarrassing as it might be, he can't seem to control. It just happened. After all, that energy cannot be destroyed, so it must be discharged from his psychic structures in some way and it radiates or ripples all the way down through the dimensions into this third dimension, where tears are one of those methods of energy release.

But the crying feels atypical, as you'll understand when and if you experience this kind of healing, or if you already have. It's not a "poor me" kind of crying at all, or even a joyous crying, but a distinct feeling of release, often accompanied by a sense of feeling deeply loved or recognized. A better way to put it might be the other way around: you recognize the higher forces surrounding you in Infinite Love. You *f-e-e-l* God/Allah/Infinite Intelligence. You KNOW it deeply, in the fibers of your being.

And any moment that you feel such an exalted thing is a moment that you're logging some new information into your Superconscious Self. You've grown as a soulic being.

By the way, laughter can sometimes perform an energy release during healing, but my observation is that it's more often tears that signal the deepest healing. And it can happen suddenly—without preamble. It happened to me once while watching the opening scenes of a Disney film set in Africa; tears and a story from my past came to me all at once in the (thankfully) darkened movie theater, as I released an old grief I didn't know until that moment that I'd been carrying.

The sudden tears and strong feelings are now familiar experiences. They let me know that I am healing some old, past-life issue. Oddly enough, I don't always know the details of what I am healing; it's not always necessary. I've got plenty of old stored-up info that's in need of improvement! I'm grateful to know that I've knocked another chip off the past-life cement clogging up my inner self. It might be as simple as hearing a story that triggers a new sense of compassion, which replaces old prejudice or ignorance. Here's where laughter as well can signify healing, especially if it's some unknown aspect of one of your old selves that you now find amusing, since your consciousness and perspectives have evolved since back in the day, whenever that might have been.

For our traveler, in addition to the conflict with his partner evaporating—seemingly overnight after this healing experience—now his high blood pressure, fear of cold, and any number of other manifestations of this negative, past-life replay also fall away. Instantly. And they will not return in future lives, unless for some ego-reason he reneges and falls back into his old habits.

I should point out that our traveler had so much trouble with this particular past-life incident because of the intensity of the self-generated, negative emotions he'd harbored while he lay dying.

So up until this healing moment, which technically required a lot of preparation between lives and could take place only at the right junction of interdimensional energies or *cycles,* up until that "instantaneous" but long-worked-for healing, our traveler was experiencing a miserable time with his life partner. But now, he's changed. And change made in this assisted way has caused him to make a huge, progressive leap in his evolutionary development. He may have saved himself hundreds of lifetimes, versus progressing in the slow, usual way.

Now he no longer oscillates with that shared past-life experience, which he and his partner had been regenerating through their numerous arguments. He's broken the electrical circuit running between them by this change he's made, and without that closed-circuit oscillation, they can no longer replay the old pattern. He doesn't even have to say a word to her about his past-life flashback. Suddenly, their relationship takes an upswing! A more loving feeling replaces the old subterranean anger and accusations.

His partner feels this change and responds positively to it. Once again, they feel like lovebirds. Only this time, it might stick. And their happiness was hard-earned in the fires of life experience.

Moreover, they're likely to treasure the harmony they've found because they worked hard for it.

Our traveler will retain the wisdom gained from his previous missteps. Perhaps his partner will gain a similar perspective, even if she's not fully aware of their past-life encounter. (Although, if she's ready and prepared, hearing about it might launch her own speeded-up journey to a greater Intelligence.)

Together, as a resonating unit, they can travel further and faster in their evolutionary progress, so long as they are supporting the positive inclinations in one another. It's another energy principle—one we've already discussed—this notion of *polarity*. It functions in relationships as surely as it does in electrical circuits. It's so important, we're going to devote an entire chapter to it.

# Chart Your Cycles

No, no, not those cycles, ladies. But seriously, do you need more proof that we're cyclic beings? Even men's lives function in cyclic patterns. And then of course, there's the biggest cycle of all: birth, growth, decline, death, rebirth.

For this exercise, you're going to chart the past-life energies that come into play in your life cyclically. How can you do that if you don't know about your past lives? Easily enough. (Again I give credit to *The Infinite Concept of Cosmic Creation* for this exercise.)

1. First, make a list of the very best things that have happened to you throughout your life, beginning in childhood.

2. Now list all the bad things that have happened to you throughout your life. Wherever possible, give a year or date, as accurately as you can, for both the good things and the bad things. If you don't know for sure, estimate. (Don't fear calling a thing "bad;" you'll distill the benefits later, but it *felt* bad didn't it?)

3. Do you notice a pattern? For instance, do these events come and go in 3-year or 7-year cycles? Or shorter or longer? See if you can identify cycles of events occurring in any pattern in your life. (Use EFT for any lingering traumas or fear.)

4. Now list your affinities—things you really like or that have drawn your interest or even passion since childhood.

5. You guessed it: Now list all the things that repulse or turn you off, throughout your life since childhood.

6. Make a separate list, or highlight in your main list, the things for which you have a *current* affinity or dislike, and make another list of your current fears. Can you find any patterns?

8. Soon enough, you'll be using these clues to identify specific

past-life associations. Be sure to write down anything that comes to mind now in your journal—you may think you'll be able to hold it in your mind, but you probably won't.

You might not realize that, when you read this book or do these exercises, you're not in your usual state of consciousness. You've actually elevated your frequency somewhat. When you return to your usual state of mind, a lower frequency, it's hard to remember (or believe!) what you've experienced in that higher-frequency level of attunement. So writing it down solidifies or crystallizes or *polarizes* it at your usual frequency, and provides a later reference you'll want to have. This is why you'll find me urging you to capture thoughts and insights and psychisms in your journal before you lose them.

Over time, you will experience higher and higher "ordinary" states of frequency if you continue in these studies. Proof of your progress! But the relative differences may remain between "elevated" and "ordinary" for a little further into your future. We've got a lot to learn and far to go to develop our interdimensional, *infinite* understanding. (Is that even possible to gain, or is it an oxymoron, I wonder?)

Since we have so far to go, we can always benefit from temporary boosts of frequency into a higher level than our usual state of consciousness, even if we're not able to maintain that elevation for more than brief periods—yet. By seeking out these transcendent experiences through study or contact with those more advanced than you, you are preparing yourself for your future lives lived in higher dimensions. Think of it as a kind of Olympic training for your Consciousness, where you'll keep breaking the record of your previous personal best.

# 11

## Building Polarity Relationships

*Twin flames, biunes, soul mates*—*everybody* wants to meet theirs. From an interdimensional perspective, I believe these advanced expressions of polarity relationship are beyond our full understanding until we reach a higher level of mental development. I know; I know; they're very popular to daydream about. But you can learn how to recognize and create relationships *right now* that will serve your needs in this and future lifetimes. Soul mates are, in practical terms, a type of *polarity relationship*.

Polarity relationships develop in exactly the way my lost traveler experienced: by working out karma with another human being. In your present lifetime, you may meet people with whom you've already done some of this work. But you also have the opportunity to build new polarity relationships for the future, and improve on the ones you have!

When you long for a soul mate, what you really want is a *polarity*, someone whom you've known for many lifetimes, with whom you've done the hard work of self-improvement through trial and error and a cavalcade of relationships. Maybe over lifetimes you've been:

friends
enemies
brother/sister

parent/child
boy/girl
man/woman
rivals
boss/employee
soldiers
co-workers
siblings again
master/slave
business partners
spouses
twins
and so on.

Energy Medicine pioneers Donna Eden and David Feinstein use their polarity power to educate and heal the world, "one person at a time."

In any of these associations, you've learned how to respect and care for one another from new angles, through different challenges.

Not with all, but with some of these individuals—those with whom you share aspirations and goals—you may develop a relativity that's easy to detect in subsequent lives. You share common interests. You're walking parallel paths. You understand and know each other so well because you've shared a long history of past-life experience. Your relationship may go back hundreds of lives! And you now treat one another as equals, a give-and-take achievable because of your unspoken understanding born of these many experiences, both "good" and "bad."

It's true that such relationships bring great spiritual and even physical benefits into your life, so our longing for a "soul mate" isn't out of order. But polarity relationships show up, not only between love partners or "soul mates," but in the most unexpected situations.

Take another look at that list above. Do you have someone in your life, maybe in your family, or a friend, with whom you share this kind of *simpatico*? Or with whom you've been building it? If so, count yourself fortunate and treasure every moment of your time together! Keep improving on that connection! If not, start now to build these positive oscillations in your interactions with others.

*Why?*

Polarity relationships can help you reach warp drive in your quest for spiritual development.

Energetically, two people traveling a parallel path through life and oscillating in this give-and-take polarity can step up the electromotive force (voltage or EMF) between them, similar to the way an electronic coupling transformer makes microphones and power transmissions possible. We, too, are electrical devices, capable of receiving, storing, and retransmitting energy. So when two individuals get together and pass that energy back and forth between them in an equal give-and-take—the same way energy travels between any plus and minus electrical polarity—both individuals will benefit from this phenomenon. It gives them a storehouse of usable energy that builds up between them, which they can and will draw upon in times of need. And it extends their reach and influence more than twice what they might accomplish individually.

Remember, energy is intelligence! Such well-matched individuals support one another in this energetic fashion *without lifting a finger physically*, by the very design of their shared and traded energies.

Of course, it may be a while into Earth's future before you'll find either a biologist or an electronics engineer who can fluently discuss this phenomenon between human beings. My initial learning resource for this subject and that of soul mates and biunes was, again, the books of Ernest Norman. Applying what I'd read, I soon discovered these relationships in my own life.

Much later, I learned how to demonstrate this electrical exchange between two human beings, using tools of Eden Energy Medicine.

**A Polarity Demonstration**

In our introductory *Energize!* classes, Joseph and I would choose two volunteers, making sure that one of them was looking fairly tired and weak (we'll call her Megan), while the other, Emily, was radiating a strong energetic field.

We'd have Emily and Megan stand side by side, but about a foot apart. So that the class could see the difference between them, we'd perform a simple muscle-test on each one's arm, demonstrating that one was weak (Megan, who couldn't hold up her arm) and the other strong (Emily, holding firm).

A muscle test, or applied kinesiology, demonstrates whether or not energy is flowing to and through the muscles in question; hence some people call it an energy test, which is more accurate. In this case, we were testing an extended arm, usually used as a general test of overall energetic strength or well-being.

Next, we'd ask our volunteers to hold hands while we muscle tested each of them again.

*Bam!* The strong one instantly became weak, while the weak one became strong!

In other words, the positive polarity (Emily, the strong individual) flowed her surplus of energy to the deficient negative polarity (Megan, the weak individual), like the water flowing into the empty glass in our illustration in Chapter 7.

At this point, we'd ask our volunteers to stop holding hands.

I'm going to guess that since you're an avid student of spiritual studies and esoteric teachings, you've experienced the kind of depletion that happens when you meet up with someone you might describe as "needy." You go away feeling tired and drained, right? You might even avoid some people who always make you feel this way, am I correct?

But if you remained in that person's energy field, here's what might have happened:

We would next ask our two volunteers to hold hands again, only this time we'd let them remain that way for a few moments longer. Then we'd muscle test again.

*Voilà!* Both would now test strong!

What happened?

The negative polarity, Megan, became charged by her partner Emily's strong energies, and thus Megan became the positive polarity as soon as Emily became the weak one. So, since energy never stops moving, that charge moved back to the first volunteer, Emily, charging her up again. A few moments of this back-and-forth, *polarity exchange,* from positive pole to negative pole and back again, and both volunteers were strengthened!

By working together, or rather by allowing their energies to oscillate back and forth, they had *stepped up* the EMF charge between them, and then both had a pool of energy from which to derive strength. They did nothing to achieve this other than to allow their personal, *interdimensional* energy systems to connect, with a shared motivation, goal, and alignment because of their mutual positions as students eager to learn in a class setting. How long this charged-up condition would last once they parted would depend upon each individual. We all encounter a million-zillion things every day that take our energy away from us—but it depends on us how fast and efficiently we *recharge* ourselves. The more resources we have for accessing this recharging energy from a positive pole, the better off we are.

This is why a long-lasting polarity partnership can become so valuable, allowing both parties to accomplish far more in their lives than either could have achieved alone. Now don't despair if you think you don't have such a partner. You have your present reasons, and besides, you actually have many opportunities to build such relationships!

**Your Many Polarities**

You've felt it, haven't you? With at least one other person in your life, male or female, friend or family? Co-worker? Study partner? Fellow musician? I hope so!

We commonly and instinctively express it as, "Two minds are better than one." Indeed. And it can happen between any two people, even those you do not intend to spend your life with. It might not last more than a few moments, or days, or years, but I believe we all experience momentary previews of what we have to look forward to in our future lives in terms of productive polarity relationships.

One day, we'll function as polarities with many people at once, as my Cosmic CoAuthors do.

Matter of fact, when I serve as their amanuensis, I am serving in a polarity relationship with them—only this is a temporary one where I am the negative polarity, receiving input from their combined positive polarity. Instead of sending this energy-intelligence back to them, when I become charged with this energy, I write or speak it, thus passing it along to other "negative polarities," i.e. the people who will be my audience. My audience, in turn, may radiate it back to me, and/or out to others.

The energy never dies, and never rests.

In fact, this is how energy is transduced down through dimensions and moved along among us. Eventually, it passes back up into the higher dimensions, never ceasing in its movement from pole to pole.

As you can see, the applications of this polarity principle among human beings are endless.

I have always looked back fondly on my years as a musician playing in an orchestra, where the joyous resonance of multiple, harmonically attuned individuals working as polarities to create art gives one an almost palpable ecstasy. At least it always did for me! Unfortunately, at my high school level we didn't often hit that precise alignment of electrical connection (which audiences would hear as beautiful music)— but when we did, it was magical! (No, no, Lianne—it was *science!*)

My next experience of the joy of polarity exchange was as an undergraduate theater major, again working with others to create art. When we hit the right alignment, we felt that thrilling upliftment, as the creative energy charges flowing back and forth among us would reach a fever pitch, hopefully in time for opening night!

Again in later years, I felt it working in other group creative endeavors where we shared a mutual goal, with that elusive elixir of polarity connection driving us on. If we were lucky, we'd feel it for a few hours or so, all total. Even so, it's enough to keep many people seeking after it by making such group endeavors their career.

I've always wanted to savor this on a film set—or at least the kind of highly-charged artistic atmosphere that must exist where a core group of the most brilliant director, actors, and artisans are collaborating peaceably together, pinging off one another. The more successful they are at achieving this kind of harmonious oscillation, the more we spectators savor their output. How many great directors of music, film, or theater have you heard crediting their ensemble for making the stellar height of their achievements possible? Those who work in a give-and-take, constructive polarity, sharing a common goal, manage to create works that surpass that other sort of group endeavor: the kind that's fraught with ego conflict.

Perhaps you've experienced the ups and downs of polarity exchange in groups you've tried to work with? Studies have even been done to prove that "one bad apple" really does spoil the bunch! One negative voice in a group project can bring down the entire ensemble, social scientists have demonstrated. On the other hand, a strong positive leader can draw up everyone else who's willing to match a higher frequency level, and from there, the polarity exchange can bring the whole higher than it could have reached as individual parts.

In fact, I recently read an inspiring book about such an endeavor, a project to build and race a solar-powered car across the Australian Outback, launched by a man who saw it in a vision and made it come true with the help of many human polarities. It's a great, heart-thumping story of vision, courage, determination, and teamwork, and I'll list it in my Resources.

*Okay, then, so what about the world's great solitary artists, builders, or other achievers in this world?*

If you look into their biographies, you can very often detect at least two polarities who work with them: (1) their Cosmic CoCreators, whom they might not mention depending on the social climate in which they lived on Earth, and (2) an individual in the physical world who serves as a kind of anchor or stability—their physical polarity.

Often that physical polarity fills the "missing" pieces in their abilities, or sees to needs that might otherwise have been neglected while the luminary spends so much time in a highly-elevated frequency exchange with his or her Cosmic CoAuthors. In these cases, the two physical individuals may indeed be soul mates, highly-developed polarities fulfilling a plan agreed upon long before their birth.

For Walt Disney, one of my favorite visionary heroes, his wife may have served as one physical polarity, but he also benefitted from a mutually supportive polarity with his brother Roy. Walt dreamed; Roy handled the business. All of Walt's animators and others worked as polarities with him, and yet you can see that very special sibling relationship furthering their accomplishments in ways that hint of soul mates, a very highly developed polarity relationship.

Particularly with those who bring through work of great importance for the upliftment of humanity, if you look, you'll find soul mates and polarities at work.

Another interesting example is Leonardo da Vinci, one of our greatest visionaries. Do you know why he wouldn't part with his slowly-created masterpiece, the *Mona Lisa*, during his lifetime? And why she is still such a mystery? Recent computer comparisons have shown that the image lines up as the reverse or opposite of his own self-portrait—opposite, as in *polarity*. He recreated her in paint because my Cosmic CoAuthors tell me that his polarity remained in the higher worlds during the Earth incarnation of this Advanced Master in order to support him from the very highest of frequencies.

This is often the case when the two souls have reached this high level of mental and spiritual development and are working together for the advancement of humanity.

Look into anyone's life whose achievements you honor and see if you can find the polarity(ies) working behind the scenes.

**Fill Your Treasure Chest**

If you're fortunate to meet someone with whom you've already done some of the hard work of developing this kind of harmony in preparation for a love-partner relationship in this lifetime, you'll know. You may have recognized one another immediately, but I also know several who didn't allow themselves this recognition until the time for them to join together was right. That includes Joseph and me, because he was too young!

Amazing how we can veil these things, working through our Superconscious Selves, when the life plan we've made requires it. But when our higher selves determined the time was right, we looked into each other's eyes, saw the familiar soul standing opposite, and there's been no turning back, lo these twenty-four years and counting!

If you haven't yet met a true polarity, whether lover or friend or family member, then know that you have the opportunity to build these relationships right now, with both men and women associates. Work on it. The hard effort of mastering your emotions and your thoughts will pay off many times over—even in your present lifetime! While you're waiting for that "perfect" mate to come along, you can be busy creating positive relationships with everyone you meet.

How to do this?

✳ Make sure you keep a balance of give and take.

✳ Learn how to listen to others.

* Learn to stand up for your right to speak, as well.

* Practice compromise where warranted.

* Flee from abuse.

* Value those who treat you with respect.

* Respect those you value.

* Share your skills.

* Seek out those who can teach you new ones.

* Think of others—but don't neglect yourself.

My Cosmic CoAuthors once told me, "Share the fruits from your tree of life, but never give away the whole tree."

A word of caution: It's easy to mistake the feeling that draws us to someone with whom we share *unresolved* past-life karma for the true oscillation of a positive polarity. Knowing someone in prior lives doesn't necessarily promise a happy relationship in the present lifetime, but negative karma can draw us to others with a powerful, magnetic force. You might think it's love, when it's only karma you've come together to resolve!

The nature of your relationships will depend on what you've already worked out with this individual in previous lives, or what you will work out together as time passes and you apply what you're currently learning, to rectify imbalances that will inevitably crop up.

Will it become a loving relationship? Or will the relationship evaporate as soon as the karma is resolved? Or will one or the other of you determine that the only solution is to walk away? Once karmic imbalances are rectified, will you become a happily-ever-after story? It's all up to you!

Sometimes, once you've resolved your reasons for being drawn together, you'll find that separate goals send you off in different directions. You've served one another as polarities for a time, but that time was short. Still, if all goes well, you'll both have grown from the experience.

What makes a couple stay together when the fires of karmic conflict are put out? A common goal and purpose is the most likely reason, usually connected to each individual's personal evolutionary plan of development.

Polarity relationships aren't made in heaven; they're made right here on earth, with every move you make toward and with other human beings. They're like a positive bank balance for your future, relationships you'll draw upon to sustain and nurture one another's positive endeavors!

∞ ❋ ∞

## Realize Your Best Relationships

1. Write about any relationships currently troubling you. How can you improve your give-and-take? Is anyone taking more than giving? Giving more than taking? Do you share common goals and aspirations? It's difficult to serve as polarities, supporting one another's objectives, when those objectives are not in alignment. If not, you may not find lasting polarity with this individual.

2. Keep notes about how you feel whenever you encounter the person in question for the next week or two. Take note of any changes that occur as you apply what you've learned

about polarity.

3. Write down any clues to possible past-life connections with the person or people in question. Don't try to draw conclusions with your Conscious Mind, merely record what comes to you, if anything. Don't worry if nothing does.

4. Step back from the current scenario and consider the generics: What's the nature of your relationship? What's the setting where you encounter one another? Is there any hidden theme you can detect? What are the hidden, unspoken emotions, if any—your own or the other person's. Of course, you can only know your own self for certain, but guessing the other's emotions or thoughts will tell you a lot more about yourself than it will about them!

5. Apply the mirror principle: what you see in another is generally true of yourself. However, don't get caught in this psychological tangle to such an extent that you fail to identify true harm coming your way. (I've seen that happen!) In other words, don't take on blame. No one's to blame if you view all relationships in terms of their continuity from one life to the next. See if you can find the roots of your current imbalance.

6. Know when to walk away. We've now given you a few more scientific tools for regarding your relationships as energetic exchanges. If the exchange is broken, beyond repair and/or without benefit to one or both of you, your higher self will let you know when it's time to break free. I'm reminded of that old Simon & Garfunkel song, "Fifty Ways to Leave Your Lover:" *Just step out the back, Jack. Make a new plan, Stan. And get yourself free!*

# 12

## Who Was I?

*I'm pretty sure that when* people ask me how they can find out who they were in their past lives, they're not expecting the boring reply that: *Who you are now is the sum and total of who you were.* You want a story. Hopefully a better story than the one you're living now!

That's one reason I wrote *Cosmic Dancer.* It's a safe way to explore the concepts of life after life, without the pain and suffering of confronting your own history. It's a story. It takes you into the higher worlds for a look at the beautiful experiences of an older soul between lifetimes, and for a lot of people, it jogs memories of their own sojourns there. But it still hasn't answered the question.

If you want to know who you were, just look in the mirror.

Ah, but the mirror changes, doesn't it? You're not as static as you might think.

One day, *Beautiful.*

Next day, *Who is that?!*

Another day, *Eh, not so bad.*

And yet another, *Hey, pretty good-looking!*

Or, sadly, day after day, everything looks wrong to you.

And sometimes, or at least for me, you look at a part of you, maybe a hand or a face or a finger, and you think, *Gosh, that's a really, really weird bit of flesh. Do I really live inside that???*

It might only last for a flash, but some part of your mind is registering that you are NOT that body. However, you are responsible for its electronic configurations, which are manifesting as flesh and bone. Oh sure, your parents got involved in the design of the flesh-body, but at your stage of human evolution the biggest influence is you. Especially the influence over the day-to-day differences you detect.

We've already talked about the choices you make in the nano-blips of life. They contribute to what you see. But deeper down, your past lives are showing up in that face. Not that you look identical to the way you've looked in other lifetimes, necessarily, but that you carry certain imprints of prior incarnations.

Some people carry these imprints literally: scars, birthmarks, dents, and deformities. And there are cases of people who do look something like they did in prior lives. Here's an example you'll find on my Pinterest page, on the Reincarnation board: http://pinterest.com/liannedowney/reincarnation/

But experience is constantly updating us, so you're not likely to be identical to your former self. Even the changes in environment, culture, diet, parentage, and work you've done with yourself between lifetimes are going to make a difference.

So let's look beyond the mirror to the external circumstances of your present life. That's where you're going to find the biggest clues:

Proclivities
Affinities
Animosities
Deformities
Weak in the knees
It makes you sneeze
And so on...

Strong emotional reactions are your biggest, easiest clue to your past-life history. But physical reactions (weak in the knees, deformities, it makes you sneeze) are also often a result of, not only present-life, but past-life experiences.

**Sometimes It Sneaks Up on You**

I recently received a new book I'd ordered about strength-training for women and it reminds me of an example from my own life.

Joseph talked me into joining a gym about ten years ago. I'd never done this kind of exercise. In school, one of my *proclivities* was toward music, so I never had to take a physical education class because I was always in the marching band. (Nice rule, that one.) Later in life, my workouts always involved some form of dancing, another of my *affinities*. Or outdoor activities such as canoeing or hiking.

So I had an instinctive *animosity* toward weight-lifting and all that sort of "macho, sweaty, unladylike" endeavor (in my humble opinion). But the gym salesman finally convinced me when he asked, "But Mrs. Downey, wouldn't you like to see your husband benefit from this?" as he glanced pointedly around the gym. Hmmm. Sold.

I maintained my nose-wrinkling resistance right up until we got into that gym, with the eager young woman who was to be our trainer. She was fresh out of college. She carefully measured our body fat percentages and we headed out for the heavy equipment.

All around us, to my horror, were humongous body-builders, grunting, sweating, flashing massive physiques and staring at themselves in mirrors. I'd never seen this kind of activity up-close and personally. My worst nightmare. And also, part of my past-life trigger.

The minute I started picking up those weights or pulling or pushing on those machines, something I'd never known about myself kicked in. I started to *compete* with Joseph, who'd done weight-lifting in high school! Me—five foot two and a half inches and still a girly kind of girl. (That was before I grew another inch taller at the age of fifty.)

Hold everything. I must interrupt my story there because real-life has taken over. Now would be a great time to caution you not to make the mistake I've just made!

### **** WARNING ****

**Let my forthcoming example be a warning to you! Past lives are nothing to fool around with!**

When I typed that last paragraph and quit writing for the day, I had no idea that within hours the reattunement would send me on an emergency trip to the ophthalmologist. But I should have known.

**Past-life energies are a part of your life-force now. You draw from them every second of every day. In a sense, they ARE your life. And they are as real and powerful as a cement truck heading straight for you on the freeway. If they contain destructive information, they can be, not only dangerous to your health, but downright deadly.**

## DO NOT INTENTIONALLY RE-ALIGN YOUR CONSCIOUSNESS TO A PAST LIFETIME WITHOUT PROPER PREPARATION AND KNOWLEDGE!

And even if you are knowledgeable (or think you are), don't take yourself back unless you have a very good, therapeutic reason for doing so.

I know how eager you are to know who you were. But it's not a subject to toy with. Fortunately this book will give you some of that protective knowledge and preparation mentioned in my warning. Nevertheless, you know the horror movies where the character is going down a dark corridor and reaches to open the door to the mysterious chamber and you're hollering, "Don't do it!!" Well, that's what I want you to picture while I tell you what just happened to me.

According to my Cosmic Coauthors, every day, millions die as particular past-life circumstances replay in their present lives. You're going to die eventually, right? So that's a great opportunity to work out extremely challenging karma. Many souls *plan* to use that opportunity when the time comes, while others may be *compelled* to relive a prior death by the principles of energy that bring those pasts back into phase, thus unleashing their full impact on the present life.

In an evolutionary perspective, death is simply a part of your journey, a very useful, persuasive, and instructive one. Still, you don't want to hasten it by unwisely directing your mind back to prior deaths *unless you have extremely good reasons to do so, and you understand how to put the past back out of phase before anyone gets hurt.* Or unless it's time to die again.

Even hypnotic regressions are a particularly dangerous undertaking, for all that they've provided this planet with some much-needed introduction to the science of reincarnation. [My Cosmic Coauthors elaborate on that in Chapter 18.]

Fortunately for me, I've already been through the past-life cycle of experience I'm going to talk about now. Several times in my present life I've crossed paths with it, and my studies of past-life therapy helped me through so that some healing has already occurred. Otherwise, I might have completely lost sight in my left eye yesterday.

Here's what happened:

**Revisiting the Past**

When I agreed to co-author this book, I didn't realize we'd be using my examples *real time!* No sooner had I written that paragraph about competing with Joseph in the gym than I had to quit writing for the day. But as we drove off for a dinner and shopping date, my mind was still on the story I was about to tell you, tracing back into all the ways this particular past had revealed itself to me, and how it had repeated at different cycles of time, years apart, manifesting in different ways.

In other words, my Conscious Mind was oscillating *in phase* with the past-life I'm about to describe. And I put my thoughts there on purpose.

*Danger! Danger! Duh, Lianne! You should know better!* —especially when physical injury is a factor in the past lifetime, and has manifested in subsequent *relivings* of it.

Remember how we diagrammed a circle as the way in which energy manifests in higher dimensions, with no separations of time and space? This is how past-life energies reside in your psychic anatomy: in timeless, vortical patterns complex with information. Intersect anywhere on those circles of experience and you are immediately in contact with every other part of the circle. (Remember the burrito metaphor?) My thoughts were the point of intersection, my alignment or *attunement* to my past.

When these energies ring in harmonically, oscillating into your present life, they are as real and immediate as if no time whatsoever has passed. The energy is timeless. If you've been on a progressive course of self-development, however, what has hopefully changed, or at least shifted slightly, is *your relationship to that past.* This shift could come about as a result of changes in your consciousness and perspective, i.e. healing, education, and self-improvement undertaken since the original incident, both in earth lives and in between those lives in higher worlds. (If your association to the past hasn't yet shifted, some healing work is in order!)

In all cases, you must remember that past-life energies, even experiences that were wonderful when they first occurred, are now by their nature regressive impulses in relationship to your present lifetime. Not to worry—you are constantly dealing with this influx from your past lives unconsciously, and generally, you are handling them quite well, either reshaping them into something more constructive, or enhancing your previous experience with new input from the present. But as we discussed in the last chapter, sometimes that's not so easy, depending on what seeds you've sown and how constructive or destructive those old energies may be.

In this instance, because I've been through several relivings of this particular past-life cycle for therapeutic reasons, my relationship to this past has changed just enough so that I avoided the full impact of the original destructive energy yesterday.

This will make more sense as I explain, but for the benefit of your learning and practice at *back-tracking*, an essential tool in past-life therapy, I'm going to tell the story backwards, to parallel the experience you'll have as your own relivings manifest in your life. I will demonstrate how I've back-tracked to draw all the lines of connection, and to mine for clues in order to determine what past has come into phase with my present life, bringing along all my old baggage.

Along the way, because of my attunement with Cosmic CoAuthors while working on this book, I have benefitted from subtle hints and insights from them as well. These are usually so subtle, they seem as if they are your own thoughts. But I've had so much beneficial experience with them over the past thirty-eight years that I've learned to recognize and give credence to their influence. They help me put two and two together, you might say. And sometimes they come right in and spell it out for me. I can now see that this is one of the past lives I prepared myself to deal with before my present incarnation. I knew it would come back around, with all its destructive influence, yet I knew I would have an opportunity to *rectify* those energy configurations stored in my psychic anatomy if I stayed in tune with my Cosmic CoAuthors. I knew I would be able to bring about some healing for myself, and at least one of my victims.

**Tch, You Opened the Door!**

Last night after I typed that paragraph and closed the file, Joseph and I went out to dinner, then drove to a nearby Trader Joe's market. When I stepped through the front door, within moments my left eye was suffused with bright rings of light and scattered black splotches. Flashers and floaters.

At first, I thought it was the fluorescent lights reflecting on my contact lenses because the flash kept spinning around, looking like the edges of my iris. But it persisted.

I was also very dizzy and disoriented, and soon quite panicked. I thought I was going to faint or lose my dinner, and all I wanted was to cling to Joseph and hide away somewhere. He suggested I return to the car while he finished the shopping but I couldn't leave his side. Fear, I suppose—not only of losing my vision, but of something else.

Floaters and flashers. A year ago exactly, this had happened to my right eye. In fact, I was due to return to the ophthalmologist this month for a final check-up. After a big scare and a restriction of my activities, that right eye had adjusted, the flashers had disappeared, and my retina had remained intact. I learned then that very nearsighted people like me are more prone to having this experience at a younger age, but that everyone's vitreous (the jelly-like stuff at the back of the eye) eventually liquefies. The floaters (black specks or swirls caused by tiny clumps of gel or cells) don't really go away; your brain adjusts to them and you stop noticing them so much. Perhaps you have them too?

But a sudden onset like this is considered dangerous. Flashers mean that the vitreous has shifted, and is pulling away from or rubbing the retina. If it does anything more radical or sudden, it can tear the retina. And if that's not treated, the retina can detach—and the only remedy is surgery if you're fortunate.

So as my doctor confirmed today, calling him right away was

absolutely the right thing to do. Thankfully, my retina looks good and healthy, in both eyes. Today, this only means I can't go ballroom dancing or start my weight training for a week. Phooey.

But I am so fortunate!! I thank the Infinite for all the work I've done so far to rectify my karma, because this relatively minor event represents a much darker history, carrying deadly energy. Here are the levels of self-analysis and self-treatment I've passed through to come to this conclusion:

**Level 1: Immediate Measures**

I did a little Eden Energy Medicine while we were still in Trader Joe's to calm my sudden panic reaction and to quell my fear. (Energy medicine is one of our most important *Survival Skills for the 21ˢᵗ Century*™, the best tool in our medicine chest.) Joseph looked at me and handed me the round, faceted lead crystal he keeps with him for another energy purpose and told me to spin it over the energy vortex that flows into and out of my left eye.

That attracted some attention from fellow shoppers, but it cleared the static energy which had clouded over the eye, which he could see and sense because these are the energy frequencies closest to my physical body. Spinning the crystal cleared or realigned the energy by mimicking the vortex's movements when normal.

When we got back to the car, Joseph muscle-tested (energy-tested some of my acupuncture meridians and my kidney meridian had gone into overdrive mode. Not surprising, because it's one of the meridians that governs the eyes, and the emotion associated with it is fear. Using what I've learned about acupressure points, I sedated that meridian while he drove us home. (In hindsight, for all of you energy healers who may read this book one day, I probably should have strengthened it as well for good measure.)

### Level 2: Mental Analysis

As we drove toward home and the energy medicine techniques calmed me down, I could think again. It was then that I realized that my eye problem did not come to me out of the blue as it had seemed. It completely related to the past-life incident I was about to describe when I had stopped writing a few hours earlier!

This was an "ah-ha" moment, so I suspect my CoAuthors were jostling my awareness, if you know what I mean.

My panic and fear completely subsided as I *objectified* the past—meaning, as I recognized that the eye problem was the result of past-life energies that had come *in phase* with my present life. This helped me realign with the present me, moving back *out of phase* with the past me.

When I realized what I'd put myself in tune with, I knew that by all rights, given the past in question, I should have lost my sight completely. But as I've said, my current status in relationship to that past lifetime has now shifted. In other words, the healing already accomplished in my psychic anatomy has taken some of the punch away from the reliving.

As you now know, past lives tend to repeat in our present lives in cyclic patterns; what goes around, comes back around. Each time, you get another crack at working something out (healing).

Hmmm, even my unconscious choice of words—*punch, crack*—reflects the past.

### Level 3: Back-tracking

Now that I knew what past lifetime was in phase with me, I started *back-tracking*, looking for clues to find what had triggered it at that particular moment, and not earlier when I was about to write about it at my computer. I essentially re-wound my mental movie to the moment I walked into Trader Joe's. What did I do or see in the moments before the flashers appeared? What was the trigger?

Instantly, I saw it in my memory's eye: a display of potted pineapple plants. Joseph had pointed them out when we walked in the door because we'd been saving some pineapple tops to grow in our back yard. In the display, each pot bore a single pineapple fruit, no bigger than a softball, at the end of a long stem. Spiky leaves poked out in all directions from both plant and pineapple. That was my trigger. They looked like weapons—but I didn't have that thought at a conscious level at the time. Only by back-tracking did I find this unconscious trigger. Any other day, I probably wouldn't have made any connection to them other than "pineapple," but that's what happens when you're in phase with a past; the simplest things can take you back.

I've since done a little research and found a picture of what it subconsciously reminded me of. It's called a mace. Used to rip open armor in hand-to-hand combat.

**Level 4: Confronting My Karma**

Yesterday, I was planning to tell you the story about how the gym had tuned me back to a past lifetime when I was apparently a gladiator-in-training. (Hm, I once named a workshop we taught, "Angels in Training." Must be why! Trying subconsciously to turn this negative past energy around!) In both past and present, Joseph had been my training (and teaching!) partner.

We've joked about it over the years, because after the healing, when the negative impact has been put out of phase, a past like that can really seem preposterous and amusing. It has less influence over you when you are out of tune with it.

But today, after my attunement to that past brought on the floaters, flashers, and later the emergency doctor visit, I revisited the seriousness of it.

I'll repeat, past-life negativity and traumas are nothing to take lightly, which is one reason we always discourage people from looking into the subject if they have only mild curiosity. You can see what happened to me! Past-life attunements can be quite risky and should only be undertaken with serious, positive purpose. My purpose today? An example for this book.

In tracing back through my years of approaching this particular past, I can see that this is one I've had to come at from several angles. It was not easy to believe and accept. It's sooo not like the me I am now! (Or so I've thought.)

Yet without acceptance of the past truth about yourself, there can be no healing because you'll never allow yourself into the right mental alignment with that energy if you don't *accept* it. It's deflating to the ego, but it's the key to self-healing.

Let me start with the first and most dramatic reliving, when I was on a honeymoon in Greece with my ex-husband, Wafic. We were visiting one of the Greek islands when I lost a contact lens from my left eye. A crowd appeared to help find whatever I was looking for on the cobbles, and by the time I found it, the old-fashioned hard lens had been stepped on and shattered.

Since I'm extremely nearsighted, especially in that left eye, this meant that for the rest of my Mediterranean visit, including a trip to Beirut to visit Wafic's family, I saw either through one eye or through a pair of very old, hastily-packed glasses which did little to improve my vision.

It was 1980. Through this constant blur, I passed through the militia checkpoints, saw the tanks of the PLO parading in the streets below his sister's apartment. I faced AK47s in airports, and I met his warmly-welcoming family. I experienced nights of laughter and good food, and squinted through a trip into the mountains of Lebanon (Me: "It looks like the Bible!") to visit a famous resort area that would soon become too dangerous for tourists like us. I squinted up at the shelled-out buildings of what had once been a beautiful city, now damaged by civil and other wars. I saw it all with one good eye, or two blurry ones.

Needless to say, the sights and places I visited all attuned me to many layers of different past lives, and put me in the midst of a scary war zone—wars prior and wars yet to come. But the eye karma predominated. And no wonder!

This was the first time in my sheltered life I'd been so close to the kind of warring violence that poor eye reflected, and the Mediterranean area in which I'd earned this karma. But I didn't have any idea yet about my eye karma. I only knew that I could feel myself as two different people when I was standing next to the Parthenon in Athens: a student of the incarnated Lighted Ones during various epochs of the Golden Age of Greece, and later, as a conquering Roman heedless of destruction.

In Lebanon, I also attuned to past lives as both man and woman, in different centuries, in various parts of the Middle East—lives both "good and happy" and "bad and miserable." I felt the layers within me.

Another little warning: Travel can also be hazardous to your health simply because of these attunements to your own history.

For the most part, I felt so inspired by visiting Greece, I wanted to move there. And so warmed by the loving nature of the Lebanese people I met, that I returned home grateful and happy for the experience.

Not so easy, however, was the loss of my left contact lens. For weeks, my left eye kept swelling and shrinking as my eye doctor tried to fit a new lens. Hundreds of dollars later, I finally asked my Cosmic CoAuthors for help. They responded immediately, making me wonder why I'd waited so long to ask!

**Level 5: Higher Help (First Pass)**

In a dream they mentally projected to me, I saw myself standing in an arena—it was too tiny for a gladiatorial arena, I thought, but that's what it looked like to me, and the crowds also looked right for an ancient arena. At the time, I knew nothing about gladiators because I'd always hated history (now I know why) so I thought they only fought in the massive Colosseum in Rome. But the dream was so vivid I knew it was true—a past-life flashback.

I was standing above a competitor I'd apparently bested in combat, with my sandaled leg on his chest, holding up some kind of sharp implement to the crowd. *Yes or no?* I seemed to be asking. Apparently they said yes, because I plunged that sword-like implement down into the eye of my defeated enemy and lifted it out for them. I woke up sobbing, of course. I knew it was me, and I knew the man beneath my sandal then was my husband now, Wafic.

Tears in a recall like this mean the release of old energy as the energetic healing takes place at the highest levels of the psychic anatomy with the help of Those who projected the dream to me. My only job in this healing conjunction was to accept the truth in my Conscious Mind, so as to close the circuit of healing. I really couldn't deny it. I *felt* and *knew* the truth.

In the days to come, I strengthened the healing by remembering that, from the first day we met, I would be talking and gesturing with my fork at a meal and Wafic would complain, "Stop waving that thing around! You could put my eye out!" And I would protest, "But it's not anywhere near you!"

Long story short, I changed eye doctors that week at my CoAuthors' suggestion. Apparently the first one had some connection with me in the past I was reliving, keeping us both in phase with it. To prove it, the new doctor fit my lens perfectly on the first try. I also told Wafic about my past-life recall and the clues confirming it. He believed me.

Three years later, when we parted company because we had different life trajectories and dreams, we parted as friends. Of course, we'd worked out the remnants of other past-life connections during our short marriage, but that was the big one. Our mission together was accomplished, benefitting and freeing us both.

Today I know that it represented only my *first* attempt to rectify the negative energies of that gladiator lifetime, and I still knew very little about gladiators. I'd been given extra help, a kind of shortcut that precluded a lot of analysis until I learned more about the energy principles involved.

Once such a healing has been achieved, most people forget they ever had a problem. The cycle moves out of phase and life goes on. Really, who would want to dwell on such a life anyway? And if you do, you're in danger of reinstating your past negative relationship to it. (Yes, a healing can fail if you will it so, by your failure to break the negative thought/energy habits associated with it.)

**Second Pass**

About eighteen years later, after Joseph and I were married, I was working at a Barnes and Noble, shelving heavy books every morning before we opened. Suddenly my neck went into a muscle spasm and stayed that way. My doctor said she couldn't do a thing about it; maybe massage would help?

Meanwhile, Joseph's shoulder kept freezing, giving him bouts of severe pain and immobility. He also had knee problems and so did I.

So I turned to my Cosmic CoAuthors for help. They often respond while I'm writing in my journal and that was the case in this instance. Their reply was almost humorous, if it all hadn't been so painful.

Previously, Joseph had dreamt about dancing and suggested that we take our first ballroom dance class together—a salsa class—and we'd been talked into performing with three other couples at the San Diego County Fair, a form of promotion for our teacher: "If these couples can learn it, so can you!" So we were doing a lot of rehearsing. All six of us were new to partner dancing, which meant we were all clumsy, awkward, and blaming of each other. Spins and dips? Dan-ger-ous!

My CoAuthors informed me that, while ballroom dancing appears to be an exercise in romantic harmony, it was actually tuning us back to warriors grappling in hand-to-hand combat!

They said Joseph and I were reliving a lifetime in the Middle Ages when we were street performers, two men who depicted mock combat, re-enacting fights as knights in armor like you'd find at a Renaissance Faire today or a Society for Creative Anachronism (SCA) event.

In that lifetime as performers, we'd actually been good friends (our polarity relationship strengthening) but we both kept getting injured. Why? Because in truth, while we thought at the time we were only pretending to fight, we had a darker history that we kept ringing in by what we were doing: earlier lives when we were fighting in earnest!

Ah, the tangled webs we weave.

With that wonderfully enlightening yet amusing insight, we both immediately healed from our *old* injuries, and we love ballroom dancing now more than ever, decades later.

We had a good laugh that first year when we showed up at the county fair in our showy salsa costumes and fancy heels, only to discover that we'd be dancing on some hastily thrown together (meaning jagged) boards, with the audience sitting on straw bales, right next to the smelly pig barn! How much more Middle Ages could you get in the twentieth century?

We also laughed at the squabbles and fights we'd been having since the first day we tried to learn salsa, especially the one where I would unconsciously grab hold of Joseph's thumb and twist it painfully while executing a turn, and he'd walk off the floor in anger and I'd fume at the nerve of him to walk away, etc., etc., etc. Typical of a past-life reliving, it turns out we were both creating that problem by where we placed our hands, making sure that Joseph's thumb would fall right in the middle of my palm! It's amazing when you start to see it, but people go to great lengths to subconsciously recreate a past-life scenario, hopefully for an opportunity to heal.

To this day as we're dancing, every once in a while we recognize the signs of an attunement to our lives as grappling enemies. Now it's pretty easy with mutual recognition to put the past back out of phase, laugh at the incongruity of it, and go back to the romantic version of a couple in a dance embrace. With the deeper healing accomplished, this is a case where laughter becomes the healing release for all those leftover bits of negative energy.

After the past-life reading alerted us, we could see that the couples we were rehearsing salsa with also fell into battle stances like men locked in combat. And it occurs to me now that our instructor, who left a dance studio job to teach large crowds of "new trainees" in a community college gym, may have been one of our long-ago gladiatorial overseers. He was so dedicated to making dance *fun* instead of competitive, and he did!

What a wonderful way to rectify the destructive energy of the past! With our joint creative endeavor, we were all literally turning that ancient murderous energy into a harmonious display of beauty, a creation others could enjoy, thus spreading the healing to our old arena audiences! They, too, would benefit from the radiant, high frequency of our healing achievements, oscillating out to them as they tuned their minds to our display by the pig barn on that hot summer day.

Of course, it's much more challenging when you don't know why you are constantly falling into arguments, or injuring each other. Ever watch *Dancing with the Stars?* Now you can view it from a new perspective.

So after weeks of pain, my neck spasm dissolved and Joseph's shoulder and knee problems cleared up within days, as soon as we learned about the mock-combat lifetime and put it in the right mental perspective. I'll bet our dancing got better, even back then, because we started to radiate more *harmony* than *hatred,* oscillating out from

*144   Speed Your Evolution*

our psychic anatomies.

This quick healing even impressed my doctor. A couple of years later when I showed up with a foot problem, she told me, "Go downstairs and get an x-ray, and meanwhile, give yourself another past-life reading." (Guess which one worked that time, too!)

But my CoAuthors had mentioned that Joseph and I had "several" past lives in which we'd both been fighting men.

A few weeks ago, I was out at a street fair representing our publishing company, for which I'd put together a little advertising posterette that said, "Where were you in your last lifetime?" Later, the framed image wound up on my glass work desk. One day, long after I'd written the first draft of this chapter, I sat down and had one of those OMG moments. I swear this arrangement was totally unconscious!

I took a photo to show you without moving a thing from this cluttered mess. (Tch, no wonder I didn't notice the picture frames sitting side by side in the very center.)

Wait, I'm pretty sure you can't see that well enough. Let me zoom in:

*Who Was I?* 145

So there we were, er, are. You know—both. What the two Society for Creative Anachronism guys in very impressive homemade armor were doing—entertaining book-fair visitors—was exactly what Joseph and I had done in a previous life! Now we much prefer the American tango we're attempting in the photograph on the left. But watch out for those *boleos* and *ganchos,* i.e., kicks and flicks! (See my Note at the end of this chapter.)

**Third Pass**

Our next past-life attunement came soon after the ballroom incident, when we decided to join that gym—the story I began pages ago when the very memory of it sent me off to the doctor with an eye problem!

You already know the punch line: it tuned me back to being, not Joseph's competitor, but a fellow gladiator-in-training. Mentally, I'd joined right in with all the sweaty muscle-men in the place!

And when I had to wear shoes for certain exercises, what did I choose? An old pair of sandals. They may have been two shades of blue, but by golly, they were Roman-style in design! We had another good laugh when Joseph pointed that out. That's how it is when you're completely in tune with your past: you don't think even the most ludicrous thoughts or deeds are out of place at all: *Of course I should be able to lift as much as Joseph,* or do it longer, or better, and so on. *I'll show him I'm strong!*

As far as my mental self perceived during those moments of complete attunement to the past, I was in the body of one of those strong, muscular, sweaty men, all visuals to the contrary. It was as real to me as anything gets.

But once again, destructive energy was also flowing back into my body. As far as I recall, my eyes were fine, but I was very soon experiencing scary angina pains in my chest and all down my left arm whenever I did cardio exercises. So off I went to see a different doctor since mine was on maternity leave. He wanted to do all sorts of tests with fancy gadgets I'd wear around all day, even though my electrocardiogram test came out normal.

Before he could arrange that, I asked my CoAuthors for insight. This time, I'll let you read what they had to say in the next chapter because their words carry the healing power of their higher-frequency mental projections to me. That's a universal healing energy that will benefit anyone who attunes to it.

Before you read it, let's review. Here's how I handled a sudden, destructive incursion of the past in my present life:

Level 1: Immediate measures to counterbalance the impact
Level 2: Mental analysis, asking, "What am I reliving?"
Level 3: Back-tracking, looking for triggers
Level 4: Confronting the karma, accepting responsibility
Level 5: Higher help, healing

Okay, on to the past-life reading. You may notice that it touches on some of my other efforts to use creative endeavors for healing, thus turning destructive energy into something constructive in the present life. There's no sharp division between past, present, and future when I'm in mental communion with my Cosmic CoAuthors through my Superconscious Self. If you've read *Cosmic Dancer,* you may recognize that I used elements of this reading regarding my mother quite literally in the story line.

To help you understand what they're talking about, my symptoms when I asked for the reading included the following: angina pains while exercising at the gym; extremely heavy periods which doctors attributed to grapefruit-sized (at the time) fibroid tumors, losing sixteen ounces of blood each month, thus causing anemia; and annual bouts of bronchitis, one of which was still lingering in my system. My much-loved father had recently been hospitalized, and I had ceased communication with my mother a year or two earlier, after she told me she wished he would "just die," which I deemed the last straw in a lifetime of harshness between us.

After you've peered into this very personal communication, we'll talk about how you can prove the truth of past-life information to your own satisfaction. How do you know it's valid?

## *Explore Your Resonance*

1. Read the past-life psychic reading on the next pages, but keep your journal handy.

2. If anything in it causes you an emotional or physical reaction of any kind, jot it down. These may be clues to your own past, and/or proof of your connection to the Lighted Ones who projected the information. (If you have no reactions, not to worry. You will learn what you need to know about yourself when you need to know it.)

**Note:** A few weeks after I finished this chapter, Joseph and I began a new Argentine Tango class. This dance doesn't really suit our current temperaments but we can't resist the challenge it presents, nor the opportunity to study with good teachers. Or at least we thought that's why we enrolled.

We were learning a new step in this complex dance that originated among lonely, rough immigrants in the Argentine brothels of old, where the man had a knife in one hand and a woman in the other. Not to be confused with the milder American tango, the Argentine version is a kind of push-pull, yes-no sort of dance with feet flicking here and there and legs rapidly twining and releasing—like a sexy Twister game set to music.

You guessed it! I strained too far to step over Joseph's leg for a serpentine move and *oops*. Took weeks for my knee muscle to recover, but thankfully it has. We'll give this style a rest for a while, but each movement we've mastered in this one represents another chink off the old block of combat karma, because Argentine tango is probably the closest replica of grappling, hand-to-hand combat we've encountered!

Yet how else to work out this particular quirk in our psychic anatomies? Sometimes you must do something equal and opposite, if you can, turning the negative into a positive. Transforming past-life trauma into art is more common that you might expect; it's an instinctive choice many people make without realizing what they're doing.

I'm aware of lives with Joseph dating back more than a million years. I didn't meet him or her in every lifetime, but it has occurred to me that with our positive polarity and our mutual love for ballroom dancing, we are serving as stand-ins for one another to resolve karma we've incurred in combat with many souls throughout thousands of lifetimes. If we ever met as enemies on a battlefield, it was undoubtedly a terrible and tragic series of bad decisions that led us there!

*13*

## *Accessing the Truth*

*The following psychic reading was* spoken into an audio recording device and later transcribed. The channel or *psychic transceiver* was fully conscious at all times and was mentally prompted with words to speak by the individuals providing the content. The transceiver agreed to speak these words fluidly, without alteration or censorship. The content was not edited during or after the transcription except to correct typographical errors.

For the purpose of this book, I've made a few notes in brackets to help put things in context.

**March 13, 2001:** "This is Lianne speaking. I have asked so many questions on so many different subjects [in my journal] that I find the list overwhelming, myself. I am concerned about my health, my working life, my writing endeavors, my eating habits, my father's illness, and so on. So I will leave it to [my Cosmic CoAuthors] to respond in whatever way they feel most suitable, and I am grateful for the help and guidance. Thank you."

**My Cosmic CoAuthors:** *(long silence)* "We have begun our transmission to you without words for the purpose of shattering the shell-like structure of negative thought-forms that have been attempting to remain encrusted, entrapping you within this armor of thought. You have added to this shell with your own concerns, fears, anxieties, and questions, which has prevented you from receiving sufficient answers in a rapid-enough manner to keep up with the deluge which has seemingly descended upon you. You find that you are unable to maintain your positive trajectory now, as the ground beneath your feet has suddenly turned to quicksand. Is this not true? And so we will begin to shore up that ground, that soil of planet Earth, with our permutations of spiritual strength and our guiding Intelligence.

"Let yourself be in a relaxed and calm state of mind for the time being, while we examine the causes of this unrest within you—and they are many, as you have already pointed out. However, none are too dire or dangerous to the point that we cannot provide some insight that will help you extricate yourself from this entanglement. We will begin first with subjects that we have touched upon lightly in your daily journal entries; however, this format [an audio recording] gives us the opportunity to speak more fully and more freely on these subjects.

"We refer to the health concerns that began plaguing you some time past, most specifically the fibroid tumor which has grown within your uterus and the attendant physical strains that growth has placed upon your system: the anemia that has weakened your endurance and threatened your very pulse of life, and the other, corollary effects which have ensued as a result of this growth. As you already know, this manifestation of a fleshy form is the result of a massive ball of energy-information wedged within your psychic anatomy, the result of many lifetimes of negative experience relating specifically to the reproductive tract, the *female* reproductive organs.

"You have been made aware of some of these elements of your past-life history, but let us, now that you are open, delve more deeply into this subject with your acquiescence. Your desire to heal this aberrant manifestation is our gangplank leading into the dark night of your past, so we shall walk this gangplank with you. Fear not, for you are in good hands as we shine our Light to reveal that which lurks in the shadowy distance!

"You have been aware of your fears of childbirth and now we take you to the bedside of one such scene, in which your prematurely activated labor pains are wracking your frail physical form. This was a life in which you were not pleased to be bearing a child into the world and hence your bodily functions rebelled and you were unable to sustain this pregnancy. However, the child's development was far enough advanced as to cause great disruption in your body's fight against this life form, which you felt to be an intrusion. You fought with the soul attempting to use this venue into the earthworld, and hence reinforced your position, your relative positions as enemies. Had the child been born, you would have carried this conflict into your external lives. As it was, this battle took place between an astral entity, and your physical *and* astral selves. You lost the battle, as did the fetus. However, the loss of life does not end the conflict.

"You ask, why has this manifestation of a five-month-old fetus reappeared at the present cycle in your life? You are still engaged in a form of battle with the individual to whom we have referred obliquely, and that is as you suspect, your mother in the present lifetime. While you have been engaged in work on your novel [*Cosmic Dancer*], which is as you have surmised a form of healing psychodrama for you, you have reactivated your awareness of the fight you have carried on with this individual throughout many lifetimes. This reappearance of a massive form in your womb is a reflection of the life form that you carried in the past cycle when you died during premature labor and the fetus also perished, being unable to sustain life at that young age.

"You have worked to understand, reform, change, plead with, cajole, entice, aggravate, irritate, anger, please, condemn, and so on with this individual in your present lifetime. You have now closed the door in one sense on your physical communication, but that does not end the psychic battle within both of you. Your awareness throughout this period of time has expanded into a greater understanding; however, we can say that the task is not yet complete and there is more for you to recognize and realize.

"Was it wrong for all the forces of your physical system to oppose the incoming life in that past era? You were responding to a defensive instinct, that of physical self-defense, and were continuing a physical battle that you had been engaged in with this individual in even prior lifetimes, one in particular in which you perished and others in which your enemy was felled by your blows—to the head, upper torso, and so on. You have also recognized certain other cycles with this individual.

"At all times, it has been a physically harmful interaction, until your present lifetime when that physical harm was kept to a minimum. Hence we can say that there has been progress, but the intense hatreds and resentment still live just beneath the surface of your polite exteriors for both of you. You, dear soul, can work on these emotions and attempt to learn compassion and caring for this individual, who is in great need at the present time. She cannot be reached directly, but indirectly you can do much to set this opposing force free and also to free yourself from it.

"Continue along the lines in which you have begun, but know that the task remains unfinished, and do not ignore this need to gain peace of mind and to heal your animosities with Love—Infinite Love, not personal, false protestations of concern where none truly exists.

"This is, of course, unexpected to you, for you had not connected the present physical ailment to your suffering—except in vague, unspoken ways. This accounts for your similarity of symptoms, not with your father [hospitalized at the time of this reading], but with your mother. The attunements that you have made to your father's impending demise are all entangled with this karmic headlock in which you have been involved with your mother. Yes, it is true; her injuries to the chest area [breast cancer/mastectomy] are the result of blows from your ax or sword and so on—fists, spears, knives, jousting implements, etc. Likewise, you have suffered your share of return blows. So the health ailments that you share [her heart problems/my chest pains] are a result of this violent exchange.

"With your continued awareness, these symptoms will be mitigated and should subside considerably. You do not need to fear your physical activities, as much as respect your mental states while you are conducting those activities. The gymnasium in which you are undertaking this exercise is a distinctive re-attunement to the gladiator arenas and training fields of your past. At any given time in this recreated arena, you can be re-attuned to one or more of these negative past involvements with weapons, implements of torture, and physical demonstrations of prowess and superiority. You need to be aware of this factor and factor it out of your consciousness with this awareness!

"Do not avoid physical activity, as it is necessary for the maintenance of your present-day health. However, this activity that you have so recently undertaken is one you had long avoided in an attempt to avoid these very re-attunements that we have been describing to you. So take it as it is: an opportunity to work out and rectify aberrant energy wave forms that have been lying dormant for many lifetimes.

"Joseph, your companion in this operation, is also an adversary and ally, depending upon which particular lifetimes you have flashed back upon. He is your best friend and your battlefield enemy at various times, which accounts for the flare-ups of temper and emotion that have engulfed either or both of you at various times during these workouts. It also explains your competitive bent, given that you are now in a relatively small, female form as compared to his masculine physique; nevertheless, you feel as if you are his equal or should be, or better yet, that you should be able to overmaster his strength and prove your superiority. These are all the emotions you have carried forward from those battlefield encounters, which you must work to divest yourself of.

"Let us turn to a completely different scenario, albeit not so in the mental sense, but in terms of the accouterments, environment, and attire. You are dressed in the black robes of priestly attainment, if we can use that word loosely, and you have been given a position of power and superiority over others. You wield the power of the Church in the same fashion that you wielded your ax or sword in the past. In other words, your political power has given you the power of life and death over others. Many were imprisoned and tortured as a result of Church rulings, of which you were a part. You are not unfamiliar with this past, and we need not dwell in the torture chambers, for once is surely enough. Let it be said that this is another factor that is interweaving in your present consciousness, as you have noted from your careful notes taken of your emotional reactions.

"Let us point out at this juncture that your note-taking in this sense is very valuable to you and has helped you to keep your nose above water, so to speak. Also, it gives us the opportunity to interject a helping thought here and there. We encourage you to keep up with your journal writing at all costs, for it will make the difference between health and happiness, or suffering and death. Yes, it is a serious issue and you are at risk, if you were not keeping up with your mental maintenance. We do not say this to instill panic or fear; quite the opposite. We point out this fact, for it is truth and it bears repeating: the soul's demise is quite impossible, but the body's termination is not only probable but definite in the future of all individuals on earth. Whether that demise comes sooner or later may often depend on how that soul is living their life and what thoughts they entertain and what pasts they allow themselves to become reattuned to. You cannot avoid your past, but you can educate yourself to remain aware, alert, and vigilant in your attempts to extricate any thoughts that carry you back down the negative wave-train into the past, unprotected by Intelligence, knowledge, foresight, and hindsight.

"All of these factors have created the present symptoms that you are experiencing: the vague aches, pains, the internal lack of red blood cells, the failure of your heart muscle, albeit in a minor sense at this point. The lack of red blood cells, as you have quickly realized, is due to loss of blood from many of these violent pasts—both your own loss and that of your victims. Bleeding to death is a common phenomenon when wounds are not instantly fatal. Also, in the disrupted childbirth, as we have mentioned, and in the torture chambers, on the battlefields, in so-called medical experiments, in the abortion wards that we have previously described to you, and so on.

"Now let us pause while you regain some mental balance, so that we may continue.

"You must, dear one, keep these facts that we have laid out for you in the proper perspective. We have been describing an amassment of negative energy, its many causes and contributing factors, and not the entirety of your psychic anatomy! As such, it is indeed a horrifying sight to behold, but you have been preparing yourself for this junction of consciousness for many thousands of years, for countless lifetimes. Even as you lived these experiences, you were learning about the many sides of Infinite Creative Intelligence and developing your will and desire to change, to grow, to become a more constructive element of life.

"We all have passed through this darkness of self-development, learning to master our destructive emotionalisms, our selfish desires and single-minded attempts to control life. But Life is not within our grasp! Nor our individual power to control—not in the sense that you and we have believed in our past. Life is far more complex and expanded than *our* minds can achieve, even at *this* stage in our evolutionary development—far, far more complex than we can even imagine! Our puny attempts to master and control this Life while on an earth planet are almost laughable, if their results had not been so destructive to that very life which we had hoped to overmaster.

"No, dear one, it is self-mastery that holds the key to spiritual advancement and the development of Infinite Intelligence—that long course of personal education in which you are presently involved, in which all souls are involved, whether they are aware or not. Your awareness clearly indicates the long attempts that you have already made in this realm of self-development. You have reached the stage at which your participation in Infinite Creative Intelligence can be more definitive, due to your conscious understanding of these beginning steps.

"For example, your writing project which is leading you in and out of many nooks and crannies of your own consciousness, and particularly into this past-life conflict with your mother: You did not intend to expose this past to yourself; nevertheless your positive motivation and desire has led you to unearth one of the large stumbling blocks that has held you back—not only in the present lifetime, but for many lives.

"We will leave you to ponder many of the interconnections and new perspectives that we have revealed with these few words of ours today, and we know that you are already engaged in this unstoppable process of linking thought to thought and emotion to emotion, as you see that your father's impending demise is all interwoven in your relationship with your mother and hers with him and yours with him, and so on, and so forth....

"It all blends together as before, but now we suspect that these interlinking connections are feeling much more *positive potential* for you than a few moments ago. A few moments ago, they seemed to be the chains weighing you down; now they are like sparking links of electrical energy surging through your veins and bones anew, and giving you hope that a small charge *here* will automatically transfer through these wires and links to connect *there,* and thus recharge *all* of your physical, mental, and spiritual life—and so it is, and so shall it be! We give you our grand send-off of Infinite Love, Light, Peace, and Truth!"

# 14

## Prove It

*Ruth Norman used to say* about past-life information that, "The proof of the pudding is in the eating." She meant that knowing about your past lives is worse than useless if that knowledge doesn't bring you some kind of positive change or healing.

You know those dreams where you're standing in front of a group about to give a speech and you realize you're naked? That's me right now, after sharing that detailed reading from years ago with the whole world. I like to think I've changed a lot since then!

But I remind myself that I incurred this karma in a public way, and so I will resolve it in a similar public arena. I am so fortunate to have received this kind of help in my present lifetime. *You can too.* Otherwise, I wouldn't have shared it.

Most importantly, *this information healed me.*

After I absorbed and accepted that reading, my angina pains went away because once the past-life spell was broken, we quit the gym almost immediately. We'd suddenly found a better way to work out. Coincidence? I doubt it. And without the past pushing me, I stopped pushing myself beyond reason. No more chest pain. It's never come back no matter how I work out and that was twelve years ago!

You never know how your "healing transformation" will manifest. Trumpets didn't blow or thunder boom, but my problem disappeared for good.

But our poor gym trainer was horrified when she saw that, at the end of our three months under her supervision, we'd both gained body fat instead of losing it! Joseph and I figured that was probably because after each workout, we went off to eat like gladiators-in-training at the nearby Mexican eatery. But next thing we heard was that our trainer had quit to take a job with a car rental agency. We never got a chance to tell her the truth about "who" she'd been working with. Do you think she'd have believed us?

As for all the other information in the reading, you can see how closely my Cosmic CoAuthors work with me when I'm writing. Hah! At the time of that reading in 2001, I thought *Cosmic Dancer* was almost done! But I didn't finish and publish my novel until 2011, after I broke through the silence between my mother and me, and after she left this world, and many rewrites and shapings and moldings later, during which the character in the book became less of her and more of a symbol.

Oh, but our healing hasn't stopped just because my mother is no longer here in the physical! As long as I'm here learning through experience to have more compassion for her, then our past-life workouts continue. (Different kind of workout than the one I was doing in the gym; that's past-life therapy lingo for "resolving negative karma.")

I so often think now, "Gosh, Mom, if I'd known *that* ..." I would have been so much kinder if I'd known then what I know now, and if I'd been kinder, perhaps she would have too. I know we will do better if there's a next time.

In 2010, Joseph and I re-published a local history book she'd written (*The Real McCoy*), during which process I swear she kept urging me, "No, no, not that color—this one!" and other psychic impressions we shared.

Every time I learn another new good thing I wish I'd known while she was alive, I send her another love-beam. Good and loving thoughts and prayers travel the dimensions, providing very positive energy for your designated recipient, wherever they may be.

*Prove It* 159

I'm sure any future encounters will be vastly improved for both of us. And frankly, as I like to tell people, we made tremendous strides together as mother and daughter this time around: she managed to get me born safely and nobody died during our long association. This was progress! (Most people don't find that amusing but I know she does.) She didn't have the abortion doctors urged for health reasons, and when a woman snatched me out of my stroller at an airport, she chased her down and rescued me. I did enjoy good times with her as well as the bad; plus, despite my vows never to be like her, her teaching and influence surely helped to propel me toward my true vocation as a writer. She was a newspaper columnist. My first writing job? As a newspaper columnist.

As for the priestly lifetimes mentioned in the reading, well, none of you think I'm dogmatic now, right? Right??? Sigh. Well, those old religious lives were my worst nightmares but hey, that's how we learn, by making big life mistakes, thinking we're doing the right thing, maybe even passionately so, then looking back at them later and, *Doh! What was I thinking??* Because what I know now is so foreign to what I enforced then in my dogmatic ways. Big sorrowful regret.

**Note:** While working on this text, I opened up this chapter for proofreading and was astounded to find two words added to this sentence (italics mine):

"But I didn't finish and publish it until 2011, after I broke through the silence between my mother and me, and after she *reached down* left this world, and many rewrites and shapings and moldings later, during which the character in the book became less of her and more of a symbol."

*Reached down???* !!! Who's been inserting words in my text? Someone who "reached down" to me? I found this addition when opening the file on my new notebook computer, which hasn't left the house and which no one else has touched.

I've heard stories of this sort of thing happening, a famous one about posthumous emails from an abruptly deceased teenager sent to his friends, containing information only they would know.

What do you think? Is our new technology literally going to reach into astral realms one day? Or does it already? ??? Didn't we just say that good thoughts and prayers travel through the dimensions, both ways? Remember it's all about energy transfers: our computer technology, our consciousness, our bodies, all of it.

Or perhaps I was unconsciously prompted to type those words, thus sending myself a message about interdimensional communication by startling myself with them? Hmmm, sometimes we are left pondering.

But this little phenomenon reminds me to tell you that, once you start working with the energy principles in this book, you can expect to have countless experiences like this, proving all that you read. Ah yes, that is the name of this chapter, isn't it? And I almost forgot to tell you about the constant little proofs that will crop up in your life now, if you take notice. Ruth Norman called them *psychisms*. You'll probably try to disbelieve them, but they'll keep happening to you until eventually you'll realize that they are NOT coincidental. Maybe this is already a part of your life?

And remember I mentioned earlier that you might start seeing Lights, as my character Amelia does in *Cosmic Dancer*. They may appear as tiny firefly flashes of color and light that blink over a page, on your hands, anywhere within your line of sight—maybe around a friend's head? Blue, gold, white, and more rarely green, red—it probably depends on your frequency relationships with the higher planes and worlds.

The colors are significant but I'm a little unsteady about this information so I'd prefer that you learn the codes for yourself. I see cobalt blue very often, and it's usually larger than the white and gold flashes

I also see. The latter often come in groups. I suspect and I have read that the colors relate to levels of development of the Beings contacting you this way, white and gold being more advanced. But it could be that you'll see them differently and I don't want to lead you astray on this! Plus, I sometimes see an oscillating *rainbow* of color, and something I can only describe as silvery rips in the fabric of this dimension, revealing the next.

If you see these Lights, greet them as the Friends they are and be glad that your consciousness is awakening to these higher levels of input! They are a delightful bit of proof that you are not imagining your connection to higher dimensions.

**No Such Thing as Coincidence**

As I was saying earlier, with so much done to assist me, I have only one job in a healing process, situated as I am in my earthly form: to recognize the truth of the information and accept it with a deep, unshakable knowing. For most of us, that requires proof. And if the science of reincarnation is valid, then it will prove itself to you.

Lots of authors and researchers have gone off to "prove" reincarnation to the *rest* of the world. I've met a few of them, and they've made Herculean efforts. But they'll never do it. No one could possibly convince you or me if we didn't *feel* the truth of our past lives within ourselves, and if we hadn't proven out the energy principles I've been talking about. No one else needs to believe us about it, either. We only need to prove it to our own satisfaction.

Healing is proof of the truth. But not all healing is instantaneous. Meanwhile, you will find other proofs of the energy nature of life, and the cyclic continuities of that life, if you look with a sincere, brave, and open-minded desire to know. You're going to develop a very finely-tuned sensitivity to subtleties most people miss. They might scoff at you for noticing them. That's okay; it's none of their business. You and I will know that the details are where you'll find Infinite Intelligence following its interdimensional energy principles and influencing your life. As architect Mies van der Rohe famously said, "God is in the details."

When I was writing merrily along and chose to use my past life as a gladiator as an example for this book, it turns out my choice wasn't as random as I'd thought it was. (Remember my CoAuthors telling us in Chapter 8 that there's no such thing as random?) Now I know that I was *already* in phase with warrior lifetimes, although I hadn't recognized it yet.

After the key event took place—the sudden deterioration of my left eye while standing in Trader Joe's—my analysis led me to discover many other clues telling me that the cycle had been in phase for some time.

That's how it is when you're completely in tune with a past: it's so close you can't see it.

But when you back-track in your mind to consider what you've been up to, the clues usually fall into place. Then you think, *It was so obvious; how did I miss it?*

Here are some of the clues I'd missed:

1. I've been writing these chapters on the eve of Memorial Day, which honors our dead, particularly those who've served as warriors.

2. Today, Joseph was doing the weekend cooking he loves to do. Every time I left off from my writing and walked into the kitchen, the smell of onions overpowered me. It happened repeatedly—until I finally laughed and realized the raw onion smell was only bothering me because gladiators ate lots of onions! Now I've learned they were also rubbed down with onion juice to "firm up the muscles." Blech!!

3. We decided this afternoon to preview one of the reincarnation films I've undertaken to screen for this book's bibliography. Turns out the one we chose (*Racing Dawn*) had a lot to do with the traumas and tragedies of warriors during the Civil War.

4. A week ago, I finished reading all three books of *The Hunger Games* trilogy. Talk about gladiators! This might have been the thing that first triggered my reliving, or it might have been that I read it because I was already in phase with the gladiator lifetime. Or perhaps I was in tune with it because Joseph was; we often oscillate with the same pasts because of our close relationship, both now and then. He read the books first and kept urging me to read them as well.

To write *The Hunger Games*, author Suzanne Collins drew directly from Roman fighting history. She even uses Latin names for her characters. The trilogy is meant as an anti-war, cautionary tale directed at young people, the author has said, not a metaphor for the trials of adolescence as some have suggested. But we will all be young people again one day, having to make those choices!

It's a terrific series, by the way, a real page-turner. I highly recommend these books (not films) for young and old, as challenging as it is to read about this subject. But because the author's motivations were educational rather than sheer exploitative entertainment, the books carry a healing frequency, and that gives them an overall positive impact on readers. At least it did for me, but then I've been working on these warrior aspects of myself for many years now.

Perhaps if an individual is not cognizant of their past lives at all, and doesn't want to be, the content of the books would be too shocking and they'd be inclined to turn away.

That can be another important clue to your history, by the way: a *strong aversion* to something.

Note that once translated to film, the story loses some of its intellectual quality and the violence becomes very graphic, altering the impact of the storytelling. If you want the positive benefits, read the books first.

You can't live many lives on this planet without being touched by war, unfortunately. At least, not so far. *The Hunger Games* are part of the thread of information always flowing to this planet in the hopes of bringing Light and peace to the people who live here. I sincerely appreciate Suzanne Collins' efforts on our behalf.

Back to my clues list:

5. Days after I finished reading *The Hunger Games*, Joseph and I "happened" to find a British documentary on our Netflix streaming list called, *Colosseum: A Gladiator's Story*. Can't call that a coincidence, although it seemed so! Must've been Joseph's higher self prompting the addition to our Netflix list, and/or our frequency connection.

Watching this documentary and reading *The Hunger Games* trilogy, I was *somewhat consciously* harking back to my own past—vaguely aware, you might say—but still didn't think much about possibly being so in tune with it that I would experience the incident with my eye!

Again, this is another phenomenon of past-life relivings: you think you're alert and aware of your life but you're really not fully
** AWARE **
in the present. We're quite accustomed to living every day in a kind of mental smog of pastpresentfuture routine. We do so much of our living on auto-pilot! It takes practice, which you're learning now, to sort out with conscious awareness the past energies infusing the present. And usually you need a good reason that jogs you suddenly
** AWAKE **

so that you start using all those unused portions of your magnificent Mind.

The *Colosseum* documentary was very informative, recently made and based on newly discovered information. After all these years since my dream of the arena incident, I learned that gladiators did indeed fight in one-to-one combat in small arenas in outlying areas before they ever got to the famed Colosseum in Rome—and the visual depictions recreated for the documentary were identical to what I'd seen in my dream!

There went my last excuse to say, "Nah, it was only a dream. Couldn't be true."

I also learned that men of the time sometimes were forced to become gladiators because it was a way to pay off debts, while others volunteered for the glory of it, or were fortunate to be offered this alternative to grueling, back-breaking work as slaves in the quarries. (Either way, they probably weren't going to live for long.) Some were prisoners of war from cultures the Romans were busy conquering. I didn't know they came to it from so many directions, or for so many reasons.

I learned that gladiators trained together in schools—like Joseph and me in the gym! They married, had mistresses, and were often fought over by rich women. Some who'd been slaves could do well enough to buy their freedom.

I have no idea how or why I became one, although I've certainly wondered. But apparently that information isn't crucial to my healing, so the facts about my particular reasons have not been forthcoming.

✳ **We only need to go back to what's essential to know for healing; the rest should be left well enough alone.**

As an example of why it's sometimes best to leave the past alone, the bloody television series *Spartacus: Blood and Sand* depicted some of this gladiator history, but in the lowest frequencies of exploitation, as is the recent fashion in cable TV series.

Nevertheless, when it first came out Joseph and I "soldiered" through a few episodes of it for the educational value before it made us both feel too ill to watch further. At the time, I was not in phase with that past, thankfully, and it had limited ill effect because I knew enough to stop when I felt the signals from my solar plexus (third chakra).

It's not only dangerous to take yourself back into the past—dwelling on it once you know about it can be even more harmful. The intention of the *Spartacus* series was far different from the *Colosseum* documentary, or even *The Hunger Games*—and intention creates frequency. That frequency affects your own energy systems as you align to it by giving it your attention, i.e., watching it on TV for an hour or more. Both the documentary and book trilogy were intended to educate as well as entertain, but the TV series, *Spartacus: Blood and Sand*, although claiming to depict some truthful elements of history, exaggerated incidents in the worst ways, seemingly with the intention to titillate the lower senses, attract viewers, and thus raise advertising rates, i.e., make more money.

In other words, the producers gave it the same appeal as the arena had for the citizens of Rome, a low frequency indeed! It's riskiest of all to tune back and regenerate your past *in its lowest frequencies*— that is, if you want to maintain health, happiness, and sanity! In fact Andy Whitfield, the actor who played Spartacus in the first season, depicting an incredibly fit and powerful physique, died from blood cancer a year and a half after the series premiered and the producers had to replace him. He was only 39 years old. Coincidence?

Back to my list again (all this persistent analysis is helping me move out of the cycle):

6. We've been watching a cute little TV show for teenagers

from Australia called *Dance Academy* on weeknights when we want to relax for a bit but don't have much time; episodes are only 24 minutes long. It's like *Glee* in toe shoes. Last night we turned on something like episode #48 after I'd written the above. Did you ever hear of a *ballet* called *Spartacus??* Me neither! I was dumbstruck! But there they were, all the kids in the ballet school with fake swords and shields, leaping around the ballet studio! And of course, the ongoing soap opera theme for that episode fell in line with the whole warrior concept.

I couldn't believe it. I wiki'd it and sure enough: http://en.wikipedia.org/wiki/Spartacus_(ballet)

Talk about ringing in a harmonic frequency! How do such things happen? It's fairly mind-boggling, even to me, after all these years of watching it happen in my own life and in others' lives.

I could go on and on, listing all the little things that I've now discerned in the present moments of my life resonating harmonically with this currently in-phase, past-life karma with warriors and gladiators. But I won't bore you. And I also wish to change the channel of my thoughts as soon as possible.

Besides, I think you get my point by now:

There is no such thing as random or coincidence. Believe it. If you study the principles of your energy self—how it moves, changes, carries information, attracts and repels, creates resonant harmonics, and oscillates between past, present, and future while traveling from dimension to dimension—you'll understand why.

But you want proof right now that what you are living in the present is a continuity of your past lives? It's all around you. Be patient. You'll soon learn to discern it.

∞ ✻ ∞

## Sharpen Your Back-Tracking Skills

When I was first assigned an exercise like this I complained because it taxed mental muscles I hadn't been using. *I don't want to look back! I want to go forward!* But I soon strengthened those mental muscles and now this skill is one of my most frequently used tools for self-awareness. This exercise will train your mind so you'll remember important details in the future with little effort. The self-knowledge you'll gain will reward you many times over!

1. Take out your journal. Think back over what you did today. What did you eat for breakfast? Snacks? Lunch? Jot down everything you can remember. (Shorthand and brief notes are fine.)

2. Think back over yesterday. What did you eat for breakfast, lunch, dinner? What did you do? Who did you talk to? What did you talk about? What stands out in your mind as significant? Can you go deeper, to things you wouldn't think to be important?

3. Go back as far as you can manage, making notes each time about what you can remember. Can you remember details as many as five days ago?

4. For the next week, sit down with your journal at the end of each day and think back over what you've done, said, felt, thought, consumed. Make a note for each thing you recall. Don't cheat by taking notes all day long; wait until evening so you can develop your back-tracking skills.

# Part III

# Speed Your Evolution

*...you can visualize yourself as actually traveling through time and space at a vastly accelerated speed as if being fired from some huge cannon. You may in a few days, or in a few hours time, actually be rebuilt or reformed to a point which would normally take you many thousands of lifetimes to acquire in the ordinary reactionary manner you have been accustomed to until this time. Should such an occurrence happen to you and at any time you should be involved in a tremendous psychic upheaval wherein there may be literally thousands of years of earth lives removed, then the various negations involved in these experience quotients are so cancelled out in their negative proportions to you as they are so contained in your psychic anatomy.*

*...This situation is not to be feared, but rather it is to be welcomed, and each particular "working out"—whether it is small or whether it is large—should be a definite milestone which marks your evolution into the future.*

— Ernest L. Norman, *Infinite Perspectus*

# 15

## The Quest for Healing

*By now we've weeded out* any reader who merely wanted to sight-see through their past lives. If you've made it this far in the book, you're serious about making significant personal improvements. You want to change who you are by rectifying who you have been and embarking on a new course through your many lives. Congratulations!

To me, any positive personal change is a form of healing.

How does one heal? I'm afraid the answer is, "That depends." There are as many ways to heal as there are souls in the universe.

But we're all engaged in a quest for some kind of healing, even if it's a quest to heal our ignorance. We seek positive transformation of mind, body, spirit, relationships, bank accounts, you name it. We want to better our lives. Some people think of this as a search for happiness. I call all of it *healing*.

And there are many levels to healing.

A doctor can set a broken bone for you, and then your body's own intelligence (stemming from your psychic anatomy) will go about recreating a solid bone, if all goes well.

But wasn't it a glitch in your *psychic anatomy* that sent the information that pushed you down the stairs in the first place? Or caused you to be in the wrong place at the wrong time, as we so often say? And how can you heal that psychic-anatomy glitch so that you don't fall down another flight of stairs in the future, or wind up in another "wrong place"—which in fact, was exactly the "right" place according to the information in your psychic anatomy that drew you to it? But now, from your present position in relationship to the Infinite, you've changed your mind about what is "right" and "wrong."

So the healing you really need is not of the bone but of that glitch in your psychic anatomy.

Complicated, eh? But not so complicated when you grow accustomed to considering all the levels of your existence and how they interact.

What we're focusing on is a complete and lasting *change* in your psychic structures. The intelligence bound into those psychic structures is software you've created, and it will direct all your future lives. If it has a glitch, you can bet that little skip will repeat over and over again. Over time, with effort, you can slowly change that fourth-dimensional, vortical pattern of energy to express a slightly (or radically!) different energy-information outwardly, into your physical life.

Of course even for a relatively "slow" healing path, we can turn to the assistance of our Cosmic CoAuthors. We also may benefit from various *catalysts* in the physical world, such as a doctor or your energy medicine practitioner, or your neighbor or friend who says or does the key thing. But we are the ones directing our course, so we are the ones who choose when and how and how fast we heal—or at least, our Superconscious Selves are. Our Conscious Minds, the part of us we on Earth tend to think of as Me, are truly the last to join in the chain of effort.

**How Slow Transformation Works**

Slow healing or positive transformation is like the path Bill Murray takes in the film, *Groundhog Day:* repetitions of same-old, same-old, until he finally decides to change a little bit here and there, gradually working himself into a major transformation.

But that film depicts a steady, straight-forward improvement. You may be more akin to the transmigrating soul depicted in David Mitchell's *Cloud Atlas* (book and film). He starts out one way, and after harrowing and wildly varied incarnations and experience, winds up caring about others, to the point of moral and physical heroism.

For most of us, things are a lot more complicated than fictional depictions because we have thousands of lifetimes and unlimited time in which to make our slow transformations, much more than the space allotted in the pages of a book or the minutes of a film.

Here's how slow transformation works:

Each time the energy of the past from your psychic anatomy presents itself in your present lifetime—recreating feelings and influencing circumstances—you may respond to this influence differently:

✴ If you "go with the flow," you may simply *regenerate* and strengthen the past information.

✴ But if you say inwardly, "No, I'm not going to repeat that mistake," or some similar mental determination, you may do something to improve the information that's stored in your psychic anatomy, and that will positively affect all your future lifetimes.

It's very much like breaking an old habit because that's exactly what you're doing—you're breaking an *energy habit*.

This is always your prerogative, and it's how most people heal or upgrade their old selves to transform into their new selves. For anyone on a progressive path, this must be a constant process of examining and discarding old information.

While you're doing this—changing your mind about "right" and "wrong," updating your knowledge or your old beliefs, coming at life from a new perspective—you're also using the pure energy Essence that is always flowing to you from the Infinite wellspring and you're adding it into the mix of your old patterns, weaving it in a new way into your software-self, enhancing and improving, and discarding that which was broken, distorted, "wrong" in your present opinion, and outdated.

Meanwhile, if you've graduated to a more advanced level, your higher affiliations, your own Cosmic CoAuthors, noting your self-determined, positive-growth endeavor, may aid you by using their knowledge of interdimensional physics to quickly cancel out certain patterns of energy in your psychic anatomy, as we described in Chapter 10's section on *What a Past Life Energy Healing Feels Like*. In my example, our lost traveler experienced a rapid, instantaneous, and very dramatic healing.

Yet healing is not always that simple. It might not be complete, and it might not be fast. Think of how many time-cycles I've transited through my karma with gladiators, each time chipping away at the negative energy in my psychic storehouse and replacing it with new understanding.

It could be that you simply change your mind about some things, and thereby slowly redesign the information in your psychic anatomy, but here and there along the way, you'll achieve some higher help that will aid you in leaping ahead with sudden, assisted bursts of insight. We may crawl and leap and crawl and leap our way to a better life.

**A Faster Way**

As always, the help you receive depends on your mental attitude; no Higher Being will interfere in your need to heal, change, learn, or grow at your own pace. But this book is teaching you how to work *consciously* with Advanced Intellects in order to speed up your healing endeavors, to eventually transform yourself into a highly aware Cosmic Being.

I don't mean making wounds heal faster (although that might be involved). I'm referring to the speed at which you can consume new information and make it a part of you, improving your mind, body, and spirit by discarding old data and replacing it more quickly. In other words, how fast are you willing to evolve into a more creative, constructive being?

With higher-dimensional help and your willingness to change, you might enter into a new level of healing: the speeded-up version of personal progress that an individual who's chosen a spiritual trajectory can obtain. You might begin a rapid advance in your creative evolution.

But all this is too abstract for my taste. So let's look at an example of how that Cosmic interaction works, and where your willing participation becomes crucial.

**You're Not Listening...**

The last time I tried returning to a strength-training program, about a year ago, I was using resistance bands, the same method we resorted to after our gym fiasco a dozen years ago. If you're not familiar with them, they're thick, heavy rubber bands, usually with some kind of fastening that you secure to a door or other solid anchor so that you can pull on them. (It occurs to me now that in this case, there's some irony in that name, *resistance* bands.)

One day I was doing a back-strengthening exercise, pulling down and toward me on the heaviest band with both hands and with all my strength, while facing the door into which the band was secured by a short cord with a heavy plastic knob on the end of it.

I'd done this so many times off and on over the years, but for some reason that day I started to think, "Gosh, if that cord pulled out from the door, it could really hurt." I kept doing repetitions, and this thought kept coming to me again and again, but for some reason I refused to give it the full attention needed. I vaguely felt that it was a strange thing to be thinking after all this time. Duh...

I've heard that your mental acuity diminishes with physical exertion.

Normally, I would secure that knob inside the door jamb, close the door, and flip closed a heavy-duty, high-security, thicker-than-normal metal latch that nothing could budge. No way could that door fly open! I did this every single time I wedged a resistance band into the door before I started to tug on it. *Every single time.*

So the persistent thought about the cord pulling out was fairly unusual. And still I DIDN'T LISTEN!! And my eyes never traveled down the side of that door in front of me to see that—

## !!!!!!! **OUCH** !!!!!!!

Oh, man that hurt! It hit me in the face, faster than I could blink. The cord left burns along my chin and jaw, and the round plastic knob bruised my collar bone and left a bump that lasted long after the redness went away.

I was so fortunate! Didn't break the glasses I happened to be wearing that day, or shatter my nose, or hit me in the eye; didn't break my collar bone. Good thing I'm pretty weak in general or who knows how much harder that tiny flying weapon would have hit me.

In fact, it did resemble a miniature version of the swinging form of mace. Or, even more, the Maori's round *poi* ball on a rope, which is now used for performance art but may once have been used to train warriors for more serious weaponry.

My Cosmic CoAuthors had tried to warn me! But I had them mostly tuned out. It was the mini-poi ball that finally got my attention.

Despite my past lives, you've probably surmised that in this lifetime I am not muscular or athletic at all. At that time, my body had an aversion to keeping muscle, and we all know that muscle burns fat, hence my frequent attempts at doing something to build more muscle.

But now that I've been dwelling on this subject with you, I can see that I've hurt myself every single time I've tried any method that even remotely resembles warrior training! And each time, I've had to give up and go back to ballet training and ballroom dancing as the most strenuous muscle workout I can manage. Or belly and Bollywood dancing. Or Latin dancing. Anything but ostentatiously macho workouts.

So I'm asking myself now, *Is this true? Do I need to give up forever the kind of muscle-building that tunes me back to past lives of masculine training, which was almost always in preparation for kill or be killed? But it's not fair!* Even French author Mireille Guiliano (French Women Don't Get Fat) *suggests that women of a certain age should lift a few weights here and there.*

Hm, but do you suppose those classic French beauties of past eras ever picked up a *hand weight?* Or pulled on a resistance band with a mock poi ball on the end?

So what was I *really* after in these attempts? (This is a key question in back-tracking, so take note; we'll come back to it.)

Actually, it's not me I'm asking. It's those same CoAuthors who tried to warn me that I'd forgotten to secure the door latch. If only I'd paid attention! But my mind was in some other zone, a dead zone, and refused to hear them. I was in tune with my past instead of my present or future. And once again, fortunate for me that some of the destruction has been taken out of that past energy. But not all.

So how much help *did* I have?

**The Help Is Always There**

The most important thing for you to gain from my painful experience is to note how the Higher Help I've enlisted through my life choices was right there to alert me. But I wasn't listening. I took the slow, painful path instead, because my higher attunement was off. That was my responsibility, and my mental choice.

As I said, how we heal and how fast we give up our destructive past truly depends on us.

Nevertheless, do you think I still had a little more help in this case? Perhaps a little flick of the plastic poi anchor ball that so fortunately missed fragile parts of me, averting severe damage?

How often is this kind of psychokinetic assistance a part of our just-missed accidents?

Or was it because I've put some of this past *out of phase* with my present; therefore, the hard round ball of the resistance band was also slightly *out of phase* with my vulnerable flesh? Hmmm??

These are the types of question I have to keep asking, because I am still learning, and always will be. I could list numerous examples in my life where I've wondered about this—I'm sure you could add a few of your own. In fact, I wrote about this very thing in *Cosmic Dancer* because I wanted to hear the answer: Did Marta miss the boulder on her plunge down the mountainside with higher-dimensional help? Or by "coincidence"? (That's a hint, but you might find it more fun to read what my Cosmic CoAuthors said in the novel's higher-dimensional setting.)

What we do know is this: The first wise step on your way to healing and living a long life here is to crystallize your interdimensional affiliation with the level of higher resources I'm talking about when I speak of my Cosmic CoAuthors. If you have an important mission to carry out, I believe there's some prior agreement made that could bring help to your side when life on Earth becomes simply too dangerous, and threatens your completion of that mission or those goals you've set. But you must keep paying attention.

Ernest Norman makes this point in his books, suggesting that we wouldn't last five minutes here without that form of help, and yet we're rarely aware of it, usually giving credit elsewhere.

But here's the catch: In our Conscious Minds, we don't fully apprehend what those spiritual goals are, and what bizarre, terrifying, unusual, spiraling, or twisting and tangled circumstances will actually help us achieve them.

Then there's this important fact that bears repeating:

※ **True healing takes place as a form of energetic cancellation within the psychic anatomy, and that higher-dimensional configuration is beyond our full knowing while we're in these bodies, unless our higher selves are Advanced Masterminds.**

Most of us are not capable of conducting the energetic repair work that goes into rectifying, through cancellation of wave forms, the actual fourth-dimensional energy signatures of the past-life traumas, shocks, and blocks we've incurred. We can slowly change that information as I described earlier. But without higher assistance, we can't perform this rapid form of healing we're discussing now. Not until we become highly Advanced Masters.

The new fields of energy medicine and energy psychology approach that level of healing, and they are remarkable and exciting for that reason. Yet by necessity, they're still based in the third dimension and so reach those higher levels by resonant association, where, again, Higher Agencies can step in to finish the healing—if the individual is prepared and willing and has made prior efforts in this direction.

So we are indeed reliant on this Cosmic assistance. However, **nothing is done for us without our participation and agreement.** Otherwise, circumstances we need to experience for our own growth could be altered and our advancement thus delayed.

**So Why Aren't You Making Progress?**

You've taken the first step. You've cultivated these associations with interdimensional healing forces between lifetimes as the first step in your self-healing plans. You need their help, and yet you know you will be carrying out your own plans for self-improvement during your physical incarnation.

If you're already on this planet, how then do you cultivate these relationships? You're doing it. By study, application, questing, and learning. By your open-minded search for truth. By all your positive deeds and aspirations which put you in mental alignment with the most positive Minds in the universe. By your thoughts from day to day and hour to hour, by your positive mental maintenance.

Okay, that's step one. Check.

Previously, we used my example to go through some of the next steps in a past-life healing:

1. Reincarnate to the scene of the crime.

2. Learn of the past.

3. Accept it based on the proof that becomes evident to you.

4. Feel remorse or a change of consciousness toward it.

Sometimes, that's all it takes. Sometimes healing *appears to be* instantaneous with your moment of recognition and acceptance of an incident from your past-life history.

But what about experiences like mine with the strength-training injuries, the ones that keep coming back around?

Or the fibroid tumors mentioned in my past-life reading, which still exist in my body?

In brief: I refused the complete hysterectomy urged upon me on the grounds that it would have a more harmful impact on my psychic anatomy than my negligible symptoms were having, which was mostly about vanity and finding clothes to fit, above and beyond the years of heavy bleeding. I decided these were not enough good reasons for inflicting further harm on that already karmically-damaged part of my anatomy. Well-intentioned or not, hysterectomy or other invasive surgeries would still destroy parts of my body, adding more destructive energy to that aspect of my psychic anatomy, where I've already got plenty of stored, psychic aberrations.

Meanwhile, I've had numerous past-life recognitions about repeated traumas in that area of my body, and countless awakenings of understanding that were prompted by this condition over the years. In other words, I've reaped benefits from my deformity.

But the rest of that fibroid healing story is still, for me, a big question mark: *Why do I still have this aberration? Why can't I heal?*

If we're not yet healed, we have our reasons. We're still not ready, despite perhaps lifetimes of preparation. And no advanced Being is going to interfere with that until and unless you ask for their help. Even then they will work to support your choices.

*Are they always good reasons for delay? Wise reasons?*

No. Not always. But this is a tangle we must unravel for ourselves. It might take an entire lifetime, and perhaps we knew that before we were born.

If you're stuck on a stubborn problem, ask yourself why you might not be ready for change, because now you know you're the person in charge. This question isn't so easy to answer. The variations on this theme are infinite, as you can imagine:

✴ Some people are learning from their infirmities, valuable lessons they couldn't gain any other way.

✴ Some people are unable to give up the energy-habits that might surround their mental or physical ailment.

✴ Sometimes the problem is a thought-form they've created for themselves, a pure-energy mind construction that becomes, with repetition, as real and tangible as any astral entity or physical circumstance.

✳ Sometimes it really is a separate astral entity or entities who have attached themselves into the individual's psychic body who are exerting a strong influence, or even a pattern of mental or physical illness manifesting in the person's exterior life. It's only in recent history that this problem has been relegated to the closet of the unspoken among the psychological and medical professions. The reasons for these attachments are endless, and at various moments in our lives, we Earth dwellers all experience this kind of mental link-up with astral entities. But the lasting, *destructive* subastral influence that we can't simply shake off by changing our attunement to a higher frequency with our positive thinking and attitudes (as Chapter 9 described)—those are the ones that create serious, stubborn trouble, such as addictions, illness, or aberrant behavior.

✳ Some people even need to die a few times from the same or similar problems before they are satisfied that certain lessons have been learned. (Remember, we older souls are more in charge of our own learning objectives. We decide when we're done.)

✳ Some people are bound to the problem in the present life by guilt associated with past-life events. It's as if they're punishing themselves for something they think they've done wrong. Or they might be motivated to cling to the problem by any other closely-held emotion. They'll do anything subconsciously to maintain the status quo.

It becomes necessary to learn a lot about yourself in order to dig out such deep, underlying *motivations*.

Remember the question I asked myself above, "So what was I *really* after in my repeated attempts to work out with weights?" I was looking for hidden incentives that were causing me to repeat the situation: Was it a lesson I was trying to teach myself? Or an emotional attachment I might be better off discarding—if I could identify it? Such motivations might lie buried in the underbelly of my subconscious, where I couldn't easily see them.

**You're in Charge!**

The variations and exceptions in the paths we take to bring about a constructive change in ourselves are never-ending. That's why we are all part of an Infinite maze called life. You will find your own unique way to resolve your unique problems. You can read a zillion advice books or consult with countless advisors, here and in higher worlds, and it will still come right down to you and your personal choices over the course of your many lifetimes.

But this gives you Power. You're not waiting for someone else to give you permission to heal or grow beyond your current limits! You're not waiting for some Superpowered Being to strike the gong, either.

If you understand the interdimensional design of your energy being, you now know that you have all the potential for unlimited growth, healing, and mental development. It's your birthright to become a functioning, godlike participant in the Infinite Creative Intelligence. It's in your hands, and no one else's. That's so liberating!

So will I go back to my weight-lifting book and try a new routine? I frankly don't know yet. I'm going to have to mull it over, and consult with my journal, where my Cosmic CoAuthors so often and so easily reach me, if I ask and listen. Ultimately, however, it will all be up to me.

I do know one thing: Once you identify a dangerous pattern, it's foolish to repeat it. I've now identified the repetitive nature of my injuries and their association with the mind-set of the weight-lifting program. I can harken back to other circumstances in my life (and in the lives of others I've known) and see that there are, indeed, many harmful things I've given up over the years as my awareness of past-life continuities and connections has set me free of them. This could be one of those instances. Or not.

The next chapter will lay out new ways for you to identify and free yourself from the resistance you might have to letting go of old entanglements, those of both past and present lives.

By the way, have you noticed that in your new perspective, the dividing line between past lives and present life has begun to blur?

∞ ✹ ∞

## Dig for Deeper Motivations

1. Do you have a problem that you've been unable to resolve or one that you'd like to begin working on? Describe it in your journal.

2. See if you can find within yourself any hidden reasons you might want to hold on to this problem. Are these good reasons or poor reasons? Can you list any benefits you've gained from having the problem? Can you list the detriments?

    The following chapters will help you with this inner research, so if the answers to these self-search questions don't pop into your mind, keep reading!

# 16

## Breaking Free

*So now you've identified something* in yourself that you want to change, whether it's a past-life remnant you've carried forward that no longer serves you, or a present-life thought-form or habit you want to break. You don't have any good reasons for holding back any longer and you are seriously ready to change and grow beyond it, speeding your evolutionary development. Or as I've termed it, you're ready to heal this aspect of yourself. So far, so good.

All healing begins and ends with *attunement.*

You feel a pain or symptom, or you identify something in yourself that you want to improve. So you *tune* back in your thoughts to engage in some back-tracking: *Where and when did this begin? What was I doing then? What, if anything, was influencing me?*

You might go back as far as prior lifetimes, or you might find something in your present life that served as your trigger for this trait or ailment. Once you've found an incident or anomaly, you ask yourself:

*What were my thoughts aligned to? What frequency did I tune into? In other words, what was my mental attunement?*

Your next step will be to change that attunement, and raise your frequency from where it oscillated in the past. This will activate all the elements of your higher Consciousness in order to facilitate healing and change and growth. By strengthening your desire for progressive change, and asking yourself these questions, you're already beginning to raise your frequency and activate your higher senses. But this is only the beginning.

At this stage it's simple. It's like when you stream a movie or video from the Internet. You choose a film to watch and next thing you know, you're watching a violent rape, followed by several assassinations and a lot of shouted profanity and more violence.

*Yikes—this is the movie I picked?!*

Your frequency discernment kicks in. Now that you've learned about energy and become more self-aware, the moment you start to feel nauseous from the lowering of your frequency to match that of this trashy movie (in your humble opinion and the opinion of your gut), you shut it down with a few clicks and choose a different one.

*Ah, that's better.*

Immediately, your frequency starts to rise again and you feel a lot better. You've adjusted your attunement. You've improved the *frequency* of your consciousness by where you've directed it.

Simple, right?

But real life isn't always so simple.

For this discussion, consider that *frequency determines quality*. Higher frequency=improved quality. Lower frequency=*ugh!*

If you're lucky, whatever you saw in those few awful minutes of the watching the wrong-for-you movie won't stick with you; you'll shed it as your frequency rises. (Ah, but as Ruth Norman often reminded me, "Luck's got nothing to do with it!" You applied your interdimensional knowledge that whatever you oscillate with, you will draw into your life in many ways, so you made a better choice.)

This is what you're looking for when you do your backtracking: What "movie" did I inadvertently download into my consciousness that triggered this pain or symptom or personality trait that I want to overcome?

Once you've identified something you think might have triggered your problem, you're going to do what you can to disconnect from it, i.e., to change the film, raise or alter your frequency, or as we used to say back in the twentieth century, to "change the channel" of your consciousness. That's not necessarily going to bring about an instant cure or healing, but it's where you want to start. You can probably find a trigger in your present life, even before you delve deeper into the subject of past lives.

For instance, this is what I did after I experienced the floaters and flashers in my eye. I looked back until I found the pineapple plants that looked like weapons. Then, with the help of some factual research in a reference book, I found a picture of the weapon, called a mace, and that led me back further into recalling my own past-life history.

By now, by studying this book, you've added a few ultra-high-frequency channels to your dial or bandwidth. When you ring in or *select* those frequencies, you're making an attunement through your Superconscious Self to your spiritual guides and teachers, who can then lend their healing assistance.

Luck's got nothing to do with it; these have all been your choices. You've exercised your *selectivity*, one aspect of your Infinite design that you'll want to cultivate in your quest for an improved life. You've selected higher frequencies for your mental attunement, and thus speeded your evolutionary growth.

So, this is why I say "all healing begins and ends with attunement." You've used your mind to tune back to the triggering cause, and you've used your mind to select a better or improved or higher frequency. You've reached for the next rung up the evolutionary spiral.

And still in theory, it all sounds very simple and easy to do. But the reality is that you're going to encounter resistance to this progressive change, and it might come at you from many directions—before, during, and after you make changes in your attunement or frequency associations.

Overcoming this resistance to change will be your next challenge.

It starts within your own self, right down at the level of the fourth-dimensional energy systems supporting your physical body.

### Prepare Your Body-Mind for Progressive Change

Change is scary. Ask your body and it will agree.

In a course I took from healer Donna Eden and psychologist David Feinstein, called "Freeing the Spirit," we learned techniques to break down both physical and emotional resistance to change.

First, we used Eden Energy Medicine tactics to calm the *energetic body's* resistance to progressive change.

In terms of the body's close-in, physical energy systems (such as your chakras and acupuncture meridians), the meridian or "radiant circuit" called Triple Warmer or Triple Heater in Chinese medicine has everything to do with our fight or flight survival response, and any kind of change—*whether for better or worse*—sends it into a tizzy.

What you feel when this happens is STRESS. You might suddenly feel really cold; hands and feet clammy like a dead person. Or if it's an extreme reaction, you'll start shaking or vibrating. You might feel sharp pains in various parts of your body, or you'll feel extremely exhausted and can't stop yawning.

These are all symptoms that your Triple Warmer meridian has thrown your body into survival mode and will actually try to *undo* any physical/energetic attempts you make to change. It tries to put things back the way they were. It's often successful.

When you try to change something, your body's energy systems don't distinguish that this change might be good for the body; it registers *any* change as a possible threat and goes into this activated survival (stress) mode. That's because your body is designed to maintain any status quo, good or bad; as long as you're alive, everything must be fine so don't change a thing!

On the other hand, if something's changing, your survival early-warning system determines that your life could be in danger! Your Triple Warmer energy meridian reacts to this energetic conclusion, takes over your other bodily energy systems, and redirects their energy to deal with the impending catastrophe. It protects essential organs this way, while neglecting others, and gets you ready to run, freeze, or fight. That's fine if there truly is a threat to your life; Triple Warmer will help you survive. But what if you're trying to break a habit? One that goes back lifetimes?

When we're trying to make energetic improvements in an unbalanced bodily energy system, Eden Energy Medicine (EEM) practitioners will first use techniques to mollify the constabulary of the powerful Triple Warmer meridian. Very often, that's the only way a body will accept healing corrections.

This would be a wonderful technique for all healers to adopt, because any kind of physical change, or medication, or introduction of a new habit is likely to set off this Triple Warmer reaction. It leaves you feeling exhausted in the short term, and it steals energy that's needed for other parts of you. Over the long term, that can damage your health. This is why modern stress is such a killer: the body responds as if the situation is life-threatening, and eventually, the body wears out from the constant strain of throwing all your gears into survival mode all day long, every day.

And that happens merely at the physical level of bodily energy systems! That's at the shallowest level of our instinctive resistance to change—in the energy systems that directly support our physical bodies as they bridge between the psychic anatomy (our blueprint) and the physical cells (our body).

Eventually, you may calm down naturally and the change you're trying to make will finally be accepted by your early-warning systems, *if you're persistent in introducing it.* Or if you've aligned yourself with a knowledgeable acupuncturist or acupressurist or EEM practitioner, you may more quickly surmount this roadblock.

When Joseph and I made improvements in our sleeping hours, for instance—early to bed, early to rise—we had to counterbalance the Triple Warmer reactions for a few days until our "early-warning alert system" calmed down and accepted the change. Fortunately, we know EEM techniques for soothing Triple Warmer, or we might have given up on our efforts to improve, thinking that our bodies weren't benefitting. We knew better, we understood the problem, and we used those simple balancing tactics to reduce the stress response until we started to feel the genuine and significant health benefits the new sleeping hours brought us.

This was one of those instances where our intellectual reach for a better life had to overcome the natural resistance of our bodies to a change in our status quo.

Frankly, I think everyone should acquire a copy of the self-help book, *Energy Medicine,* and learn many easy ways to calm stress and work constructively with the Triple Warmer response. But since I'm supposed to be overcoming my past-life dogmatic tendencies, I won't insist.

**Psych Yourself Up**

Next in the "Freeing the Spirit" class, we learned methods from the new discipline of energy psychology to calm *emotional* barriers to healing or change, or what David called *psychological reversals.*

I remember the first time Joseph worked through the self-checking questions with me, when we were practicing an advanced energy psychology method developed by Donna and David. At the beginning of our session (Joseph as healer, me as recipient), we went looking for any psychological reversals that would block my success.

First he had me say, "It's safe to get over this problem," while he muscle-tested my arm. That is, he used a technique of applied kinesiology, more accurately known as energy-testing. If my extended arm had fallen as he pressed on it, meaning no energy flowing through my muscles, that would indicate that I didn't really believe that statement. But in this case I did believe it. My arm stayed strong.

Next I was to say, "I'll be okay no matter what happens," while he tested me.

*Ka-flump!!!* Down went the arm!

*Really?* Really. Apparently I didn't believe the statement at the level of my energy systems! My Conscious Mind, ever the trickster, was perfectly willing to claim it *did* believe the statement, but my true belief was revealed by the energy test. I was lying to myself!

When I did the prescribed countermeasure to calm my energy systems into feeling safe no matter the outcome of my healing experience, I started to cry, proving that I'd touched on a deeply embedded fear. Tch, embarrassing! Glad it was only we two in the room. But they were healing tears, a release of the energies comprising whatever fears were embedded in my psychic anatomy, fears that would have blocked my acceptance of any kind of healing change.

Bizarre, right?

For this healing modality, I did not need to know exactly what those fears comprised, although I had vague ideas. This is one of the wonders of energy medicine and energy psychology: your physical energy systems can be sorted out and balanced without full conscious awareness of what caused the problem, and your emotional and physical body will fall in line, at least temporarily.

As we've said so many times, permanent healing is a matter between you, your preparation, and your higher resources. But an energy medicine form of temporary aid sometimes triggers the full-scale, permanent healing.

That could be because, since you're working with invisible (higher-dimensional) energy, albeit at relatively lower frequencies closer to the third-dimensional body, you may be in turn linking harmonically to the higher-frequency aspects of the psychic anatomy more easily than, say, a chemical drug that suppresses symptoms. The energy-healing tactic may then become your catalyst for permanent change in your psychic anatomy blueprint, rippling all the way up to its highest frequencies of the Superconscious.

A difference in motivation might also play a role in your experience: taking a drug that suppresses symptoms versus seeking a change in your energy patterns and habits, even at the lowest levels.

So as I repeated the countermeasure technique a few more times, my energies calmed down and I was able to say the statement with conviction. I muscle-tested strong, meaning I believed now that I would be safe, with all parts of my accessible consciousness.

We went on to a third statement and I passed that one, so then I was able to proceed successfully with the energy psychology session I'd embarked upon.

You know that if I remembered what that session was about, I'd tell you, right? Honestly I don't, but I will say that, next to my experience with past-life therapy, energy psychology (and energy medicine) have yielded wonderful results for both Joseph and me. That includes both the self-help tapping methods, such as the Emotional Freedom Technique (EFT) developed by Gary Craig, and the practitioner-assisted method taught by Donna and David in their advanced classes. You'll find many useful self-help techniques as well in *The Promise of Energy Psychology*, co-authored by all three of these extraordinary individuals. It's easy to learn the basics!

Energy psychology has been particularly beneficial when the change we wanted to make in our relationship to the external world (our attunement or frequency association) was relatively minor. But it also serves as a wonderful accompaniment to other healing endeavors, such as past-life therapy or medical treatment. And around the world, practitioners are compiling very impressive success stories with victims of post-traumatic stress and other psychological conundrums. Expect to hear much more about this form of treatment in the future!

**Revisit Your Hidden Resistance**

Ironic, isn't it? The thing that's really good for you and is evolutionarily wise—progressive change—sets off warning alarms in your body, both energetically and psychologically. We are wired to maintain that status quo, *whether good or bad.*

This is why change, or what I've called healing, is such tricky business. We have so many defense mechanisms that prevent growth or healing: fear, guilt, self-deception, rationalization—we humans are amazingly competent at coming up with ways to avoid change!

But let's take a look at other methods for overcoming your natural resistance to change in order to create true, lasting improvements in your life.

As you can see if you haven't skipped ahead to this chapter, *there's no one else in the universe responsible for our predicaments but us.* We are the Power—because we hold the keys to the contents of our psychic anatomy, the software program that directs our lives.

Now's the time to go a little further with your journaling practice. You're after a new level of reflective honesty. No one else needs to read what you write, ever. But if you can't learn to dredge out your true feelings and thoughts, you'll always be in the dark about what's actually lurking within you that might be the root cause of your troubles.

Inside your mind are many trap doors. What's behind them can often be subtle, unconscious motivations you've hidden from yourself. If you are brave enough to open those doors, you might untangle the worst messes you've made in your life by discovering WHY you've done it, and why you continue to repeat the same pattern, even though your Conscious Mind awareness claims to be absolutely and completely sick of it! Whatever "it" is!

Motivation. Intention.

What's behind the choices you've been making? Honestly? If you attempted the exercise at the end of the last chapter, dig deeper now, and keep digging. Write it all out. You'll probably be amazed if you've never done this before. The more you write, the more intelligent you become—

*Hey, wait a minute, is that just me? Or are my spiritual advisors coming to my assistance?*

Well, they might be. What's your motivation for writing? Are you venting? Cursing? Accusing others?

Or are you sincerely trying to heal yourself, change and improve?

Again, your motivation will determine your frequency, and your frequency will determine whose mind you're aligning yourself with.

It's good to vent but be careful not to dwell in griping and grumbling. You do want to understand your emotional state, so don't suppress, but remember the energy principles at work: whatever frequency you resonate with, that's what you'll ring in. Whether it's a friend, family member, or astral entity, whether you're talking or writing, don't give anyone the opportunity to chime in on some negative emotional state and reinforce it. To get to certain neighborhoods, we must sometimes drive through the unsavory ones. But we don't linger.

Same thing with your journaling: Don't squelch your feelings—after all, you're trying to get to the truth of them and this is your place to feel free! But stay aware and be sure your motivation remains one of self-understanding, not blaming. That positive intention will put you in touch with the Minds of advanced development who may offer you some truly valuable insights while you write. (Or sketch!)

Resistance may be futile in a *Star Trek* world, but it is always persistent. Your hidden motives might be harboring secret, internal resistance, or creating a subtle influence that causes you to short-circuit the changes you've already made. Use your new powers of honest analysis to sift carefully through the sands of your many thoughts about the change you're embarking upon.

Now, it's very easy to write in a book that you need to ferret out all your self-deceptions, but it's next to impossible to do. Seriously. We all have dark areas and blind spots, because you simply can't heal every aspect of yourself all at once. They may be a kind of self-protection that we need until we're ready to deal with whatever's next on our healing agenda. Or we might not be done with the lessons involved in our so-called problems. So do be honest, but gentle with yourself. The pace of your growth is entirely at your discretion.

**Family, Friends, and Former Associates**

Were you wondering when I'd get to this?

In addition to your internal physical and emotional resistance, inevitably as a changing, improving, and growing soul, you will encounter external resistance.

I don't like to dwell on this because it's too easy to veer over into the blame game. But Joseph has pointed out to me that the subject must be breached, because often our internal resistance attracts other people who will mirror that resistance back to us. It's not that they're on the attack, necessarily. It might only be that we've let them in the door, allowing them to mirror some little doubt or unresolved hang-up we're having about the changes we're making.

Then again, if you're steadily improving, you can also rile up those who don't like to see that change or what it represents. As the Japanese say, "The nail that sticks out gets hammered down."

First let's talk about the natural evolution of relationships that's going to occur as you grow.

Raising your frequency from its former state means you're no longer oscillating in the same harmony as before with those who persist at your former frequency. I'm not going so far as to say you're not going to relate to them at all. That's so dependent on many factors! But you're likely to encounter a shift in your relationships with others as you speed along your evolutionary growth.

I like Ernest Norman's analogy for this inevitable adjustment, although he wrote it decades before personal computers and Facebook entered our lives. If you find that a few former friends no longer fit with your new life and values, don't feel sad about it. Remember how close you were with your second- and third-grade pals? And how easily you moved away from those relationships as you grew up, went through changes, and entered adulthood? Even family members may need to stretch and shift their interactions as they grow beyond the nuclear family.

Not only in this life but over the course of lifetimes, you'll form associations you'll need to leave behind in order to evolve. In many cases, it happens naturally and without resistance. But sometimes it's painful and difficult, like ripping off a bandage: feels much better and everyone completes their individual healing after it's over, but the process can be challenging. We've talked about this in the chapter about polarity relationships, and we'll talk more about it in the family healing chapter.

But now we must discuss the people who remain in your life for whatever reasons who will resist your efforts to change, to improve the status quo. You might encounter individuals or entire groups who oppose your self-improvements.

Two things to remember:

1. You cannot change them; you can only change yourself.

2. You must not allow yourself to be hampered in your progressive momentum.

It's not easy to remain cool, calm, and collected in these situations. But if you let them get your goat, as they say, you will have lost your battle for a higher frequency and they will triumph in their efforts to keep you at their level.

Also, the further and faster you travel in your self-development, the more subtle the attempts to halt your progress will become. By that time, you've learned to identify and counterbalance garden-variety resistance, in yourself and in others. It's when you start getting cloaked and disguised resistance that your mental agility will be tested. You'll have learned by then how to identify the subtle manipulations of astral forces that might want to waylay you, or impede your positive influence on others they've made their own, in a possessive sort of way. You have to use all your powers of frequency discernment then, to break down these interactions into their component frequencies and identify who or what the driving force behind this resistance might be: Is it your own self? The lower self of the individual voicing the words or performing the actions? Or a subastral influence attempting to reach and stop you through this individual, by triggering all your own lowest reactions and thus defeating your efforts to rise above your former station in life?

Throughout the course of your many lifetimes, you've undoubtedly formed associations with people, groups, and powerful astral influences who now will seem counterproductive, if not downright abhorrent to you. They do not want you to grow beyond their influence. They will indeed try to stop you, particularly if your positive example is going to pull even more people out of their grasp.

Not to get too dark with this subject, but it does happen and it pays to know about it. Sometimes that computer failure causing you to lose vital information might come through your own lower self—your inner resistance, untamed, making you subconsciously strike the wrong key. And then you must recognize and address that resistance before you can complete your positive project.

But sometimes there are larger forces at work. The individual who made the remark that took all the wind out of your sails. Was that coincidence? Were they motivated by their own jealousy? Or by an astral force who knew exactly what to prompt them to say and exactly when?

Either way, the solution is the same so don't spend too much time wondering about the who's, how's, and why's. You are still in control—you control your emotional reactions.

"Don't let the bastards get you down," and "Forewarned is forearmed," as I was told in my interdimensional infancy. Or perhaps you can recall the infamous scene from *Star Wars* where Luke is being tempted to join the Dark Side by Darth Vadar: "You have controlled your fear. Now release your anger…only your hatred can destroy me."

Yeah, right. Nice try, Vadar. Drop your frequency to a lower level and you've lost your personal battle for progressive states of mind, thus joining the Dark Side so that you can be controlled by even darker forces, as Vadar was. So raise your frequency back up as quickly as you can and get back on the path of Light you've chosen.

No one's perfect; sooner or later someone's going to get to you. But to quote another Japanese proverb, courtesy of Joseph, "Fall down seven times, get up eight."

The bigger your self-improvement project, the stronger the external resistance, coming from multiple dimensions. We've touched on this here and there throughout this book, but when you feel it directed right down at your little evolutionary attempts, you're going to become engaged in a battle for your Spirit that will test all that you know. And you will triumph! Because you've been forewarned, and because you have new knowledge and understanding, new tools, and new friends and polarities who've got your back, as they say.

In this chapter, we've been talking about the resistance we must overcome in order to pursue our creative evolutionary development, but it's also good to remember the benefits of resistance. Without resistance an incandescent light bulb won't glow! And we wouldn't develop strength in our convictions, or Power in our Spirit. Every time you resolve to pursue a positive course and apply all of your knowledge and experience to the task, you're making your Spirit glow a little brighter.

## Soothe Your Stress Reactions

Try this simple method I learned from Donna Eden the next time you want to make a change and can feel, with your new sensitivities, that your body is going into a Triple Warmer survival, *anti-change*, resistant, fearful reaction:

1. Place the palm of one hand over your forehead.

2. Place the palm of your other hand over your navel, covering a few inches above it as well, over your solar plexus. (I like to center my hand so that I'm touching points both above and below my navel, but do what feels right to you.)

3. Hold this position while you bring to mind the change you want to make, or whatever else is making you feel unsettled. Remain holding these points for a few minutes or longer, until you feel a shift within you or your thoughts can no longer stay focused on the problem and spontaneously jump off to another subject. This works well with anything that's giving you undue stress!

4. If you should be among those whose Triple Warmer is worn out from too many years of stressful living, so that it goes weak instead of going on alert, you might feel tired after you perform this exercise. Next time, try simply holding your forehead and forget the hand over the navel area. This will still calm your stress. Then go have yourself checked out to see if you're suffering from adrenal burn-out as I once was! (If you feel exhausted after you eat, that's another clue you're

headed for trouble. Time for a check-up!)

Many more easy, quick, energy-balancing techniques are available to learn through the resources I've listed in Appendix A. Now that you know that you are a pure energy being, take the time to learn as many as you can. They often take mere moments to perform, and I'll wager you soon view them as vital tools that make your life so much more enjoyable. That's certainly been our experience.

Remember: Your life begins in your energy systems, from the top (psychic anatomy/higher dimensions) down (physical body/third dimension). Any energy adjustments or improvements you're able to make, even at the nearly-physical level like this, can only help resonate a balancing influence up and down your entire system. No side effects, no harm done.

# 17

## Higher-Dimensional Learning

*Never underestimate the variety of* ingenious ways your Cosmic CoAuthors will find to get information to you, to guide without interfering. Mastery, indeed.

When you've absorbed the concepts of interdimensional consciousness to understand how you can live from life to life, and how you live between lives, carrying with you all that you are and ever have been, you may begin to have past-life flashbacks, dreams, or insights, generally fostered by the higher-dimensional forces working with you.

Record them. Write or draw them into your journals. Pay attention. Believe what your instincts and inner teachers tell you, because quick as a flash, you may begin to deny that such-and-such could possibly be true, and that will cause you to forget what you've been shown! These insights are often so subtle and natural-feeling that people have labeled them "intuition," as if it were something that came from you alone. Too many fail to take them seriously.

Even if that's all you ever use it for, your journal could become your most important healing tool. Matter of fact, I've been dreaming more vivid dreams recently after improving my sleep habits. I've had dreams that gave me warnings of wrong steps I'd been taking; dreams that supplied scenes from prior lives; and dreams that bore remnants of my visits to higher worlds.

I am going to get up from this computer and put a dream journal next to my bed right now before I forget. I like to use a separate one because my regular journal gets moved from place to place as the whim takes me, so this one will always be there where my sleepy hands can reach it.

If you decide to do the same, in case you haven't yet begun to record your dreams, I will applaud you for joining me in this difficult quest. I say difficult because too often we must leap out of bed to be somewhere or to fulfill someone else's schedule. But with very little exertion of will and effort you may find that, if you've made your sleeping environment optimal, you'll dream richly, and then awaken shortly before your alarm goes off so you can linger in that fertile, hypnagogic state, part way between dreaming and waking. In that half-in, half-out-of-body level of awareness, your dreams will remain with you and many other inspirational jewels may come to you. Grab the journal and catch them before the morning's activities make them evaporate like dew in the rising sun.

What is an optimal sleeping environment? Sufficient food and water during the day, with blackout drapes in the bedroom and any electronic sensor or other lights taped over or extinguished, so that your hormones (serotonin, melatonin, cortisol, and all the rest) have the complete darkness they need to do their proper nightly exchange. Studies have shown that even the smallest light amid complete darkness—a fiber-optic at a location behind the subject's knee—stopped melatonin production.

Add some fresh air by opening windows a crack if you can, and give yourself two hours before bed to wind down naturally. That means turning off all electronic screens that emit blue-green light which would disrupt your vital hormonal shift. Yep, that's your TV, computer, e-reader, tablet, phone, etc.

As energy beings, we are highly photosensitive, as much as any plant! We are designed to respond to the changing color of natural daylight as we progress from the bluish tints of morning to the golden tints of evening. Our amazing hormonal dance takes its cues from these light changes and literally keeps us sane and healthy. Unfortunately, most modern electronics mimic early daylight, tricking our bodies into waking up instead of calming down. And we all know it's not nice to fool Mother Nature; she tends to make us pay for it later with insulin resistance and other serious ailments.

Hard to do? Only at first. Worth it? Yes!

You'll discover that candlelight showers and baths are wonderfully restful, and so is your quiet time with journal, sketch pad, musical instruments, conversation, or novel (the paper kind). Favorite TV shows air late at night? That's what recording devices are for.

Don't neglect to address your chosen lighting devices throughout your home. Certainly you won't want fluorescents for a multitude of health reasons, and beware of tinted incandescents. Learn about any LED's or halogen bulbs you use. You do not want daylight-mimicking light bulbs during the hours that such lighting is unnecessary. Save them for lighting the work space you use during the natural day.

I've included items in the Resources section for more information on this fascinating aspect of our energy-design.

As you might guess, this is my latest de-stressing, health-enhancing tactic. So far, so good. The truly unexpected benefit has been the restoration of dreams that I know are deeply meaningful to me. So, forgive me while I take a moment to move my dream journal into place. I'll be right back!

...

Okay, now that's done, and we can talk about the greatest benefit of a good night's sleep: your nightly sojourns in the higher worlds. This is where you raise your frequency to the highest possible levels during your physical incarnation.

My heroine in *Cosmic Dancer* has vivid dreams of her life between lives. Actually, she leaves her sleeping body behind and "travels" to the sparkling worlds of Light mentally, where she continues her education in classes such as "Remedial Reincarnation 101 for Earth Dwellers," or in conversations with her teacher Coriskancsia. I really don't want to give away her story here, or reveal all of her higher-world teachers. So let's talk about you!

Each night when you drift off to sleep, you are self-hypnotizing into a suspended state of consciousness. But that's only with regard to your Conscious Mind. Your true mind remains active, as your dreams indicate. This is when you can make the most of those higher-world connections with your Cosmic CoAuthors.

Younger souls may have limited opportunities between lives and during their sleeping hours, simply because they haven't yet developed their minds to grasp much beyond the "here and now," tangible aspects of Earth. They may experience a form of "darkness" or senseless-seeming chaos or subconscious unravelings until they are reborn or wake up from sleep.

I'd already written this description when I read *Proof of Heaven* by neurosurgeon Dr. Eben Alexander. He confirms this notion as he describes passing through this state during his extraordinary near-death experience. He called it the "Realm of the Earthworm's Eye View," and described it as "Darkness, but a visible darkness—like being submerged in mud yet also being able to see through it. Or maybe dirty Jell-O describes it better. Transparent, but in a bleary, blurry, claustrophobic, suffocating kind of way." And, for many reasons, he soon found his way or was led out of this state and into higher realms. (It's a terrific book, by the way.)

His habit of regarding the world and his work as a surgeon as a purely physical endeavor probably landed him at that low level first, oscillating at a lower frequency. But his higher associations and even prayers and thoughts of his loving family directed toward his comatose body soon brought help to his awareness, and that assistance enabled him to break free of this subastral realm. It's also possible that this courageous man chose to endure a whole spectrum of possible frequency associations as he left his body in clinical and brain death, strictly for the purpose of coming back to tell us the whole story. His circumstances were so extreme and unique, I'm guessing that even Dr. Alexander suspects he might have planned it all prior to his birth in the present lifetime in order to bring back his illuminating report.

Even if you did start out with the earthworm's view after death or during sleep, as Dr. Alexander demonstrates, you're not bound to stay there. If you've developed any kind of higher-frequency connections at all, if you've got friends in high places or even friends on Earth who have made those connections and triangulate a little prayer or thought in your direction to help you make the link, or if you've been touched by a bit of knowing that there's more to life than "eat, sleep, television, and sex" as Ruth Norman often quipped, then your experience between lifetimes and during the nighttime hours carries the potential for something quite magnificent.

**Night School**

Higher dimensional worlds or planes or realms are as boundless and changeable as the Infinite. While your body lies sleeping, you might travel into the shimmering gardens of your higher-world teachers, visit their glittering energy classrooms and temples, learn while sitting in on an Advanced Master's presentation, and then return to your body before morning.

Will you remember? Not likely. The energy frequency of these locations/visitations is so high, it might not be compatible with your conscious, waking state of mind. Particularly if you've not sought much information about higher-dimensional worlds, it might completely freak you out if you suddenly awakened with a clear memory of them!

So we tend to bring back bits and pieces, flashes of gorgeousness, and most importantly, the inner knowings that our night classes have fostered.

The more you learn about these higher-dimensional places, Beings, and associations, the more chances that you'll bring them back to mind clearly during your waking hours. But don't be disappointed if you don't remember! That doesn't mean you're not continuing your studies every night you allow yourself that kind of deep, restful sleep.

I frequently find myself remembering the more mundane dreams I experience as I wind my way back down toward an Earth-based frequency, but they often indicate that they've followed after one of those higher-world night classes. They're often set in a "schoolroom" or instructional setting that's more like an Earth-based university or boarding school—complete with teachers who seem sooo familiar, although I've never met them in life. Perhaps I'm wrong about those being only mundane "dream locations." They *are* higher-dimensional because I'm dreaming them, and I learn a great deal when I wake up and think them over. So—no limitations!—higher worlds can appear to us to resemble anything, especially anything that will make us feel at home and comfortable. After all, they are designed by the Mind-energies of our teachers for our benefit while we're living on earth. It's what we learn while we're there, and the frequency at which they oscillate, that makes all the difference in our lives if we pay attention to them.

My morning dreams often contain important symbolism or insights that I'll be needing that day, which makes me think that my spiritual mentors are still working with me up to the last second before waking so that I'll remember. I learned a tactic of asking elements of a confusing dream what they symbolize to me in particular. For instance, while striving to complete this book, I've had quite a few dreams about newborn babies! That symbolism wasn't too difficult to figure out. (If I'd consulted a dream-symbol dictionary, it might not have been accurate *for me*, so trust yourself in this, and believe your first impulse or insight.)

Don't be discouraged if the dreams you recall seem routine. That doesn't mean you haven't been in Night School during your deepest, forgotten hours of sleep! And they might mean more than you think.

Even monsters and battlefields can be created for an important lesson, or to help you with the fears you've determined to overcome. Or they might symbolize the subterranean implications of something in your life that appears innocuous during waking hours. And so on! The speculations are endless, but your dreams will be unique and meaningful specifically for you. You grow spiritually as you analyze and consider these nightly sessions.

Truly, we learn in the higher dimensions first. Everything in our third-dimensional world happens in higher dimensions initially, then manifests down through lower and lower frequencies, oscillating down those harmonically linked, spiraling vortexes of energy until it reaches this world and re-emerges in third-dimensional, sine-wave based oscillations, which our five senses detect as all the elements of the world in which we currently function.

The same is true of your creative evolution. Your educational input begins in the higher worlds: You learn a thing in your true Self while in a higher-dimensional state. Then you come here to prove and test it in the third-dimensional world, where you've enrolled in Earth school for now. For an older soul, this continuing education begins between lifetimes, and doesn't stop during your physical incarnation.

So the next time you think you want to stay up late, remember the classes and experiences you'll be missing if you short your sleeping hours!

**Beautiful Destinations**

It helps to have some destination in mind when you go to sleep (or make a more lasting departure from your body).

Around 1955, Ernest Norman's Cosmic CoAuthors took him on a visionary tour of seven particular, higher-dimensional teaching worlds or centers, beginning with the higher astral planes of the planet Venus. These aren't located in our third-dimensional spectrum, and in fact the people who live on Venus range in frequency all up and down the scale. So if you've been reading about Venusians, you might have encountered those at the so-called lower planes (which are still far higher in frequency than Earth), or you might be discovering the higher level Beings he met who work for the benefit of humanity in the areas of physical and mental healing. Their work isn't limited to helping the inhabitants of only one planet, but Earth maintains a close relationship with Venus because of our population's frequent visits to its healing wards.

During his tour, Mr. Norman was shown such things as a ward full of glowing "bassinets," containing the tiny remnants of suicide victims' psychic anatomies. They were being bathed in love-energies by advanced healers and more highly-evolved "family" members to repair some of the damage they'd done, and to supply these souls with the means to, one day, reincarnate in order to attempt resolution of their difficulties. Otherwise, their self-destructive act, which shattered their psychic anatomy, will have halted their creative evolution.

Venus is the home of the skilled psychic EMTs who rescue all sorts of malformed and maladapted psychic anatomies and bring them back to these special realms for corrective and healing therapies. That is, if the lost or damaged soul has some link or means by which he or she can relate to such assistance.

But those are the most extreme cases of astral obsession, suicide, murder, sudden death, cancer, and so on. The plane of Venus offers wonderful learning opportunities and magnificent temples and gardens for all of us to visit during our nightly journeys, and its permanent residents include many of our most cherished spiritual leaders and teachers, as well as personal guides and mentors. In fact, if you wish to become a healer on Earth, you've very likely spent time learning your trade on one of the planes of Venus to which you've formed some relative connection. You can read more about it in *The Voice of Venus*, first book of Ernest Norman's five-book tour, called the Pulse of Creation series.

I understand that visionaries further back in history have described similar locations in the language of their time, as in the works of Emanuel Swedenborg. I haven't read those books yet; perhaps you'll tell me about them one day? Also, numerous contemporary individuals who've had near-death experiences (such as Dr. Alexander) have brought back scraps of visual description, and so have mystics from many cultures and orientations.

The seven enormous teaching centers described in Ernest Norman's series each have their own point of focus, loosely described as Healing, Science, Philosophy, Education, Arts, Leadership, and Devotion. A determined soul might spend thousands of years pursuing their interests through these seven planes and all their lower, associated realms of learning.

For example, let's say acting is your thing. You will probably visit Muse and/or its lower-frequency "subsidiaries" to study and expand your artistic expression between lives and during your nightly visits. If you're a physicist, you might find yourself on the scientific plane of Eros or its subplanes. Visiting Elysium? You'll meet some of this world's finest spiritual thinkers and doers. And so on.

You can see how helpful it would be to spend learning sojourns through several of these planes, for instance studying leadership in order to make your scientific or artistic accomplishments more useful during your subsequent lives.

This is why we're not limited. Such between-life scholastic endeavors depend on what you're after, and how long you've been at it. We have guidance, of course, but once you've reached a certain level of mental development, your soulic education is truly in your own hands. But as with any university, you have to earn your way into the higher levels through your oscillating frequency and your personal associations, objectives, and achievements. That's another reason to constantly strive for higher-frequency states of mind: it matters not only during your present lifetime, but also after this life ends.

In other words, the same energy principles of harmonics, frequency, and polarity that you're learning in this book will take you where you need to go in your interdimensional education, far into your future.

Since you and I are still at the level of needing to incarnate in a physical place such as Earth, as students of the Light we are given some assistance for our visits to these higher-frequency worlds at night. Otherwise, our little energy bodies might burn up in these high-energy atmospheres which are beyond our current levels of attainment. So, for instance, your Cosmic tutors might build an energy bubble to protect you, using their mind forces. Or you might be led into a protected area "for visitors only." Most likely, it will be suited to your own conception of what such a place or protection should be so that it will feel familiar and comfortable to you.

My visionary author friend Thomas Youngholm wrote a novel based on his notion of a "celestial bar," where the bartender is quite a knowledgeable character and things aren't exactly what they seem and it seems to be a landing spot for a troubled earth guy who's looking for spiritual guidance. (See Resources.)

While writing *Cosmic Dancer* and other books, I've been shown a number of fascinating, higher-dimensional locations, as I'm sure other visionary writers have experienced. I've also experienced my own healing, psychic visions of such worlds and Beings. I let my character spend lots of time there during *Cosmic Dancer* as an excuse to do a little exploring myself and together we had some fascinating experiences and met some unexpected teachers.

**Infinite Landing Sites**

When they leave their bodies at the end of their earth lives, some people keep doing what they'd been doing on Earth before their transition, not fully realizing they've made a dimensional change. They might be surrounded by the accoutrements of a life that feels familiar to them, with all the structures and tools they remember. Sooner or later, someone might alert them and take them to a healing location or school. By now you probably realize that "healing" and "school" as separate ventures are earth concepts; education and healing go hand-in-hand in the higher worlds we're speaking of.

Or the individual could carry on living much as they did on Earth, until they find or are automatically drawn into the womb of a compatible mother who gives them birth again.

At such a level, the individual is making very slow evolutionary progress, either for reasons of soulic youth, or because of some hampering trauma they've experienced. Undoubtedly we've all been there in our many life-learning attempts: we might have lingered in an unaware state when we were very young souls; or we might have left our bodies behind in dire circumstances so we floundered for a while in the lower frequencies of the subastral until we were reborn to try again on Earth. We do have many opportunities, so a few lives of confusion are to be expected, I think. I've certainly had them. It's another way to learn, but one you wouldn't like to repeat.

What we call "subastral" is also a relatively "higher" frequency dimension than the third dimension you currently reside in, so endless subastral nightmares are also a potential after-death landing site for you. If you have religious beliefs that train you to expect a certain type of afterlife experience, you're likely to have it—unless someone comes to show you an alternative, or something changes your mind and perception. You don't have to remain, but you might start out there.

The nonphysical worlds you visit at night and between lifetimes present infinite possibilities. Where you wind up depends on:

✳ What you know

* Where you've directed your consciousness via thought

* Your basic frequency oscillation

* Who you know; what higher (or lower) associations you've made during your waking life

It's all up to you, in other words, but not in the usual sense of, "I get to decide now." You're deciding at every moment of your energetic, permanently inscribed life.

My *Cosmic Dancer* heroine goes to a place that was probably familiar to me—makes sense, no? It's spectacular in my inner vision, filled with light and color, everything appearing as if made of pure crystal because it's all energy—sparkling and brilliant—and it's full of the kinds of surprises I would like and the learning opportunities that would appeal to me. Ah, the privileges of authorship! But your inner and higher-world experiences might not look like mine.

Our lifetimes-long endeavors may one day earn us a full-time "scholarship" to a higher-dimensional world where we'll continue our education and serve our younger brothers and sisters coming up behind us. We'll no longer need the lessons of a third-dimensional, Earth-type world, but will be incarnating into progressively higher planes of existence, working our way up the creative, evolutionary spiral. Until then, it's wonderful to take advantage of the special learning opportunities that have been created for the benefit of humanity coming and going on Earth and elsewhere.

In fact, without these night classes and between-life experiences in higher worlds, our planet would not globally experience its leaps forward, its inventions, and its gradual or rapid improvements. Individuals who pass through these educational centers bring new knowledge with them as they reincarnate on Earth, or return from their dreaming state. Thus, they supply the steady infusion of Light

Intelligence that becomes available to the planet as a whole.

Can you think of people who must surely have learned elsewhere what they've brought to this world, much to its benefit? They may not be famous, but their contributions bear the distinctive touch of a higher input, if you look for it. I call these individuals Visionary Heroes and I've been fortunate to meet several of them, working in a variety of fields.

You and I can share in this global healing effort every night that we tune up our minds to reach the higher worlds. How much we bring back with us depends on what we've prepared ourselves to achieve in this lifetime. And we can always improve as we go along! This is where your daytime studies will truly pay off, supplying skills and knowledge that crystallize your nighttime education into permanent additions to your psychic anatomy, while supplying the means to pour what you've learned overnight into this needy third-dimensional world.

One thing we can all bring back: a beautiful, uplifting LOVE energy that we've soaked up during our night classes! That alone will enhance the lives of those around us—not to mention our own!

∞✶∞

## Where Will You Go?

1. Have you ever stopped to think about where you'll go after you leave this lifetime? Or where you go at night? Journal about it. Visualize it. Ask your spiritual Mentors about it.

2. Think about the afterlife scenarios you've been told about or read about. Do they really appeal to your sensibilities? Will they feel familiar to you and will you be comfortable there? Or would you rather be somewhere else to feel at home, like my friend Tom's *Celestial Bar,* or a place of your own

invention or memory? (And who's to say if "invention" or "imagination" isn't actually "memory.")

Clearly Mark Twain (Samuel Clemens) spent some time musing over this because he left behind several versions of an unfinished manuscript he tinkered with over the years. As always, he used humor to point out some, *ahem,* discrepancies that might arise if a soul were to actually arrive at a place that resembled the popular notions of Heaven he'd heard bandied about. Only six months before he went out with Halley's comet himself (as he predicted), Twain finally published an *Extract from Captain Stormfield's Visit to Heaven,* in which his ship-captain hero gets lost while racing a comet on his way to the pearly gates. It's hilarious and insightful, but not all that Twain wrote on the subject. The most complete version I've found was compiled by his first literary executor from Twain's notes and published in a now-rare, 1952 volume, *Report from Paradise.* The shorter *Extract* is available free online. See Resources.

3. If you have memories of attending night school, or if you've ever had the experience of waking with the answer to a problem or the ability to perform some feat that you'd been unable to accomplish the day before, now's the time to write about it. Or draw pictures! I overcame a problem with pirouettes overnight when I was studying ballet in my late teens; Ruth Norman learned to type overnight; others have solved math or work problems. Has it ever happened to you?

# 18

## Psychic Readings Good and Bad

*If you have a broken* leg, a crutch is a wonderful thing. But if your legs are in fine working order, you'd never walk with one, right?

Asking another person to make a psychic link for you, or relying on information someone has volunteered via their psychic connections—that's a crutch, sometimes one we need. But remember always:

* **You are an Interdimensional Communicator, a psychic transceiver by your very design. You do not need intermediaries when your consciousness is functioning properly.**

The truth is, you may not be communicating *verbally* back and forth between dimensions but energy-information is constantly passing through and to you and back again, every second of your existence.

Unfortunately on this world, and for a very long time, articulate interdimensional communications have landed some people in hot water; er, maybe I should say in rather fiery circumstances due to the general ignorance about this subject and, in some cases, enforced opposition to independent thinking. (Think Joan of Arc for a famous example.)

But that's all changing now. Honing your psychic or clairvoyant intuition with regard to your own life, to whatever degree you can, is a vital survival skill for the twenty-first century!

What I'm going to say now might seem strange if you haven't already guessed it, considering all the trouble I've gone to, validating the contents of the psychic reading I shared in Chapter 13. But even the cover of this book proclaims that some of the work here is not of my own mind. That includes my psychic reading, for which I served as my own psychic transceiver.

That's right: I was the channel who brought it through. I'd been unable to write in my journal fast enough to capture the information quickly flowing into my mind. So I turned to my standard transceiving technique:

First I asked my question into the tape recorder, quickly, in my own words and voice. (And back in ancient times at the dawn of the twenty-first century, I was still using magnetic cassette tapes—now I couldn't even remember how to spell cassette!)

Then I took a few deep breaths, calmed my mind, discarded mental distractions, tuned up my mental dial to contact my Cosmic CoAuthors, and listened. I spoke what came to me, as the introduction to Chapter 13 explains. I didn't edit it later, much as I would have liked to omit some things! But alas, that wouldn't have omitted them from my akashic records, aka my psychic anatomy. If only it were that easy!

You can also learn to become your own psychic transceiver, which is another reason I've included this reading in the book. I want to encourage you to break away from any dependence on others for your information. (I discuss this further in Appendix A, "How This Book Was Written.")

So what are the chances that I "made it all up"? About that, which is a common self-doubt, all I can say is that it has passed the most stringent "pudding" test. ("The proof of the pudding is in the eating.") The reading brought me positive, healing changes.

So in one sense, psychic readings are not necessary. But sometimes they can be extremely helpful. Then again, sometimes they can be downright dangerous and destructive. Between those two extremes stretches a vast landscape of experience. In this chapter, I'm going to share examples from either end of those two extremes. My objective is to help you learn how to discern good readings from bad readings, and decide how and when to apply any information you receive from psychic readers—the traditional type who contacts someone on the other side to gain information for you. My motivation for including this chapter is the simple fact that when many people think of past lives, they think of readers and fortune-tellers.

However, there's a new breed of clairvoyant coming on the scene, a development we've been looking toward for a long time. I love the descriptive phrase *energy intuitive* for these skilled individuals who are able to sense into what they often call your "subtle energy body"—that is, the system of electronic structures closest to your physical body—to determine weak spots, imbalances, illness, or to read your basic "life colors," meaning the frequency that emanates from your psychic anatomy into this dimension, appearing to the practiced eye as physical color surrounding your body, indicating traits and proclivities. (See Resources.)

Modern energy intuitives are often trained in various forms of energy healing or other conventional and alternative therapies, combining their intuitive skills with their professional training. They can be wonderful helpers when needed! And the best among them are, like Joseph and me, eager to teach you to develop your own sensitivities to the energy fields in which we live, and to promote your own connection to higher resources so you don't become dependent on their skills alone, but learn how to awaken your own.

By the time you finish this chapter, you should have tools to help you determine what type of clairvoyant you're dealing with, and how safe you are relying on their information. But first we need to sort out the good, the bad, and the ugly among old-fashioned psychic readers who contact their guides and tell you tales.

**What to Do When You Need Crutches**

In my early years of interdimensional study, I did occasionally receive readings from others. I was so "blocked off" at that point, I needed their assistance to break through. I didn't know then that I was in training to become a psychic transceiver myself, but so it was. I needed to free up my mental constraints before I could recognize this (with much surprise on my part when I discovered it). Maybe I'd been training to do this work for lifetimes but in the present life, my pipes were definitely clogged by karma that needed to be resolved first, and knowledge that needed to be restored to my conscious awareness. This may be your situation as well! The next few chapters will provide additional ways to clear away blocks in your psychic intuition, so that any information about past lives will flow to you naturally, and at exactly the time you require it, should such a situation come about.

Meanwhile:

*What if someone else tells you who you were or what you were doing in a past lifetime? Can that be helpful?*

Of course. But the degree of helpfulness depends on what you do with the information. First thing is to validate the truth of it.

As we all understand, psychic readings can be as fallible as human beings. And even if true, the information may not prove useful to you in your present state of mind. We'll talk about working with cosmic cycles in a little bit. But for now, start with basics, adding them up:

* *Does it ring true in your mind?* Your journaling practice should make you more sensitive to your true feelings and will help considerably in making this judgment. Don't be fooled by an ego that wants to disbelieve, however. Be honest with yourself.

* *Did you have any physical reaction to the information?* Did you break out in a sweat, tremble all over, get goose bumps,

feel dizzy, cold, or any of the other million ways we respond physically to energy-information?

* *Did you have an unusual emotional reaction?* Did it make you cry, feel sad, depressed, ecstatic, angry, homesick, or any of the other million strong emotions we are capable of feeling?

* *Did it answer a question you've been asking,* or explain something about you that's always been a mystery?

* *Did it provide an insight into a physical ailment that speeded your recovery time?*

* *Did it provoke change in your life that happened spontaneously, almost without conscious thought?*

Any one of these by themselves still might not prove the "truth" of it, but it's much more likely to be true if you've experienced one or more of these reactions. Not always, though.

If a past-life psychic reading leaves you feeling nothing or has no relevance to your present lifetime, leave it alone. (Don't discard it yet, however; we'll explain why in the chapter on cosmic cycles.)

If it causes distress or harm, or drains your pocketbook by calling you back for repeat sessions with the psychic, run for your life.

I've seen people who appear to have been healed from past-life readings alone and it always seems miraculous. But keep in mind that there's been prior work done by that individual, and agreements made between that soul and all the helpers who've brought the information to the forefront. By the time the "instant" healing took place, perhaps hundreds or even thousands of lifetimes had passed in preparation!

What we see in this dimension is only a tiny fraction of who we are, and the actions we take here are but minute expressions of the fuller picture of our interdimensional life. The truth is, a past-life reading is only one piece of the puzzle. If you realize some benefit from a psychic reading, it means you've done your spiritual homework before, during, and after. The reader and the reading have merely served as a catalyst for you, triggering all that you've prepared for.

By the way, it's advisable to reread a written version of a past-life psychic reading several times, over a period of time, once you've determined that the Source is reliable, i.e., that it was inspired by your Cosmic CoAuthors. You'll be amazed at what you missed the first dozen times through. And even if you've proven its value by experiencing positive change (the ultimate proof!) keep it and reread it periodically, even years later, for the additional benefits it might provide when your mind is more open and you've grown spiritually.

I should add that a few individuals I've known have had difficulty accepting a valid and truthful past-life reading, or even present-life advice from their Cosmic CoAuthors, when their egos weren't ready to accept this truth. I'm sure that includes me somewhere along the line. Who doesn't have a stubborn ego?

And yet others have beaten themselves up for years over something in a reading that was purely fabricated, i.e., not true, thus compounding their insecurities instead of healing and growing.

You see? It's all going to come right back down to you, even if you borrow those crutches for the time being. Only you will know the truth, and only when you are ready and able.

### Reading the Akashic Record

You may have heard this term, *akashic,* an older term for that part of the psychic anatomy that contains past-life information. We've termed it the Mental Consciousness.

It takes a person of truly advanced mental development to *directly* access this information. Instead, most psychic readers work with individuals in the (hopefully) higher astral worlds who can perform this service, which is then relayed, usually vocally, through the psychic to the individual questing for information. It may be that some psychics believe they are directly accessing the akashic, but it's more likely that it comes to them through intermediaries, even if they're not aware of this assistance.

This is how my past-life reading occurred, with the exception that I served as my own psychic medium between me, the quester, and my Cosmic CoAuthors, the providers of information. It makes no difference. A conduit of pipe can be any shape; it's the quality of the water coming through that matters.

There have been times when one of us was ill that Joseph or I would step in to serve as a conduit of Cosmic CoAuthor information to help the other, but only because we were too physically weak to voice the words ourselves, or didn't trust our objectivity despite our training to speak whatever comes to us.

Most often, though, we rely on our own inner knowing and don't require a formal "reading" to connect with our best Sources. We ask inwardly for help and information, and it comes to us naturally, maybe without words. Over the years the process has streamlined considerably so that now we function in this connected way without giving it a second thought. But if we're stuck, we might ask each other or someone else for insight—then test the information using our own mental faculties in all the ways you're learning here.

Many of my dearest friends have developed their innate psychic abilities to use as a tool to serve others. But you also have this potential by your very design, and this interconnected consciousness is a tool that can be used in infinite ways! Perhaps to make art or music, or repair a cracked foundation in your house, or pass an oral exam, or perform before a group of people, or bake a spectacular dessert, or rescue someone lost in the woods—you get the idea. No limitations!

Have you ever watched a performance or event of any kind that brought you to a tearful state? It's likely those whom you were watching were tuned in to their highest resources, funneling healing energy into this world. I watched two young siblings, thirteen and seven years old, dancing a classical Indian dance in a talent competition and the energy they brought in with it blew me away and left me in tears. That is true psychic transceiving! But they were using their bodies, faces, and movements, with not a word spoken. They gave evidence of lifetimes of training (and between lifetimes) to achieve that level of interdimensional communication.

Because of our design, anyone at the height of their expression, whatever it might be, is likely to bring through much more than ordinary earth-energy. Solving problems in school or at work? How often have solutions suddenly come to you?

Over my lifetime of exploring past lives, I've met good psychics and confused psychics, had helpful readings that vastly improved my state of being for all time, others that left me cold, and some that didn't mean anything to me until many years later. Here are two opposite stories from my storehouse of experience.

**A Cautionary Tale**

When I was writing for a small newspaper in northern California, one local psychic reader contacted me and insisted that I should write about her. *Why not?* I thought. It might be an opportunity to open some minds if my paper were willing to run the story.

I did the interview, took the photos, and wrote the feature article, which was duly published. But she didn't go away. Instead she tried to insert herself into my life with repeated phone calls and bits of "information" her guides wanted me to know, and she tried to train me to do a form of "meditation" that would put me in touch with my own "spirit guide."

I tried it and I "saw" what she'd instructed me to see—but even with my limited knowledge at the time, the "spirit guide" seemed less than elevated to me, despite the fact that I was supposed to meet him or it at the top of a visualized elevator. Okay, you could say he looked like something out of a horror film, all red and flame-y! That was thirty-four years ago. Today, I would describe this entity as "sub-astral." And he/she/it didn't give me any single bit of useful or intelligent information.

Thankfully, some as-yet-untrained instinct (or inspiration) convinced me to quickly abandon this "meditation," although I didn't tell the psychic that.

You might say she was trying to snare me into becoming a repeat customer. Truthfully, it was not she, but the astral individuals whom she'd allowed into her consciousness who were trying to lure me in, as I understood later.

I was very young at the time, and vulnerable at that early stage in my studies of interdimensional science. Fortunately my true advisors—my Cosmic CoAuthors—came to my rescue and devised a way for me to see clearly what I'd aligned myself to. I was inwardly prompted to take this woman to meet a metaphysical teacher I admired (a student of Ruth Norman). During the visit, I was astounded to watch the pushy psychic reader completely flip out when this wise teacher confronted her with a few pointed questions and a very positive, radiating energy field.

Before my eyes, the psychic lost all composure and transformed into a swearing, spitting monster of rage when confronted with this "threat" to her control over me! I'd never seen anyone possessed before, or at least not so obviously to my eyes—like something out of *The Exorcist!*

Whew! Close call!

About a year later, after I'd left my husband and moved to a new city, my ex told me that she'd come around and aggressively pursued his affections (shall we say), despite the fact that she was married herself. He managed to put her off, but told me that the poor soul had wound up in a mental institution shortly afterward with a so-called nervous breakdown. That's a modern medical euphemism for astral possession. She had truly lost her mental balance by allowing these astral influences to take over and rule her life.

As for her psychic readings, one vague bit of health information she'd given me ("you'll have trouble with this area later") proved true decades after, when the fibroid tumors developed visibly. But I was already suffering terrible menstrual problems so it wasn't a challenging prediction for her astral friends. The rest of what she told me could have taken me right down with her, if I'd been more gullible and had not formed positive links previously with the Higher Minds who came to my aid.

I wish I could say this was a very rare incident, but I've heard and witnessed too many cases like it. Your very best protections against astral meddling are your understanding of interdimensional science, and the development of your own higher associations.

It is a frequent occurrence that psychic readers are associated with astral entities who are somewhat like the do-gooders you encounter in the physical world: they mean well, and they may be very sweet and dear people who are disembodied, but they might also appreciate an audience, especially a repeat audience. They can sometimes be helpful up to a point, so I don't discount them entirely. Of course, a few have worse motivations and there's the danger. But I think I've made my point: you must be the one to "test the spirits."

**A Happier Experience**

Years later, during my studies at Ruth Norman's learning center where I engaged in a speeded-up course to clear away my psychic blocks, I was sometimes offered information that had been obtained for me through a psychic reader other than myself.

For instance, twenty years ago I was having difficulty as a public speaker and teacher, unable to overcome a life-long vocal insufficiency. ("You sound like a three-year-old," is how my teacher put it.) This, despite my dogged pursuits of college drama, acting, and speech classes. So Mrs. Norman asked one of her advanced students to use his transceiving abilities to ask my Cosmic CoAuthors for deeper insight into the problem. I wasn't present and didn't know she'd asked, but our teacher-student relationship was such that it was perfectly in line for her to do so. I had already given my permission long before I was born, you might say.

What the reader turned up—much to my shock and dismay—was a hidden, *present-life* experience!

The reading said the trouble was that I'd been raped by an uncle when very young and had completely blanked out the memory!

What a scary thing to learn about your mind's abilities; makes you doubt your sanity in the present. My Cosmic CoAuthors explained in the reading that my childish voice and figure were a result of this psychic shock in the past, which had been holding me in a suspended state of childhood.

Why I'd want to remain suspended in a state in which I was abused still confuses me, but apparently that's how our bodies sometimes react to trauma. They simply freeze right where they are. Fight, flight, or freeze.

I was stunned. I'd been given the reading in a sealed envelope and encouraged to take it home and read it in the privacy of my own room. I reread it several times. For a few long moments, I could only think of one uncle, my father's brother. I could see him clearly in my mind and there was no way…

And then I remembered that I had another uncle I'd forgotten about, my mother's brother. He'd lived with my grandmother well into his adulthood, and she'd lived next door to us when I was in early elementary school…and that's about where my memory failed. I couldn't see that uncle in my memories!

In my mental images, he'd vanished from every family gathering where he should have been, or at least where my intellect reasoned he should have been. I used to walk past that grandmother's house on my way to and from elementary school every day; in fact, I remembered visiting her after school—well, I reminded myself I'd done that, but I could only see myself sitting at her electric organ on a screened-in porch with my back to the rest of the house.

I couldn't see the inside of the house as it was when my grandmother lived there, but I could see it clearly from earlier memories because I'd been born while my family lived in that house. I can see my parents and older siblings there with me until I was five—but nothing after we moved into a new house down the hill and my grandmother brought her son and her belongings to the place. And nothing at all of this man, my uncle, living there with her.

That realization—that I couldn't even remember what the man looked like—made my stomach drop. Could any of this bizarre reading be *true?*

I sat and mentally paged through my adult history, harkening back to the moment when I should have been experiencing my first physical relationship with a man—and he'd insisted kindly that he wasn't the first. Again, my heart thudded as I remembered that moment of shocked denial. I thought of many other clues: emotions, fears, reactions. I got up and called my sister, who is about seven years older than me and now lives in another state.

She told me that when she was in her thirties, she'd had a spontaneous recall of being molested by this uncle as a child. Until my phone call, she'd failed to mention that recall to anyone else in the family—including me!

I called my mother in another distant state. She claimed to know nothing about this brother of hers molesting children but said she'd confront the then sixty-year-old guy. I tried to discourage her. Too creepy!

Much later, I recalled that this uncle had married eventually. After my grandmother remarried, her new husband connected this errant son of hers with a woman from his church. They'd married and moved to the East Coast to have a family. I remembered someone telling me that he'd named his daughter after me because he thought my name was pretty. I don't think I saw him again after that. But I don't trust my memory now!

The amnesia alone seemed to indicate that the reading might be true. Why else would I have completely erased this uncle from memories of every family occasion where this man would have been? I could only remember that he wore white socks inside his brown sandals, a sight I've always abhorred on anyone who would wear such, and that he used Ivory soap, a smell that gags me still.

As Mrs. Norman pointed out later, I'm fortunate that I can't recall being raped or molested. I only have the restored knowledge that this uncle was on many occasions my solitary baby sitter at two of my grandmother's homes before he moved away.

And apparently further detail wasn't necessary for healing.

Within a day or so of receiving this psychic reading, I had a very vivid dream. I know it was projected into my consciousness by my Cosmic CoAuthors, it was so clear and true.

I saw myself as a young girl or woman who was standing in an area that could be nothing other than the opulent surroundings of a rich man's harem in either a Persian or Arabian setting. Somehow a workman had gained access to the forbidden women's quarters. He not only saw me changing clothes, he managed to touch me. Only a touch. But in that lifetime, I reported him. And was forced to watch as they dragged him out, threw him to the ground, and cut off his arm with a long, curved sword. I awoke from that dream still hearing his screams, with the scene resonating in my mind.

No wonder I made myself forget, rather than tell anyone in the present lifetime! No wonder he might have wanted a kind of revenge in the present, or came in with some twisted ideas about touching young girls!

And—oh my gosh, this proof cascaded into my mind after I was fully awake from the dream—I'd completely forgotten that this uncle's most distinguishing characteristic was an arm so damaged and shortened by polio that he always carried it as you would carry a stump from an amputation!

How could I hate or resent this man who had been so harmed by me—in my own opinion, very outrageously so? I could not. And along with my symptoms of being trapped in a childish body and voice, so vanished my anger instantly in the present.

That's how powerful a past-life *knowing* can be. The reading was one thing, but this past-life knowing resonated through every crystalline bone cell in my body. The knowing was so much a part of my very structure because I had actually lived the events of the past, and my conscious mind had finally tapped into this network of truth in my energetic being, the vortexes of my psychic anatomy. I can't describe the feeling to you, though. You will one day feel something similar for yourself, I hope. And you'll be changed.

Over the next few days and weeks, as I proved and validated the information to my own satisfaction, my voice "miraculously" changed to a deeper pitch and stayed that way, *effortlessly.* Nothing I'd tried before had accomplished that! Even my body reorganized itself into a more womanly form, and my bra size went up to prove it.

Amazing what our body-minds are capable of! But this is what I mean when I say healing can seem instantaneous. I was attending a past-life therapy class full of witnesses to this sudden transformation; many of them were so inspired by my experience, they sought their own past-life readings from the same psychic transceiver.

Actually, awful as it seems, I must have been fully expecting this encounter before I was born.

Skeptical? You've read those articles about fake repressed memories? Here's one last bit of proof:

Last year, 2011, this uncle who must now be in his eighties wormed my phone number from a relative who didn't realize our history. I hadn't spoken to him since I was a child and fortunately he lives as far from me as possible on this continent, in what sounded like some kind of nursing home. I froze for a moment when I saw the caller ID. Then I picked up the phone. Was this my opportunity for full resolution?

After hello, he began by saying that many years ago, my mother had indeed confronted him about certain things and he thought perhaps he didn't answer her truthfully because he'd denied it all. So he "called to apologize"—and then launched into some details that turned out to be another way for him to relive whatever happened. Yuck!

I quickly diverted him by asking about his own children. His answers told me that he'd likely not reformed, and perhaps had abused the daughter who'd been named after me. He said she was "all messed up" and claimed that some other man had molested her when she was a child. And so on.

I could hear the man, now a widower and estranged from his children, struggling to both protect himself and confess. He was telling half-stories and half-truths. I didn't say, "I forgive you," because it's not my place to forgive him; that will be his own task one day.

But during the call I decided, *What harm could it do if I tell him the deeper truth? About past-life karma? He won't understand it most likely, but that truth and my healing carry a healing energy that might help him when the time comes that he must face and rectify his own karma.*

It was my little way of furthering the closure of my connection with this soul. So I told him what I could in words I thought he might comprehend, seeing as he's always been a regular churchgoer and was now trying to get me to contact some evangelistic organization he's a part of. I used simple words.

Still, I got the creepy feeling he was more interested in reliving the past, which he kept repeating in what became a new form of verbal sexual abuse. So I got off that phone as fast as I could.

*Shudders.*

And then he called my older sister and pulled the same trick on her before I could warn her. She didn't dawdle around about hanging up on him, she told me later, adding that her little sister never had to listen to any dirty old man who called her on the phone ever again.

Still, the phone call told me as an adult something I never discerned when I was young: that this uncle was mildly mentally retarded. The family had apparently covered for him back in the 1950s, perhaps because (a) he'd been a polio victim they felt sorry for, or (b) retarded people were not treated well in those days. (Today we wouldn't even use that term.)

One of my brothers has since told me that he heard our grandmother expressing sorrow that she'd not called for help sooner during my uncle's difficult birth, a tidbit my brother offered to confirm my new realization about this uncle's mental challenges.

One last thing: In my 1992 dream of the past lifetime when his arm was cut off for touching me, he'd been some kind of "workman" doing repairs or maintenance around the harem quarters. In the 2011 phone call, I asked him what work he'd done in this lifetime. He told me he'd spent most of it working as a janitor.

That was a long story, with many proofs, and I still have not recited them fully for this volume. I shared it because it proves my point that sometimes a psychic reading can help you break through a very stubborn block. In this case, I knew the information to be coming from my Cosmic CoAuthors, but through another individual because my own consciousness was so blocked to this particular piece of my history, because of the protective mental amnesia I'd created as a child.

That's when a psychic reading can serve you best: when you've done your utmost to gain insight into a serious problem on your own and you truly need this kind of assistance.

Once my Cosmic CoAuthors broke through my amnesia with the present-life reading, I was able to receive the rest of the information from them in my sleep state, the part explaining what past-life connection caused us to intersect in such an awful way in the present. That information meant much more to me because it came through my own inner faculties. Yet, as with all past-life information, I still had to complete the healing work myself, accepting the dream and insights; doing my research and analysis.

The healing the past-life dream brought to me was the dissolution of any victimized attitude I might have developed from the present-life incident(s). It gave me perspective and compassion for us both. My uncle may have carried anger or entitlement into this life; I had carried a guilt that kept my lips sealed and placed me in jeopardy.

Happily, all of that has now dissolved in the healing energies provided by my Cosmic CoAuthors, sufficient that I could now go so far as to share this story publicly for the first time!

**Develop Your Energy Intuition**

As with hypnosis, which we'll talk about in the next chapter, it's easy enough for spurious influences to enter into a psychic's work, so as always, you must be wary of the source of information and the possibility of being misled. It might be pure error that trips your psychic up, or it might be the work of a malicious or mischievous or even greedy entity associated with the unsuspecting psychic. Most all working psychics are good people who do not know they are being deceived when it happens. It's a dangerous occupation.

So if you do consult a psychic reader, keep your wits about you and test the spirits. If it proves useful and valuable to you, well and good. But be cautious about who you're dealing with, in this world and out of it. It's easy for spirits living outside the limitations of this third dimension to dazzle and impress.

*How can you determine when you're being taken for a ride by astral meddlers?*

Apply all the tests you're learning in this book. Ask yourself this hard question, "Is my ego being flattered or built up?" If so, you're probably not getting a story that's going to benefit you. It's a common ploy of the subastral to lure an individual along with frequent ego-boosts. In your mind, question everything you're told, just as you would if a stranger approached you on the street.

The best protection is to make your own connection with Higher Minds who can assist you by reading your akashic record or Mental Conscious and relating the information you need directly to you, within your own mind. Only rarely should you need intermediaries.

The good news is that the more you extend an effort to learn about your psychic design, the more your interdimensional communications will naturally improve. You can receive all you need to know via dreams, flashbacks, insights, and so on.

That's how a normal, healthy mind should function: in concert with other, more developed individuals who are ready, willing, and able to extend their Minds to yours when they can supply information that you're ready to receive.

If you choose to pursue further studies in the fields of human energy-beings, such as you're reading in this book, or in the fields of massage or healing touch or psychology or social work or conventional medicine, and so on and so forth—in fact, in any field in which you are dealing with human beings—you may find that your new knowledge of the hows and whys of interdimensional life will improve your conventional skill set to such a degree, that you, too, might consider yourself to be an *energy intuitive*. One day, we hope that the use of one's ability to sense and discern energy frequencies and flows will be commonly understood and accepted.

Already, many alternative schools and teachers have sprung up to teach the development of one's sensitivity to the quality, quantity, and form of interdimensional energy flows, which was once the unspoken province of artists and musicians.

I can't tell you how many famous actors, directors, designers, musicians, architects, and other visionaries I interviewed during my career as a journalist who would allude to their psychic sensitivities when pressed (gently, of course). But at that time, it wasn't generally accepted to admit to higher-dimensional help, or psychic sensitivity.

The fuller understanding of your interdimensional design and connections that you've gained from this book will speed your intuitive development. I hope you'll seek many opportunities to develop your skills, but you may discover that you're far ahead in your knowledge of how it all works—from telepathy to futurism, from spirit contact to medical intuition—now that you're gazing through an interdimensional lens. How does a dog detect cancer in a human being? How do bees accomplish their amazing feats? How can a human being know who's calling before they look at the caller ID?

It all makes more sense from an infinite perspective, doesn't it? No limitations!

## Test the Spirits

1. If you've received psychic readings in the past, retrieve the printed copies, or if they were strictly verbal, replay them in your mind. Use your new tools of analysis to journal about them. Did this information heal you? Help you break through a block? Convey something you did not know before? Can you prove the contents in any way, or if that's not possible, does it "ring true" for you?

2. Alternatively, did anything in one of these psychic readings cause an inflation of your ego? Hold you back? Keep you attached to the psychic reader?

A truly inspired cosmic reader will assist as needed, then encourage you to develop your own psychic faculties and urge you on your way. Don't settle for anything less.

# 19
## Future-Life Therapy

*No matter how you arrive* at the awareness and belief that you've lived before and will live again, the most lasting healing benefit will be the change in your attitude. You are creating your future lives right at this moment, and every moment of decision-making.

Once you've validated even one past life to your own satisfaction, your choices will forever be influenced by the knowledge that *everything you do today will remain with you infinitely, eternally, until and unless you do something to change that energy-information in your psychic anatomy.*

You can't actually "heal" the past. It's done and gone, and best left in the dust behind you. But the change in your perspective brought on by a sincere understanding of your endless life will inevitably cause you to transform yourself for the better, thus "healing" your present and future lifetimes by the choices you make today. This is what I call Future-Life Therapy.

In the exercise at the end of this chapter, you'll experiment with another way to independently access the hidden knowledge of your prior lives. Perhaps you won't need psychic readers or hypnotists or guided regression therapists when you apply this and other methods woven throughout this book, but sooner or later you might wonder about using hypnosis to access past lives. Hypnotic regression has been attempted by skilled and highly credentialed psychologists, as well as curious amateurs, ever since a dabbler in hypnosis experimented on a friend in the 1950s, a housewife who became infamously known as Bridey Murphy (see Resources).

Although her story was discredited later, the search was on for past life memories that began cropping up among patients hypnotized for other reasons, individuals who seemed to be healed of a variety of problems by their recall of prior lifetimes. By the 1970s, this kind of experiment almost became a fad among those who believed or wanted to believe in reincarnation. Many books were published as a result of hypnotic regressions and research that used the technique as a primary method. (I'll tell you my own experiences with one such researcher in a moment.)

But oddly, the world did not stand up and applaud that "proof" of reincarnation had finally been discovered. Why not? We'll need to examine hypnosis itself through an interdimensional lens to explain the problem.

**An Interdimensional View of Hypnosis**

Hypnosis (from the Greek *hypno*, or sleep) is the practice of placing an individual into a trance state that is, by design in a therapeutic setting, susceptible to suggestion.

In fact, we self-hypnotize every night when we put ourselves to sleep—Ernest Norman called it an autosuggestive trance, where we suspend our Conscious Mind connection voluntarily and by trained habit, something we've developed over the course of our normal evolution as a human being. He also pointed out that no one else ever hypnotizes us—nor can they. They merely direct us in how to use our consciousness so that we hypnotize ourselves; i.e. we voluntarily suspend one half of our mind function.

In the mid-nineteenth century, after Franz Mesmer's healing theories had become quite the fad in Europe, the Scottish surgeon James Braid expanded on Mesmer's work, discarded the parts he felt to be too "woo-woo," and coined the term "neuro-hypnotism" for what he termed a form of "nervous sleep." He discovered that he could focus a subject's mind, using an object or jewel like you've seen in old movies, until his or her awareness of external factors and distractions appeared to be suspended, and their eyes glazed, taking on the trance-like stillness. In this state, the subject became highly susceptible to directive guidance or focus on specific ideas and suggestions conveyed by the hypnotist. For therapeutic use, the hypnotist's power of suggestion was the aim and tool.

Now let's look at this in light of The Psychic Anatomy diagram from Chapter 6, which shows how your brain and psychic anatomy exchange energy-information. Here's a thumbnail reminder:

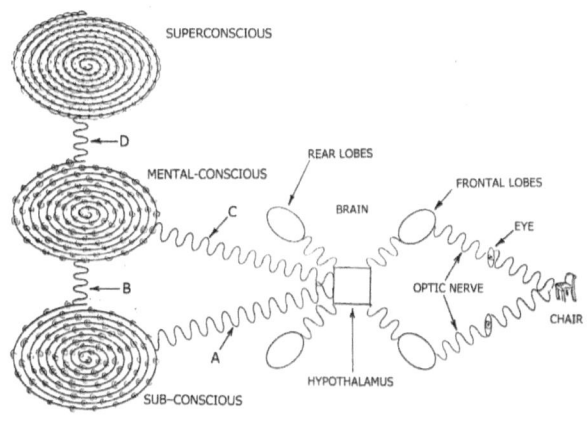

The Psychic Anatomy
*Image © 1970 Ernest L. and Ruth E. Norman*

In *The Infinite Concept of Cosmic Creation*, where this illustration originated, Ernest Norman explains in greater interdimensional detail how hypnotism suspends normal consciousness, but I'm going to simplify it for our purposes.

In a normal cycle:

1. You take in energy-information through your five senses;

2. This energy-information passes through your brain circuitry to connect with frequency-matched, higher-dimensional information from your psychic anatomy, including that contained in your Subconscious, Mental Conscious, and Superconscious, which is also your link to Infinite Intelligence;

3. This combined energy-information, filtered through and by all of your experiences, then pours back into your brain and thus into your Conscious Mind awareness, influencing your actions and decisions and completing the interdimensional circuit of Consciousness.

But "hypnosis" suspends this normal cycle of thought. Under hypnosis:

1. You can still take in energy-information;

2. The energy-information can still oscillate with the higher-dimensional information stored in your psychic anatomy;

3. But until you are brought out of the trance, you cannot release the newly combined information to your Conscious Mind, so the circuit or cycle of consciousness remains incomplete or open, with the energy-information dammed up like a river. Conscious Mind function thus remains "suspended."

During such a state of suspension, one's electronic consciousness is highly susceptible to influence from others—a hypnotist or any other individual present and talking to you. In a clinical setting, you might be given the suggestion to stop smoking, or that your stomach is smaller than it actually is (a form of virtual gastric bypass), and so on.

Then, when the trance is ended or you wake up, the dammed-up energy releases, and the function of consciousness completes its normal electronic circuit. All the energy/information held back by the suspension then floods the Conscious Mind, including any suggestions made or instructions to remember what you "recalled" during the trance.

Perhaps you've seen a stage hypnotist? For entertainment, they'll plant suggestions such as, "When you awaken, you will feel rested and relaxed, and you will remove your shoes and dance on your left foot." The physical comedy is great for laughs, but it's also a psychically risky endeavor to allow someone this access to your unconscious self.

Looking from our interdimensional perspective, we must include the potential for influence from roaming astral entities, or the aspects of the hypnotist's subconscious that you really don't want to make your own, which you'll be open to because of your mutual electronic design. You'll be under the influence of anyone who comes along and speaks to your mind during this suspended state.

It is a well-known (in certain circles) brainwashing technique to first induce a form of autosuggestive trance, say by repetition, and then plant information you wish the subject to act upon or believe. Ever seen a TV commercial? Listened to repetitive music? Used a meditation technique? By aligning your consciousness to the repetition, you are self-hypnotizing, and in that state, you are most easily influenced. (Other methods besides repetition can be used to put you into this receptive, hypnotized state, such as certain forms of concentration or focus. Or torture.)

Naturally, this tactic of creating receptivity to post-hypnotic suggestion can be used for either positive (quit smoking) or negative (blind allegiance) purposes.

If you look again at the psychic anatomy diagram, you'll also understand why information recalled under hypnosis can be unreliable or confusing.

Many third-dimensional scientists who've studied the phenomenon have discovered that subjects, eager to please the authority figure asking questions or planting suggestions, will compile bits and pieces of information into a new fabrication that becomes a memory once they've awakened, a very powerful memory which they've determined to sometimes seem more real to subjects than actually experienced events. But through research, they've discovered these "memories" to be bogus—often taken from disparate parts of the subject's life or imagination or exposure to information. Sounds very much like that other form of hypnosis, the dream state, when our minds perform a similar function.

Looking at the diagram, let's imagine you've allowed a hypnotist searching for past-life information to put you into a trance. With the direct access granted by the suspension of your Conscious Mind, the regression therapist would be (unwittingly) directing you to extract bits and pieces of the non-chronological information stored in the fourth-dimensional vortexes of your psychic anatomy—from both your present (Subconscious) and your past (Mental Conscious) life experience.

If this should be happening without the guidance of your Cosmic CoAuthors, the information selected from the trash heap of your entire psychic anatomy by a hypnotist's arbitrary questions might be fragmented and unrelated, resulting in a mash-up that no longer resembles a coherent, actual memory. Of course you have lived previous lives! But this hypnotically retrieved information could also be influenced by and include ideas oscillating into your mind from the subconscious of the hypnotist, including your own fleeting encounters with information you've contacted in either your present life or your past lives, maybe a book you've read, a TV show you watched, or a class you've taken—all rolled up into a new package.

You could easily wind up more confused about your past lives than when you began. You have certainly lived before—but now you've got something that feels like "memory," but you can't necessarily validate it as your actual experience because it's become unrecognizable, or because it's not what you actually lived.

That's not to say you couldn't benefit from the experience. It might be the first thing that makes you feel as if your prior lifetimes were real, and that alone could lead you into a form of Future-Life Therapy, causing a major shift in your life choices and releasing you from the natural fear of death. That would be healing!

It's also possible that the whole experience could serve as a healing catalyst, bringing about a change you'd been working toward for a long, long time.

And it could even be that you would connect with a true and accurate past-life memory, if all things rolled out in your favor and your Cosmic CoAuthors used the opportunity to help guide the process and relay past-life information that is pertinent to the present and useful in your healing.

But as we've been saying, you don't need a hypnotist for them to reach you with this information. You have so many more natural and reliable ways to foster this interdimensional, Intelligent communication through your Superconscious connections.

**My Noble Experiment with Hypnotic Regression**

Despite all my concerns and skepticism about hypnosis, I nobly volunteered for hypnotic regression once—in the name of journalism and science. I became a volunteer for author and psychologist Dr. Helen Wambach (1925-1986) in 1978, after she'd published her first book, *Reliving Past Lives: The Evidence Under Hypnosis*. We met as journalist (me) and subject (her) at one of the group-research workshops she was conducting for her next book, *Life Before Life*, during which she hoped to tap into subjects' experiences prior to birth.

By that time, I'd already experienced direct input about my past lives through my own, fully-functioning consciousness, with the inner help of my Cosmic CoAuthors, which resulted in healing of both physical and emotional issues. So I would be able to compare recall under hypnosis with the non-hypnotic, past-life recall and analysis we're focusing on in this book.

I'd read Dr. Wambach's first book and was working for that small newspaper in northern California when I learned of the workshop in nearby Sacramento. Naturally it interested me, and my editor thought it would make a great feature story. All I had to do was overcome my personal apprehensions about hypnosis!

From my interdimensional studies, I understood all that we've now discussed, and the prospect of allowing someone this mental access scared the heck out of me!

I've always shied away from any influence that would disrupt my normal flow of consciousness, creating the potential for outside intrusion. I like to stay in mental control of myself. Even if I hadn't been required to fend off the backstage, inappropriate advances of a stage hypnotist who'd performed at my high school, I believe I would have been unwilling to try hypnosis. So Dr. Wambach's workshop presented me with a personal challenge. Would my desire to explore and write about past lives overcome my fear of her primary research method?

I sought the advice of a trusted teacher of interdimensional science, who pointed out that, since my motivation was positive, I would undoubtedly be under the influence and care of my Cosmic CoAuthors throughout the experience. Moreover, my article might help promote Dr. Wambach's research. I agreed. So I took a deep breath and made arrangements to meet her, and to participate in her workshop for the sake of my story.

During our breakfast interview, I told Dr. Wambach about my fear of hypnosis. The enthusiastic psychologist assured me that I'd be fine. The workshop would only require three brief hypnotic trances. After each one, she'd ask us to complete a questionnaire about our experiences. If the hypnotic suggestions caused me any trouble, I'd simply go to sleep, she explained. She also said that a lot of people cannot be hypnotized. I silently decided that I must be one of those!

Since I asked the kinds of questions other reporters probably didn't, she also told me fascinating, off-the-record stories about her experiences and inspirational resources. On the record, she told me that her research began when she had her own spontaneous, past-life recall. I liked her, which did a lot to assuage my concerns.

Resigned if not entirely reassured, I followed her to the hotel ballroom she'd rented for the workshop. I soon found myself lying on my back on the carpeted floor with fifty other volunteers, convinced nothing would happen but a nice nap.

**Not Likely!**

She explained to the group that she would guide our three trances in escalating measures of depth. In other words, first a light trance to get us used to the questionnaire process; then a deeper trance; and finally, the deepest trance to see if any of us could access our birth experience from our present lifetimes. Apparently, most people in her workshops fell asleep instead, especially if they'd had any trauma during birth. But those few who were able to report their experiences would provide material for her new book, *Life Before Life*.

To my surprise, no sooner did she begin talking us into trance than I started to spin horizontally on the carpeted floor. At least, that's how it felt: as if I'd become a giant pinwheel! At this point in my studies of consciousness, I had no idea of my own psychic sensitivities. I had never allowed myself any form of out-of-body-ness other than weekend experiments with marijuana when I was in high school and college—a long discarded social endeavor by that time, because it, too, made me very uncomfortable.

I reached out instinctively to my Cosmic CoAuthors for reassurance.

They were still new to my conscious awareness, although I had some idea that they might be helping me write my newspaper column and feature stories. That diverted my attention from the spinning sensation and helped me calm down enough to start following Dr. Wambach's directions.

She wanted us to observe things that could later be verified by historical research: what kinds of eating utensils we were using, what we were wearing, what the room looked like, what we looked like, that sort of thing. She gave us hypnotic suggestions that we would remember these things clearly enough to write them down after we woke up. Thankfully, this trance was brief and we were soon awakened. The moment she asked about our experiences, my hand shot up.

"What was that spinning sensation I experienced?"

She smiled at me. "Oh, that means you went into a much deeper trance than I intended. Some people do."

Great. It turned out I was an excellent hypnotic subject! Maybe that's why I had an instinct to avoid it? Apparently my between-life studies had taught me the principles of energy surrounding the process of thought, and the wisdom to stay in control of my own consciousness at all times.

I may occasionally serve as an audio channel for my CoAuthors, speaking aloud the words they prompt, but I never relinquish my Conscious Mind awareness at someone else's command. In other words, I do not use hypnotic trance as many channelers do, including the famous Edgar Cayce. My ego steps aside to allow my CoAuthors' words and ideas through, but I do not let anyone, not even the most Advanced Beings I know, take over my mind (not that they ever would)! I remain solely in charge, but I've trained myself to allow their clear access.

Except on this day, and for the sake of research.

What did I see during that first trance? Fragments of a "past life" that I have never validated.

# Future-Life Therapy 245

I don't recall all the details, since I couldn't find personal, therapeutic benefit in them at the time, but I remember seeing a row of colored bottles on a high basement shelf. (*Apothecary? Poison? What's the significance here?*) I was a woman, I believe, and apparently I knew a woman then who has been a friend to me in the present lifetime since we were five years old. But she and I have known one another for many lifetimes and I couldn't see the importance, if any, of this scene.

That's the problem with being directed to past-life information out of context by another individual, when it's not a currently in-phase lifetime you need to know about for personal healing, and it has not been directed into your conscious awareness through your own Superconscious Self. It means little, and has no current purpose. I couldn't entirely dismiss it, however, because I have no proof of either its falseness or its truth. The few details I recall might one day become useful to me, if later I have some experience that proves their truth.

Hmmm…thirty-five years later, last year, this same friend sent me this hand-blown, opalescent perfume bottle as a birthday present, rather apologetically saying she didn't know why it made her think of me. Coincidence? I still don't know.

The fragmented scene of that first trance reminds me of the kind of quick-flash recall I've experienced during an energy medicine treatment, when someone was clearing my chakras. I've heard it said that massage or energy work will sometimes release past-life information, but in my experience, the information has come in quick, unrelated images, less useful or coherent than the full-blown psychic recall I've experienced in other ways. However, sometimes that's all you need, so I don't dismiss anything.

Next trance I saw more, and from a different era. In some ways it has been more useful to me. But it also brings up a common mistake that people new to the subject of reincarnation can make.

In my younger years, I was completely bored with history and avoided it whenever possible. So when Dr. Wambach directed us under hypnosis to see ourselves and our mode of dress, I saw a portly, eighteenth-century figure. But in my mind's limited storehouse, I immediately connected my attire to a familiar icon of childhood history lessons. Even while under the trance, I decided I was making things up because he was a handy figure to bring to mind for that era. Something culled from a textbook and stored in my Subconscious, perhaps? I couldn't rule that out.

During the trance, as Dr. Wambach guided us to various parts of this lifetime, I saw myself as this individual in two different countries, with slight variations of attire. I was looking out through the eyes of this man, whoever he was. Was this information accurate? Guided by my Cosmic CoAuthors? I don't know. It healed and changed nothing, so it has not to date passed the "proof of the pudding test."

Then she asked us to go to our deathbeds. Now, that has been useful to me!

Hazily through this man's eyes, I saw what must have been family gathered around my bed. I sensed or knew I was dying of a lung ailment. I felt intense distress over a book I had not finished writing. The scene was real to me, as if it were my own death. Easy as could be, and irresistibly despite the book I wanted to keep writing, I pulled up from my toes and rose up out of the top of my head. (Years later, a present-life doctor told me that my x-rays revealed scarring consistent with serious lung diseases I've never had in my current life, and I've since learned of other, verified lives in which I suffered lung problems.)

So vivid was this death experience that it became the model for a character's demise in chapter three of *Cosmic Dancer*. And it has vastly reassured me about the literal process of dying. It wasn't difficult at all.

The rest of that trance—the confusion about my identity—I chalked up to some spurious influence. Since I have no validation for such a life, the most useful piece of information to date was the vicarious experience of death.

**A Common Mistake**

It's easy for newcomers to the subject of reincarnation to make mistakes about famous people. The ego ever tempts, and an easily-influenced trance experience could provide a neophyte with plenty of excuses to believe it.

Often what we know about history is only what we've read about the main players, or those who were given ink at the time (or parchment or stone). So when we have an affinity with a particular time period, we might think we were one of those we've read about because that's what seems familiar.

But as Joseph is fond of pointing out, how many people who were teenage fans in the late twentieth century will one day reincarnate and think they were Madonna, or Britney? Or William Shatner? Or maybe J.R.R. Tolkein? We still put a lot of our attention on public figures.

Or suppose you were a servant for a whole long life and deeply admired the life of your employer, desiring with all your heart to live as richly as they did, while you had a very close-up view of every detail of that coveted life. When a century or two later someone hypnotized you and asked you to tell them a story about your life in another era, which would you pick? Your dull life as a servant? Or a life you perceived as much more wonderful? You might even tell them about a life you read about in a novel in your previous life. That could be much less deflating to a certain ego type than admitting they were a "nobody."

But I'd say that being a soul learning about life the hard way—whether famous, infamous, or unknown—becomes extremely important, thus making every one of our lives into a "somebody" who means a great deal to us, and to those who know us.

We store everything in our psychic anatomy—including what we read and what we watch. Now, if someone proved that you'd read the novel in an earlier lifetime, the hypnosis might still prove the validity of reincarnation, but it wouldn't tell you much about your own life and karma, now, would it?

And then again—you might have been someone whose name history recorded. But to you, that life might have been one of your most difficult, and one in which you incurred karma on a grand scale, being an individual who influenced huge numbers of people. How'd you like to have the karma of a king?

Be careful what you wish for! And be careful when determining who and what you have lived before.

**Life Before Life**

The third trance of the workshop startled me with a sense of accuracy. Ironically, I was one of the few who were able to revisit their birth into this life without falling asleep.

First Dr. Wambach took us to a time before our conception and asked where we were, and if anyone was helping us make decisions or plans. I already believed this idea, but if I hadn't, her question might have planted the suggestion in my mind.

Then she took us to our mothers before the birth and asked us where we were in relation to our mother, her womb, our body, and so on. Then she took us through it, all the time reminding us that if anything became uncomfortable we should go to sleep and wake up feeling refreshed. Most of the people in the room went to sleep.

Right up until that moment, I'd completely forgotten that mine had been a Cesarean birth. That was a rather unhappy surprise!

I saw my mother in a hospital bed before the birth, looking young and beautiful as she did at the time. I seemed to be hovering around and outside of her, concerned for her well-being and that of the little body in her womb. Right before the time came for my birth, I slipped into that body (again, through the top of the head) and wiggled its arms and legs wondering how on earth I would get along in that tight fit.

But I didn't have much time to think because some lunatic, bloodthirsty doctor was cutting into my mother's stomach! I was horrified! They were hurting her! And then I was frightened by the closeness of the "knife" to my own body.

*Barbarians!* I thought as I was yanked out into a painfully bright room by a group of people wearing white. *Why are they all grinning? They are so ignorant! They have no idea where I've just been!*

My disdain was almost furious. I was shocked by how cynical and adult this inner voice was! I suppose I thought they should be sad for me, coming into this world, by comparison to the beautiful higher dimensions where I'd been surrounded by Light Beings mere moments before. But this third trance experience rang very true to me.

In more recent years, while listening to the audio version of *The Biology of Belief* where Bruce Lipton describes how our experiences in the womb have affected the subconscious beliefs we hold today, I could harken back to this hypnotically recalled event. It gave me further insight into present-life fears and concerns. They originated in past lives, and extended right through that harsh introduction to my current Earth life.

So this trance experience met the "proof of the pudding" tests: it rang true to my inner knowing, and it helped me understand and ultimately, heal.

Did Dr. Wambach prove the existence of life before life? Did she prove in her earlier book the validity of reincarnation?

It's very subjective. If you know reincarnation to be valid, deep in your bones, then you would probably say yes. If not, then you might say it's still conjecture and hypnotically retrieved information proves nothing.

For me, the experience did not yield a past life I could prove my own connection to at the time—even if the silverware or the wigs were recognizable historically. It did, however, allow me a taste of my own deaths and rebirths that felt true for me.

I still applaud Drs. Wambach, Fiore, Weiss, and many others for their efforts to enlighten the world on this subject. They've used the best tools they could find in their attempts to prove the continuity of consciousness from life to life, despite criticism and threats to their professional reputations. Perhaps future documentation of past lives will depend more on self-obtained information and healing results rather than a method as uncertain and easily influenced as hypnotic trance.

**Trust Yourself**

In her book, *Across Time and Death: A Mother's Search for Her Past Life Children,* British author Jenny Cockell describes a harrowing experience with a series of free hypnotic regressions that left her depressed, anxious, drained, and overly obsessed with the past.

The hypnotist—an amateur, not a therapist—wanted to research the reality of reincarnation. He repeatedly took her through scenes painful and distressing to recall. Yet she felt driven to continue, with the past more and more overtaking her awareness of the present. Ultimately, it drove her into a depression so deep that she felt she had to take chemical medication for it.

What she termed depression was more likely a simple matter of full re-attunement to her past-life state of mind, which she couldn't shake off when her hypnotic sessions ended, until she eventually sought medical treatment.

Finally, she realized that the hypnotic regressions hadn't helped much in locating the eight past-life children she'd always remembered leaving behind (due to an untimely death, twenty-one years before her present-life rebirth). She'd been driven to try hypnosis by the guilt she'd felt when dying and leaving her past-life children with an unsuitable and dangerous father, and she felt an urgent need to find them while they still lived.

After she recovered from the depression, she continued her search for them on her own initiative, following her inner guidance—a much healthier and more successful choice for her, especially since she'd always had spontaneous past-life memories. She eventually found her previous family.

Generously, Mrs. Cockell wrote of the experience: "Perhaps the biggest difficulty with the hypnosis was that I had wanted to find out more about Mary [her past personality], whereas the hypnotist had wanted to research hypnotic regression. The result of any enterprise where there is a conflict of interest, even when each party is trying to help the other, is that neither is served particularly well."

Mrs. Cockell's success at finding her past-life children came later, when she relied solely on her own inner resources, intuition, and vivid memories. But she'd come dangerously close to losing herself completely to the past, as have many unfortunates who currently reside in mental institutions. Even if your past-life regression therapist promises not to require hypnosis, continually reverting your thoughts to your past lives is not going to serve you well in your present life, as we've already pointed out. I hope that you'll always use caution and common sense, no matter what method you're using for past-life recall.

Another reluctant hypnosis subject, perhaps even more famous, was the novelist Taylor Caldwell. If you've read any of her historical novels, you can feel how "true" her retellings are. She'd clearly lived in many of the eras she wrote about! Many times during her career, medical doctors swore she'd done extensive research or had training in medical settings in order to write the realistic scenes she recreated, but she hadn't. A cantankerous artist, she nevertheless hints in some of her later books that she, too, had at least one Cosmic CoAuthor. I consider her to be one of the best psychic historians I've read. She tunes right in and takes you back to what really happened.

But her friendship with author Jess Stearn drew her into a lengthy experiment with hypnotically-recovered "past-life" information. She was a somewhat willing subject, but remained stubbornly unconvinced. The book he wrote about their collaboration (*The Search for a Soul*) concludes with her disclaimer. However, she then set out to write about one of those "lifetimes" discussed under hypnosis—a book that feels "real" enough to send chills up your spine (*Glory and the Lightning*).

Trust your inner resources. If you need to know details about your past lives, you will find a way when you're ready. In fact, the following exercise will help you take another step toward a more general past-life awareness, the kind that doesn't require detailed recall in order to reap the benefits of Future-Life Therapy.

And if details come to you through any method whatsoever, remember to always, always test and prove them to your own satisfaction before further involvement.

One last question:

*Is it possible to contact future lives through hypnosis or any other method?*

How could that work, since you are making your future at every moment you breathe? You might be able to extrapolate from past experience a possible future, about as successfully as making economic or weather predictions, I suppose. But such circumstances would only come true if you made no changes to your psychic anatomy whatsoever in the intervening time. Better to use your time and energy to create the kind of excellent future you'd like to live, by what you're thinking and doing today.

## The Truth Is Right Here

1. Make a list in your journal of people close to you—family, friends, and/or coworkers.

2. As you find the time, slowly and thoughtfully consider your connection to each one of these individuals. Answer some of these questions:

   ✴ For friends and coworkers, did you feel an instant rapport or animosity or other strong emotion upon first meeting?

   ✴ Do you share specific likes and dislikes, such as a fondness for a particular culture or an era of history?

   ✴ Do you always connect around a certain kind of activity?

   ✴ Do you ever switch roles? For instance, if you're thinking of a parent, do you ever feel like they're the child and you're the parent, or as if you are siblings or friends rather than parent and child?

   ✴ If you're currently friends or coworkers, do you ever feel like family?

* What gender do you feel like when you're around this person? Is it the same as your current gender?

* Do you have a leader-follower relationship? Who's in charge? Can you place that interaction in any other type of setting, unrelated to your present-life roles?

* Do you have a consistent argument or source of conflict? Do you have something you particularly enjoy together?

* Does either of you feel owed something by the other, or, conversely, do either of you indicate a sense of guilt in the relationship unexplainable by your present-life experience? (These emotions might be so well-hidden, it will take some introspection to find evidence of them.)

* Can you identify any other kind of imbalance in the emotional exchange? Has this changed over time (which might indicate a slow healing underway)?

* Have you experienced any kind of flashback regarding this individual?

3. Let me caution you regarding leaping to conclusions about past-life connections and informing the other person of what you've determined. Don't do it unless you're rock-solid certain, and with ample proof. So often the guesses we make with Conscious Mind are wrong! What I hope you'll gain from this exercise is a more tangible sense that you've known all these people before—some more intimately than others. Often, that's all you need to speed your healing progress. And they might not need to know at all in their Conscious Minds for their higher selves to kick in and help complete the work.

## 20

## *Unmasking Your Creativity*

*Are you as creative as* you'd like to be? Even if you make your living in a creative field, do you find yourself blocked now and then?

Considering our Infinite design, with interdimensional Intelligence pouring into, around, and through us at all times, the inability to funnel that energy into constructive projects is rather astounding—almost as astounding as it is a common affliction!

We all want to express more freely, but we all hit stumbling blocks here and there. By now you can guess that the roots we're tripping over go back countless lifetimes.

One of my editorial clients told me how the nuns at his school used to rap his knuckles if his fingers were held wrong during piano lessons. They also fiercely criticized his penmanship. He became so insecure about his writing that he developed a serious lump on his index finger from gripping his pens so tightly. That made writing physically painful—right up into his middle years, when he decided to become an author.

In order to record the marvelous first novel rattling around in his head, he first had to get past the trauma those nuns had reinforced in his present life. Fortunately, his desire to write was so powerful, he hit on a solution: he would hire an editor to help him with the writing phase.

It wasn't quite that easy, however. His first choice of editor (karma had other ideas!) turned out to be yet another devout Catholic who turned this aspiring author's delicate, fun, and visionary ideas into something dark and common, far removed from my friend's original vision. I had the privilege of coming along later to help him save the book.

I quickly saw how this first editor had completely diverted my client's good storytelling instincts. We cleaned up the mess, deleted whole sections of the other man's additions, and put my client's pen to paper once again, as it were. That novel won him a whopping advance, opened many doors, and was translated into fourteen languages. He's always telling me how he meets Italians in some unlikely place—say, on a trail in Sedona or Machu Pichu—and they soon reveal that they not only know of his book, it's at home on the night table! (I've already mentioned it, Thomas Youngholm's visionary tale of *The Celestial Bar*.)

Only later, as we began work on his second novel, did we unearth the *past-life* traumas at the root of my friend's creative blockage. One of those lives did indeed involve a prior run-in with the Catholic church. Holy moly—that one involved *me!* The short story I wrote to help work my way out of some heavy karma with this former client I will publish one day. But here's the happy ending:

My client regained his writing confidence, overcame the negative past incidents (in this life and others), and now has no problem spewing out wonderful stories, both written and spoken, without editorial aid (except, like all writers, at the proofreading stage). The lump on his finger disappeared when the first book appeared in print, and he's currently writing a new book all on his own. No doubt he's rectifying karma with every word.

Did I mention that reincarnation is one of his themes?

In fact, he's doing so well, he recently helped me over one of my own creative blocks!

Joseph once wrote a poem called *Incarnation* about how, when he came into this life, he'd "set the treadmill on ten," its fastest setting. He was bound and determined to work out karma as fast as possible by setting up some whopper challenges for himself. This is what older souls do!

For all the creative artists I know, overcoming psychic and physical hurdles in order to carry out creative tasks demands their monumental determination. That's because we've chosen endeavors that will challenge us to work out karma. The blocks we're facing began in prior lifetimes and we've purposely set out to dissolve them.

So why should it be different for you? It's not!

**Why You've Set the Treadmill on 10**

Take a deeper look at your creative projects. Buried in them—their character, quality, setting, and style—you might find hints of prior-life traumas and the goals you've set for this life.

This may be true of anything at all that you are attempting to achieve in this lifetime, whether it's going smoothly or not. But if you've stumbled to a halt, you've probably come up against the karma that set your entire objective in motion.

One of my karma-conquering friends recently told me, with wry humor, that the massive project he'd spent millions of dollars and two decades achieving was something he'd probably considered from a lofty height while still in the higher worlds, when he must have said something like: "I can do that! It'll be *easy!*"

We had a hearty laugh over that one! We humans would be so amusing, if we weren't so pitifully egotistical.

Ego is the biggest block of all. When ego takes over, inspiration dies. How can we bring in something new, when we think we already have it all?

To become a clear channel—that's the goal. To bring in a higher frequency from worlds that lie beyond. This is what Ruth Norman called "the effortless way." Open the mind, and let it flow. It does sound simple, doesn't it?

Breaking through people's creative (and other) blocks was a specialty of Ruth Norman's, who opened her learning center for students of her late husband's work when she was seventy-five years old.

I had the good fortune to study with her between 1983 and 1993, until she left us a few weeks short of her ninety-third birthday. She was such an inspiration to me, both as a personal mentor and all-round amazing woman, that I've never been able to describe her adequately. But I can tell you about her crafty and successful methods for cracking open the hardest of human shells to find the richness within. Me included!

Mrs. Norman never taught in a classroom. She left that to one or two senior students who felt they had something to teach about Ernest Norman's interdimensional science. Instead, her favorite approach was to encourage and facilitate creative activities to bring out the best in people, to fully develop their talents and proclivities.

On evenings and weekends, you'd find students at her school involved in every sort of building, painting, writing, singing, music-making, sewing, designing, sculpting, dancing, filmmaking, and even play-acting. No limitations! Everyone was encouraged to take part in creative activities. What a dream for someone like me who loved music, dancing, and theater! (Writing? Nah, that was just a way to make a living, I thought at the time.)

But very often this activity led us straight into a brick wall of personal impairment. She knew this would get our attention better than anything on a chalkboard.

*Your painting's not going well, dear? So—you've hit a blockage in your inspirational flow, which by the way is the natural state of a healthy consciousness. So what did that painting tune you into? What past-life incident has cropped up to shut down your natural link to the higher worlds, where all the best creations originate?*

That was her strategy. Encourage our creative proclivities. Provide all the opportunities to express: classes, equipment, materials, loving attention. Then point out the discrepancies when they arose. And heap praise on those who broke through their blocks to achieve more than they'd ever believed possible. How? By working with the Cosmic CoAuthors Ernest and Ruth Norman introduced us to, each of us in our own way.

This is what she meant by "the effortless way." Freed of ego, fear, trauma, and any other negative emotional associations from prior lives, our minds would naturally open to let in the Light of an Infinite Intelligence. Perhaps we would never achieve fame and fortune, but we could achieve a personal overcoming that shone a special brilliance into the project at hand, radiating with the love-energy provided by our Cosmic mentors as we worked through old, even ancient issues of personal handicap.

As a group, we shared the desire for self-improvement in order to take up our station as conduits for this higher-dimensional, healing energy that could funnel through us to bathe others in Light. We all wanted to become healers of the world! Or artists of one kind or another! We had such lofty aspirations!

But we soon learned that you can't heal anyone else until you overcome your own blocks. What a deflation! And ego deflation is the secret precursor to inspiration, I learned. The way was "effortless" only after you'd slain the demons within!

The work I do now with my Cosmic CoAuthors is a direct result of this training, although my perception of what it means to "heal the world" has vastly changed because of the experiences I had at Mrs. Norman's school. I'll be fortunate to heal myself this lifetime!

Essentially, by embarking on creative projects, we tricked ourselves into looking at past issues our conscious minds would have preferred to avoid. In the psychic reading I've shared with you in Chapter 13, my Cosmic CoAuthors spelled this out for me:

"For example, your writing project which is leading you in and out of many nooks and crannies of your own consciousness, and particularly into this past-life conflict with your mother: You did not intend to expose this past to yourself; nevertheless your positive motivation and desire has led you to unearth one of the large stumbling blocks that has held you back—not only in the present lifetime, but for many lives."

In other words, my creative effort was like the farmer's old-fashioned hand plow, unearthing and healing elements of my past lives as I pushed the project along. It's one of the best tricks I learned for keeping my consciousness afloat and progressing spiritually, this habit of keeping a creative, constructive project going at all times.

**Positive Projects**

If you're going to challenge yourself to work out past-life karma, then you, too, will need this lifebuoy to keep you from sinking under the weight of the inevitable ego deflations. Trust me on this. You *will* need it to restore your self-esteem now and then when the going gets tough on your spiritual quest.

You can begin as we did, when Mrs. Norman would ask a new student, "So, dear, what are your hobbies? What do you like to do?"

Embark on a project that, to you, feels purposeful and meaningful. Bonus points if you have that wonderful sense of "lost time" while you work on it—meaning that you've truly discovered one of your passions, as popular literature terms it. You lose awareness of the passage of time and your thoughts are lifted right up out of your self-centered world, elevated to a level where your inspirational CoAuthors can work with and through you.

Don't be surprised when you hit a snag, if you do. You'll have all the tools you're learning now to help you uncover the deepest roots of the trouble, and to dig them out and render them harmless. You'll be motivated by the desire to complete your positive project.

Once you've embarked on it, the project will also serve as an easy way to elevate your thoughts whenever they threaten to drag you down into any kind of depression, or other negative emotions which inevitably crop up in the course of life.

I recently watched a wonderful film that illustrates the positive project principle: *Salmon Fishing in the Yemen.* Seek it out if you haven't seen it! One man's unlikely vision inspires a host of positive changes in himself and others, knocking down problems all along the way.

But there are other tools of the past-life therapy trade that I learned from Mrs. Norman. She used to say, "You have to get in to get out!" Meaning: For serious past-life therapy, you can't dilly-dally around the edges of knowing about your prior-life experience. If you're prepared and ready to go into this dark tunnel to learn about your personal history, *dive in all the way.* And she had a whopper of a way to help you do it.

**Experiments in Group Psychodrama**

To speed up the process of overcoming past-life, psychic blocks in order to attain a healthier, more creative state of being, one of Mrs. Norman's inventions was the use of filmed psychodrama, a kind of play-acting used in conventional psychotherapy—although her application was far from traditional. In this case, the objective was *past-life* therapy.

In the 1970s and early 1980s, Mrs. Norman herself participated in these costumed events to "up the stakes," so to speak, by portraying some of her own past lives alongside her students. Many of the individuals attracted to her center were those who'd opposed any kind of spiritually progressive movement in the past, including some she herself had led. Because of her students' respect for her (and tendency to worship), this became their opportunity to face, identify, and rectify some of that global karma—global, because their actions had affected so many others by blocking their access to new ideas.

To make this clear, think of the Dark Ages and the suppression of more enlightened ideas by various factions. This went painfully on and on for hundreds of years on Earth—until the higher-dimensional teaching centers rained Advanced Minds onto the planet, luminous Beings who were willing to incarnate here to help bring through our most recent era of Renaissance.

Even then, a few destructively-minded individuals still opposed the forward-moving activities of the Enlightened Ones, thus unwittingly incurring their greatest karma. Nothing is worse than opposing the progressive development of humanity, on Earth or anywhere else!

Of course, some of us didn't realize that or figure out that's what we'd been doing until we were in the higher worlds, looking back at our physical lives. We had thought, of course, that we were doing the "right" thing—until from that expanded perspective after death we saw with horror where we'd gone wrong.

So this group psychodrama opportunity was a very intense and personal study—not for the timid, nor those without that sort of heavy, global karma. In fact, that included karma from lives on other planets! Yes, indeed. My novel *The Liberator* is all about the Earth population's extraterrestrial history, and I'll give you this past-life "reading" for free: You probably lived on other planets, too, hundreds of thousands of years ago.

The organization Mrs. Norman founded still exists, albeit with a different emphasis these days, but they still conduct one of Mrs. Norman's interplanetary psychodramas every year in mid-October. If you want to take part, I recommend arriving early to help in the days of preparation in order to get the most therapeutic benefit. Of course, the local media thinks it's all a joke, or a dead serious cult activity, but actually it's neither. It's therapy for folks with interplanetary karma!

Some of those very early, videotaped psychodramas from Mrs. Norman's learning center can still be found airing on public access cable stations around the country. While they helped many who participated back in the day, without explanation now they must seem

*Unmasking Your Creativity* 263

very strange indeed to the casual channel-surfer.

I didn't arrive at Mrs. Norman's school until 1983, after eight years of studying Ernest Norman's books at home. By then, the directing of videotaped psychodramas had been left in the hands of apprentices who were using it as their form of creative expression, their own "positive projects." Inevitably, that meant that their motivations would skew here and there toward personal ego, creating an educational experience for all involved—but not quite as expected!

Don't get me wrong. Even at the age of eighty-three, Mrs. Norman was still an incredibly inspiring woman who left skeptical news reporters tongue-tied with admiration for her, and who could and did put such sarcastic naysayers as David Letterman in his place without batting a glittered eyelash. During that time, I interviewed a local physicist who told me of the deep respect he gained watching her on TV. (I could swear his popular books on quantum physics were colored by contact with Ernest Norman's visionary concepts, but then quantum physics itself has made rapid advances in recent years toward proving those concepts in conventional, acceptable terms.)

Nevertheless, Mrs. Norman had left the rigors of film production to students eager to prove themselves and who needed something to fill their time constructively. It has been said that one of her finest teaching techniques was to "give an individual enough rope…" Sooner or later, his or her troubling ego would hang itself.

Such was the case during my nervous first week at her school.

Immediately, I was "volunteered" by one of these individuals to perform in a psychodrama he was directing and filming. Instead of being given an opportunity to choose a role I thought might be helpful in ferreting out some twist of my previous lifetimes (as Mrs. Norman encouraged), I was instead arbitrarily assigned by this student to stand in a corner in a bikini, wrapped in plastic wrap. I was supposed to portray something like a human doll, a "prize" to be awarded in the pseudo-orgy scene he intended to film that weekend.

Being very shy at the time, and also very new to this buzzing group of individuals, I bravely did not protest too heartily. I'm afraid that's as far as I went in my personal courage, thinking it was brave to say yes I'd do it, rather than realizing how brave it would have been to say, "Are you crazy!? *No way!*"

(Lesson number one for me. Remember what I said about how we're always personally responsible for the messes we get into?)

But you see, I was already *tuning in* to the group-mind that was actually directing this psychodrama. It was a very unusual mental experience, even above and beyond the strange physical setting and costume. Once I'd agreed to participate, my mind began to oscillate along the same group plane, you might say. Put simply, I was already playing the role assigned to me: the mindless object, the brainless Kewpie doll standing in the corner. The one who didn't have enough sense to say no! Perhaps I had something to work out after all.

The evening went ahead as planned, with video cameras rolling and flash powder flashing, the grapes consumed, the gluttony and drug-taking portrayed with only G-rated intensity, by students in pop-star attire who seemed comfortable with this sort of tune-back to past lives of decadence. Meanwhile, I stood at my post on the fringes of the action, staring dully ahead. It was all extremely mild by today's standards, I assure you—not even approaching modern network standards (or lack thereof). But the attunement was enough.

Mrs. Norman, by the way, was not present. I have no idea how much she knew about the work underway in the video studio at her center. And I'm not sure now why that particular scene was deemed necessary. I believe it was part of a larger film the students had been making. They told me, the puzzled newbie, that their purpose was to extricate the parts of themselves that had so willingly participated in the debaucheries of the past. (And they still seemed gleefully willing, as they decked themselves out in scandalous attire culled from bits and pieces—very small pieces—they found in the costume room or brought from home.)

Me? I was in a key location on the outskirts of the set to observe the scene as it unfolded, and mutely at that—a safe, mild introduction to this frenzied group of past-life therapy students.

A little too frenzied, I'm afraid. As you might guess, this particular filming turned out to be a disaster.

The set caught fire from the flash powder and incense burners. Participants were so in tune with the drugged-out past they'd been miming with oregano, cornstarch, and grape juice that they barely noticed, moving in slow motion to respond. It was all duly recorded by the video crew.

Fortunately, no one was badly hurt and the studio did not burn down. The next day, after she'd been shown the recording, Mrs. Norman left no words unsaid when chastising the group for its careless use of a powerful technique of past-life recall.

Which is the only reason I've shared this inglorious tale! We made a really great bad example.

**Intention. Motivation. Purpose. Goal.**

Somewhere along the way in the preparation of this so-called psychodrama, the original objectives had been diverted. Egos took over and the old mind-set of the orgy-goers clicked in, to the point that they forgot that they were trying to dislodge and discharge the past—not bring it back to life and live it up!

They forgot that they were there to *rectify,* not *regenerate,* the energy of past lives. It's a tricky balance!

Many participants became physically ill after that debacle. They had all sorts of excuses and rationales. But the truth is, even in that school where past-life healing was supposed to be the ultimate goal, taking oneself back to previous lives turned out to be more complicated and risky than they'd previously perceived. Most of the people involved learned that lesson, much to our embarrassment.

During my brief years at the school, I participated in other, more sanely conducted psychodramas. When orchestrated correctly, they provided a way to allow oneself, for the moment, to reattune to the past in a protected environment and to speak and act as if you were the person of your past incarnation, even to interact with others who were likewise portraying their former selves.

This accelerated method dramatically exposed your ancient, deeper self, often uncovering elements hidden within your protective mechanisms that could help you heal in the present—if you had the courage to admit the truth of it. The video captured it all for your later review. The experience gave you the shocking sensation of thinking as the person you were in your prior life. But would your heart and mind believe it when you returned to the present? That was the key to genuine healing.

Naturally, the psychodramas affected us in different ways at different times, and as often happens in peer-pressure settings, we probably all had our moments of ego-bluffing our way through. On the other hand, I witnessed some very moving demonstrations of on-the-spot, tearful release and healing.

Moreover, some of those filmed group psychodramas have served as an introduction to past-life healing for new audiences, and in that way, you might say they provided the original participants with a means to re-purpose past-life, negative energy into something new, artful, and constructive. A tiny way to begin "healing the world," perhaps? By healing ourselves first, of course.

As with ballroom dancing, what a nice way to resolve some of one's karma with humanity!

It happens all the time as we watch films and theater, or visit theme parks. The actors work out karma, while we observers get the benefit of safely exploring past-life themes we're readying ourselves to address more directly at some future time. (I'm speaking of the best films and theater, of course; certainly the wrong thing can intensify and regenerate a negative past, adding to your karmic burdens. But only you can determine what's "wrong" and what's "right" for you. Intention. Motivation. Frequency. Attunement. Education. Experience. )

**The Unmasking**

Perhaps the most successful psychodramas at Mrs. Norman's learning center were those involving simple masks and costumes, dispensing with the elaborately designed sets of earlier years.

The Unmasking Psychodrama would take place in one of the thrice-weekly classes taught by students. In those classes, we usually read and discussed the concepts of interdimensional science you're beginning to study with this book. But for this rare event, an individual who wanted more help to shed a sticky past-life trauma or persona would volunteer for an unmasking. The idea was to discard the past in a dramatic, self-convincing way. As always, the reality was a bit more complicated.

The student would stand before their classmates wearing a self-designed mask and costume depicting the life they'd chosen to address. It was often something that kept coming round and round again, a history that wouldn't stop haunting their present, making it difficult to simply "change the channel."

In other cases it was a lifetime they'd been told about, or imagined for themselves, but still didn't believe in the fibers of their being, which is why they couldn't get free of it. The psychodrama would either prove—or disprove—that supposed past life once and for all. If you really *weren't* Cleopatra, you'd demonstrate it very quickly for all to see!

By the way, I've heard it said by wise psychics that Elizabeth Taylor could truly and rightfully claim that dubious honor for herself, so all the rest of you can lay that idea to rest; it wasn't you. But was Richard

Burton really Mark Antony?

I swore I wouldn't put winky faces in my book…which means I must make another side note about thinking you were someone famous. How about a list, to reiterate what I've said in previous chapters:

1. You probably weren't if the idea appeals to you.

2. You might have lived during their time.

3. You could have been jealous of their life so now you want it for your own.

4. You may have known this individual or served them.

5. If you've truly lived a prior lifetime that attained any level of favorable or ill repute, or even of total anonymity, YOU WILL NOT WISH TO CLAIM IT for your own.

6. All genuine past lives will feel downright yucky to you now.

Nobody *wants* to learn about their real past lives. Not even me. I got hooked and snookered into it because I wanted to learn the interdimensional science of life. Unfortunately for me and you, reincarnating humanity is part of that big picture.

I will say that a few people come to the study of past lives because they have flashbacks, and a few because they are desperate for answers. We all have our reasons. But bottom line:

✳ **Whatever you've actually lived before now feels repugnant in the present, whether it was a lovely happy life, or a sour and awful one. Be suspicious if it doesn't.**

Why? Because of the energy principle of polarity. The past now poses a negative polarity in relationship to your positive, forward-moving present. It is regressive. It pulls you backward. It feels suffocating. You can relive those energies—and you do—for brief periods of time, but if you're stuck in them for longer than that, you will start to shrivel and die inside, spiritually, physically, emotionally, and intellectually.

Ever had a relationship or job that started to make you feel that way? That's because your connections to it involved energies stemming out from your prior lifetimes. At first, all was lovely and magnetically attractive. But as time passed, things started to fall apart.

So this is why we brave students of past-life therapy were willing to humiliate ourselves in front of our classmates (and a video crew!) by volunteering to perform an unmasking psychodrama. We were eager to shed the suffocating past. And since we all shared similar aspirations, we felt ourselves to be in a safe, supportive environment.

The healing aspect of the psychodrama usually began the minute we started to put together our costume, encountering all the usual creative blocks and stomach churning anxiety.

But once you began to speak to the group from behind the safety of the mask, improvising your words and essentially "acting" out the role with a lot of nervous tension, the truth started to leak into the process. If the past was one you'd actually lived, real words began to pour from your mouth. You'd be stunned to hear yourself saying those things, behaving like someone else, even thinking like another you—someone you are not now.

With the *intention* of past-life healing (a key factor), you had realigned your consciousness to the energy-information buried in your psychic anatomy, undoubtedly with your Cosmic CoAuthors standing by to lend a healing projection of higher-frequency energy when the time was right.

For those of us observing, the atmosphere electrified when someone authentically connected with their past-life persona. You knew it was real. But did they?

In the revelations that ensued as they spoke, the individual might unveil what had been hidden within his or her personality, right up until the present day. Very often, deep *motivations* for actions taken in the present or beliefs carried over from the past were exposed as well. And by putting on the persona of the past, it often brought us a better understanding of our choices, and with that, the all-important elements of self-forgiveness and compassion.

For instance, if I did an unmasking about a gladiator now, I might be able to answer *why* or how I became one—if that was important for me to know as a part of my healing. That knowledge might stop me from making a similar mistake in the present, if I were so inclined. Even as a woman, that past still lives within me and comes around in phase at the most inconvenient times, as you've read. It's not hard to imagine some circumstance in which I could lead myself into physical harm, or someone else, if I were unaware of this prior lifetime and simply prone to carry on with that old energy oscillating in phase in my present.

You can look around in the world and see people doing this sort of thing everywhere, with all nature of results.

Ultimately, the time for the physical unmasking would arrive, when the student had spent themselves utterly in portraying their former self. They'd had their fill of it. They'd learned all they could. They'd said all they wanted or needed to say. That feeling of suffocation the past always brings was beginning to descend upon them, and the need to reassert their present Self had become urgent.

Having encapsulated so much of their past lifetime in that physical mask by animating it with their words, gestures, and actions, the mask now personified all that they had been—and all that they no longer wished to be! Often with words of hope, commitment, aspiration, relief, or joy, they would shed the mask in a flourish! And with it, they'd let go of the past.

Tears usually followed or suffused these solitary performances, and one can presume that healing for that soul was underway, the old energies falling away with every teardrop. But even without tears and instant transformation, the drama and rarefied atmosphere created an unforgettable experience. If the performance didn't do the trick for you, since you were so in phase with your prior self, then watching the video later added another chilling opportunity.

And as I mentioned, in some cases the healing involved ridding oneself of an erroneous idea, which is another way of getting yourself stuck! You can create a thought-form, imaginary past life that will haunt you every bit as destructively and persistently as a real one. Asylums are filled with these sad cases. So the only failures in the unmasking attempt would be those who never managed to let go of the mask, whether they were clinging to a real past, or a self-created one.

During these events, one's Cosmic CoAuthors participated to whatever degree the student would allow their inner input, from the planning stages right through to the (hopefully) healing conclusion. Even in cases that didn't appear successful, the student's willingness to participate had propelled them forward, another level of resistance removed. At their next pass through the cycle in question, they might well achieve the healing freedom or truth they sought.

Psychodramas are certainly not a requirement for rectifying past-life, negative energy. But as extreme therapy, and under the right conditions with the appropriate motivation, they can provide great benefits.

My favorite form of psychodrama is a milder version I also learned at Mrs. Norman's learning center, something I call the Family Psychodrama. It doesn't require masks or costumes, and a version can even be accomplished in solitude, if necessary. Joseph and I have introduced it in classes we've taught, with stunning results. Who doesn't have issues with members of their own family, right? Next chapter, I'll show you how it works.

∞ ※ ∞

## Make Your Mask

Even without access to a classroom of fellow students, you can engage the helpful energies of the Unmasking exercise. But it might be best to wait until you have gathered supportive associates or a healing partner. As I've said, psychodrama is not necessary, so there's no hurry to take this on, but if you do find the courage, it can be a powerful aid in self-understanding.

1. Ask for higher help before you begin any sort of psychodrama. Then choose an era or character for which you have an instinctive affinity or sense of need. You might want to journal about this to help you decide and determine how to proceed.

2. Design a mask for the character. Choose a costume. Be as elaborate as you like in these choices.

3. If you plan to enlist the support of additional friends or family who will understand your quest, do so. A supportive audience can never hurt, and they too might benefit from your courage. This might be something you try with a friend who is similarly studying the principles of reincarnation so you can become audience for each other's unmaskings. They can also assist with the recording tasks, which might otherwise distract you with twenty-first-century technology.

4. If you have an audience, stand before them. If not, use a full-length mirror or face the camera. Video or audio recording is important because you won't be in your usual state of consciousness, so it's essential to be able to watch it back or listen to it later. Otherwise, don't be surprised if you don't remember what you've said.

5. Whether alone or with associates, choose a time that you will not be interrupted—which could make a hilarious story later but it's not your objective this day. (This is not a Woody Allen movie!) On this day, you are going to embark on a serious healing endeavor, with the help of your most advanced spiritual mentors! So, arrayed in your mask and costume, let yourself be inspired to speak aloud as this character you've chosen to portray. Keep talking for a while to give yourself time to get into the role. Speak until you know you're finished.

6. Be sure to end the Unmasking by removing your mask with a flourish, and making positive statements to bring yourself firmly back into the present. Say something definitive and affirming, such as, "And now I discard this old personality and take up my new station in life," but with words that have deep meaning to you. Any healing partners present will help bring you back, since their presence should serve as present-life reminders and anchors. Tune in to your Cosmic CoAuthors when you're done, as another way to realign to your current Self.

7. Next day or in the following days, play back whatever you've said to and/or about yourself. Take notes on any reactions or insights you've gained. What did you learn? Are you more convinced, or more confused? Do you think you actually

lived such a life in your past?

You might *not* have! Surprised that I would say this? I was one of those who performed a complete Unmasking in front of a crowded classroom, apparently as a way to prove to myself that I was NOT the person in question. Of course that wasn't my conscious intention!! But when it all came to pass, and had been video recorded so I could watch it back, there was absolutely no conviction in my portrayal. Why? Because I wasn't who I'd thought I was, or more specifically, who someone else had told me I was!

Yes, that was embarrassing, but the point was self-education, right? And I got that. Mission accomplished. I divested myself of a wrong idea that might have seriously hampered my spiritual progression.

So fear not! Whatever you choose to portray, if you feel inspired to do it, you will have your reasons for doing so.

By the way, don't many of us do this every Halloween? *Mwa-haha*—you'll never view that holiday the same way again! Look back at prior years when you weren't self-conscious about your choices. You might find more truth in them than you'd bargained for!

# 21

## Powerful Family Healing

*This chapter is for people* who have challenging family situations holding them back. You can dig around in ancient civilizations through books, films, plays, and psychodramas, but sometimes the hardest truth is staring at you from across the dinner table. It's the starting place for many of us who are seeking to free ourselves from the past in order to move ahead in our personal, creative evolution.

Begin with questions:

* *How did we become members of the same family?* Through past-life associations.

* *Are we together to resolve some difficult and maybe even awful injustices or injuries?* Very often.

* *Do I need to know the details?* Not always. Sometimes love is enough. A lifetime of learning to love one another as family members could do the trick. But sometimes the debts and residue are simply too much.

* *But what if this troubling family member is not on the same evolutionary track or level as me? What if we're so far apart in

our chosen course of spiritual development that there's no way we can sit down and talk it out? Or what if they're no longer living in this dimension? That doesn't put an end to your unfinished business, you now realize, because life doesn't kill karma when it kills your body. Your unresolved karma endures, your imbalances remain. You will meet again in trying circumstances—unless and until you do something to rectify those past-life energies stuck in your respective psychic anatomies.

✷ *But here's the really good news:* As long as at least one of you remains in this third dimension, it's not too late to work out karma and heal your relationship!

So for the sincere student of creative evolution comes the tool we're calling the Family Psychodrama. It was first introduced in a class at Mrs. Norman's healing center conducted by her student Charles Spiegel and orchestrated by everyone's Cosmic CoAuthors, as always. What took place seemed magical, albeit firmly grounded in principles of interdimensional science.

As with the other psychodramas at this particular school, the family communication exercise—which you might encounter in conventional self-help settings—reached the rather uncommon level of *interdimensional connection*. And we were all assigned to give it a try.

**Soul to Soul Communication**

For me, the problem I wanted to address in 1989 was an alcoholic, mild-mannered father whom I deeply loved, in addition to the alcoholic mother whom I loved but with whom I had a troubled relationship. Typical of their station in society, neither would admit that their so-called "social drinking" was a problem. But of course it was slowly destroying their minds, bodies, and personal relationships.

In both cases, my heart was breaking for them, though it was my father I most wanted to reach at that time. How could I "heal the world" if I couldn't heal my own father, right?

But there was no way I could have the heart-to-heart conversation I wanted to have with him. Although at the time he still lived in his physical body, my ideas about life and death and rebirth were too different from his own. He couldn't hear me! So I chose a volunteer from the class to serve as his stand-in for my psychodrama.

It happened to be Joseph I picked, an unlikely choice since he was about the youngest guy in the class. He'd never met my father, on that we agree, but we can't remember if we were dating at the time or not yet, since today it seems like we've always been together. But now I know Joseph was the ideal candidate for my psychodrama for many reasons.

I don't think Joseph realized what would be required. I doubt if the class instructor even realized what would take place. I certainly didn't!

We sat side by side in folding chairs and I began to talk to my "father," pouring my heart out about how much his drinking pained me, and how it was killing him.

That alone would have been therapeutic. But then something amazing happened.

He answered!

In the refined atmosphere created by individuals who are gathered in full knowledge of the interdimensional, continuous nature of life, the frequency rises significantly. At this higher frequency, not only are you attuned to your Cosmic CoAuthors, but the events that unfold take on a larger significance and resonate up into the higher levels of your psychic anatomy. When Joseph spoke back to me, "pretending" to be my father, I recognized the words coming through him as my father's own frequency! Joseph was serving as a psychic link to my father's higher or Superconscious Self.

I fully believe the reality of it to this day, because the things spoken could only have been said by my father. I was given the opportunity to converse with him, Soul to Soul. Thrilling.

By the time we finished, the Infinite L-O-V-E radiating through that classroom brought me to tears—copious, healing tears. I was touched and transformed, and I believe my father was, too. I understood him so much better! My emotional pain over the situation never vanished completely, but now I had a new perspective—his— and that helped me cope and accept during the last years of his life.

**The Never-ending Conversation**

Jump ahead a few years to March 19, 2001 (six days after the psychic reading I shared with you in Chapter 13). By then, Joseph and I had married and remained in San Diego, California, while my parents had sold the family home in southwestern Michigan and moved to Colorado to be near their grandchildren, my oldest brother's children. Their drinking and health problems continued, and my father had been hospitalized with numerous, serious system failures. His prognosis wasn't good; he'd been in a Colorado hospital for some weeks.

One night at 3 a.m. my eyes popped open. This never happened to me; I was a very sound sleeper. But I was suddenly wide awake with feelings that everything in my life was *amazingly wonderful!*

Gratitude overpowered me! I could only weep quietly in joy, so as not to awaken Joseph, for all the goodness in my life. I could not go back to sleep. For three hours I lay awake, sobbing with love and gratitude for so many things, and marveling at this tremendously powerful feeling of Infinite Love that had me in its grasp!

I got up feeling refreshed and fabulous, went about my business as usual, and then, later that morning, I received a phone message from my oldest brother. My father had passed out of this world—at 3 a.m. my time!

Later I learned that my father had with sign language insisted that the doctors remove the tubes and contraptions keeping him somewhat alive and transfer him to hospice, but my distracted and distressed siblings on site forgot to notify me. I didn't know his time was so near, and even if I had, I might never have associated it with those beautiful feelings that had suffused my nighttime hours.

To put it poetically, I must have been caught up in the sweep of angel wings that took him out. I'd been swept into a tide of beautiful, interdimensional Love—of his own expression, and of the Light Beings and family members who came to help him along on his way to higher educational centers. His mother, my grandmother, had been a spiritual comforter to me many times before and I'm guessing she was among them, as well as my own spiritual teachers and mentors.

Soon after, I saw my father in a dream, being cared for in a higher-world "rehab" center. In another dream weeks later, he called us up on the telephone from upstairs in an unfamiliar house where all my siblings and I had gathered. He spoke to us of many things, regrets and joys—mostly joy. He was reassuring and comforting. Most surprising to me was his biggest regret: that we'd all spent too much time doing "chores" and not enough time fishing! He should have put his foot down about that, he told us.

**Unexpected Assistance**

Three years after that, Joseph and I were in the midst of moving to a house we'd bought in West Michigan on a wild and crazy whim, the state where my family had been brought together in this life but which we'd all abandoned one by one. Suddenly a host of "grandparents" showed up (psychically) to help!

It was while I was driving as Joseph slept during the last few hours of our long, cross-country journey from San Diego to Michigan that suddenly a chorus of relatives announced clear as a bell in my mind:

"We're all here, including Granddad!"

??? I didn't have a Granddad. Only a Gramps and a Grandpa.

As soon as Joseph woke up I said, "Who's Granddad?"

"Granddaddy? My grandmother's second husband. He was my step-grandfather. I always called him Granddaddy."

Mind you, I never considered myself to be that kind of psychic—seeing dead people! Or in this case, "hearing" them. Working with Cosmic CoAuthors residing in the highest planes and dimensions was one thing, but this was new. Today, I believe it doesn't require training to experience—maybe only to give such contacts credence and accept them as real? In other words, this kind of contact could happen to you or me or anyone with not-actually-dead relatives on the "other side."

How did I know they were all there, speaking to me? I'm not sure. Somehow they let me know instantly that I was being addressed by the whole group. And both Joseph and I felt and heard them from that moment on, usually one at a time, depending on what we needed them for.

We eventually decided this infusion of deceased relatives into our lives must have happened because

(a) we had no jobs and knew no one at all in the Michigan community we were moving to in the dead of winter, and

(b) we needed a lot of very practical, earthly help!

We knew almost nothing about furnaces and wood stoves and chimneys and putting antifreeze in the windshield washer fluid so it wouldn't freeze the wiper blades in a snowstorm and not letting the pipes freeze and how to claim recompense from the insurance company when a flood before we arrived in Michigan destroyed the carpeting in three rooms and a staircase. Neither of us had owned homes for long because we were always moving, plus Joseph had grown up in sunny Southern California and I'd left Michigan for that sunny climate after a year of college. That was barely enough adult-time to learn the required responsibilities. I think the Grandfathers and Grandmothers were appalled by our ignorance!

We survived thanks to their promptings and insights about the most mundane but necessary tasks. We'd never before appreciated how important it is to have parents and grandparents on hand, offering their advice or instruction! That alone was an insight worthy of the term "family therapy."

The silence around us in our new house in the woods would have been deafening during those first weeks, if not for our psychic family's sudden appearance in our lives. We had no physical friends or acquaintances, and we'd unknowingly chosen to live in a small part of Michigan where the local society is particularly closed to outsiders. (The area I'd grown up in was far friendlier, so this was quite a surprise!)

We'd also taken a pretty bold financial leap, with no jobs waiting for us and a new mortgage to pay, and no *earthly* excuse for Joseph to quit his excellent job as we uprooted ourselves from San Diego, other than our conscious thirst for adventure and change. We were a bit nervous about this crazy choice, to say the least.

So a few weeks later, as we shopped for the endless home supplies in a Michigan chain store, I felt myself being urged off toward a different aisle, leaving Joseph out of sight. I came back with a new tool chest and informed Joseph that, "Granddaddy says you need this."

He laughed as he told me that his rusty, beat-up, metal tool chest had been a gift from his Granddaddy many, many years before and that's why he still had the ugly old thing. His grandfather had found it by the side of the road and fixed it up for his grandson. We felt his love pouring over us both as we realized he'd just done it again!

Turns out Granddaddy was a wonderful craftsman and maintenance man, ex-Navy, and full of excellent advice. When Joseph was three or four years old, Granddaddy had taught him how to hammer nails, although he didn't realize he was also teaching his grandson to swear like a sailor while he worked, much to his grandmother's dismay!

I've since learned what a character this man truly was, after he played a few other practical jokes on us. Shortly before Granddaddy left his body, Joseph had visited him in the hospital and they'd had a little discussion about the afterlife. Months later, Joseph dreamed that he visited the (higher astral) construction site where Granddaddy and his old Navy buddies believed they were working on a house-building project. He and Joseph shared a few words, but he was in a hurry to get back to work. Joseph thinks his Granddaddy hadn't yet figured out that he'd died, but sooner or later a Lighted One would show up and gently break the news to him.

I suspect that's what had happened by the time he met up with us in Michigan, so to speak.

Life after death isn't the huge change that you might think—many people go right on doing what they've always done, until and unless someone comes to show them a new way to improve on their customary expression.

Or if they really haven't prepared themselves for life between lives by learning about the spirit worlds, they'll quickly oscillate to a womb with which they have a frequency relationship and re-enter this world and the life they knew.

For older souls, they'll often find a school that suits their current level of psychic, mental development and continue their education between lives. "Finding" it means that they'll resonate right to it based on their personal frequency rate of vibration.

Your own family members might be at many different spiritual levels, so their after-death experience will vary according to their evolutionary development. This is why you're working so hard to improve your understanding of the interdimensional aspects of life—you're insuring that your own after-death experience will be the best that you can conceive.

Granddaddy was Joseph's step-grandfather, but we've learned that you don't need to be blood relatives to serve as important family members—especially not when you take reincarnation into account. How many times have you known one another, and in how many roles?

Some of the Grandfathers and Grandmothers who stepped in to help us out felt as if we'd known them in prior lifetimes.

For instance, I didn't have a Lebanese grandmother in this life, but I did once have a Lebanese mother-in-law, now deceased; I swear she still helps out in the kitchen. She'd been close to me from the minute we met and I now believe she had once been my physical grandmother, long, long ago. And the Grandfathers who led us through the darkening woods when the winter sun dropped too quickly for our California sensibilities? Definitely from another century! So when our new crew of Assistants had announced that day in the car (in my mind), "We're all here," they meant quite a crowd indeed!

Before we left Michigan four years later, we'd also met a number of past-life family members and friends *in the flesh*, much to our comfort and relief. We had to advertise for them, though. We needed to find kindred physical spirits in this unfriendly community, and what better way than to set up classes in subjects close to our hearts? Frequency relationship—that's what makes successful "families"— whether bonded by blood or spirit or past-life experience.

Now that we're back in California, our urgent need for the Grandmothers and Grandfathers has subsided, and so have their visits.

**Karmic Resolution Defies Death**

It was also in Michigan that my father and I continued the Soul to Soul conversation I'd begun with the Family Psychodrama exercise.

Before we moved, Joseph and I made a brief week's visit to Michigan to choose the house we would purchase. We landed at Chicago's O'Hare airport in the middle of a January blizzard. My Wisconsin brother picked us up and loaned us a car: a hand-me-down from my parents that he'd fixed up with new tires for us. Joseph was driving in snow and freezing rain for the first time, so we were inching our way from Wisconsin to Michigan to meet our realtors when suddenly, standing across a snowy field in the sunset light, we spotted a herd of deer. All at once I felt as if my father were sitting in the car with us. Tears rolled down my face. Somehow I associated him with those deer.

I learned later that I wasn't the only one he visited. That same brother had spent many hours buying and flying small planes with my father in earlier years. The summer before, my brother was touring a famous air show in Wisconsin when his new girlfriend said, "Who is that man walking beside you, looking at the planes?" She then described my deceased father perfectly.

She hadn't told my brother she was psychic for fear of scaring him away. She told me that my father insisted she tell my brother of his presence, and she couldn't get any peace until she did.

Her fears were unwarranted. My brother was pleased and excited, and definitely a believer. He says it was exactly the kind of thing my father would have done in life, sizing up the airplanes with him. And he also told me later that my father did tend to show up when anyone drove his old station wagon, as we were the day I felt his presence.

We also sensed my father looking out for my mother during her last years of declining memory and health. And he made it clear to me in many ways that he wouldn't be satisfied until I'd regained some measure of communication with her. Eventually I did, via my oldest brother's cell phone calls from the nursing home in Colorado, for which I'm very grateful.

But now that both my parents have gone over, and have both done what they could for their children, their thought-presence is less frequent—as it should be!

Schooling in the higher worlds is an all-consuming endeavor, from what I've sensed of it. You wouldn't want to keep your loved ones from their beautiful experiences and their new challenges, readying themselves for the next incarnation! Please don't call them back to this dimension, but welcome their subtle waftings of thought-presence if and when they come to you.

I believe our loved ones are given assistance to make these brief thought-contacts as part of their schooling. I've been touched this way by many friends and family members, especially shortly after their transitions out of this world. They are usually brief but distinctive jolts of identity and hellos and reassurances. It usually takes a few weeks before a new arrival shows up in my mind, and I think this is because they are adjusting to their new surroundings, dealing with any physical impairments they'd had before death, and making the connections with their own Cosmic Teachers that make this communication possible.

Matter of fact, this happened to me last evening with a friend who'd gone over several months ago at a relatively young age. She'd spent many years in past-life therapy classes with me, studying this very science. I suspect she had on her mind a teensy karmic leftover reason to connect with me. For her benefit, let me add: *It's all good—we learned from it!* And I know she'll get that message. Moreover, she spent her last months, unbeknownst to me, scanning and proofing a digitally-lost children's story I'd written years ago that her children had enjoyed, making it now possible to publish. Her friends sent it to me after her transition. *Thank you, dear one! Enjoy your new life!*

I've already mentioned my father's after-life contacts. My mother's after-life contact came several weeks after her transition, while my mind was thoroughly distracted watching a DVD movie with Joseph. Suddenly I heard her say, "Hi, Honey," in her very characteristic intonation. I "saw" her sitting propped up in a bed, surrounded by caring, loving Beings who'd done something akin to handing her a telephone to make the call. (Just like my brother had done when he handed her a cell phone in the nursing home!)

"I'm doing fine," she added.

And that was it.

But I knew I was supposed to pass this along to my siblings and I did. My mother and I had engaged in so many "discussions" about my beliefs that I think she knew I'd hear her and believe it!

The experience also showed me that she was getting help for the ailments she'd suffered before her transition, including the alcohol addiction. I felt her presence strongly again years later, while I was working on republishing her book, but I just realized that book's significance to this story—you'll see in a moment.

These contacts are not at all like a séance or other Earth-initiated contact. They're more like a gentle touch of love from a recognizable source, a happy moment to help us all know that life is eternal. And perhaps, by recognizing their thoughts when they've been directed your way, we help our loved ones lay some concerns to rest.

Please believe me that I am not the kind of psychic who cultivates relationships with the deceased; these contacts have only occurred as a result of my closeness to the individual, or to the individual's loved ones, and they are brief, purposeful, *unsought* visitations. I would not consider calling any one of them back to this life or plane!

So it was more than a little unusual that my father became a strong presence early in Joseph's and my Michigan sojourn. This was, however, during the time that he was keeping a close watch over my still-living mother in Colorado; he'd moved on, but not that far.

**Old Hunting Grounds**

What had attracted Joseph and me to the house in the somewhat unfriendly community was the fact that it sat amidst beautiful white pines, on the edges of the Allegan woods. "Coincidentally" that was one of the places my father had loved to go on hunting trips when

I was growing up, but I'd never visited the area before. (Our family home had been a few counties further south.) Once we decided on Michigan, Joseph and I simply pointed at a map. We fell in love at first sight with the woods around the house, which blinded us to a few flaws in the structure itself.

Soon after we moved in, clues started to show me that I had past-life connections to Michigan that I'd never recognized during my eighteen years there, before I migrated to California to finish college. Now I understood that where I grew up was too far south for the full attunement I was experiencing, plus I hadn't studied reincarnation until my early twenties.

To better understand this little pocket of western Michigan and its unexpected hostility to outsiders, I started reading history books about the area. I discovered that we were now living smack in the middle of old tribal hunting grounds, shared by three loosely united tribes: the Chippewa (Ojibwe), Ottawa, and Potawatamie.

In fact, as those tribes had done a century before, I soon longed to move farther north to Traverse City, away from the European settlers who still dominated the scene with their prejudicial ways, even in the present century! Joseph and I went so far as to take a scouting trip north to test out the idea and consider how we'd support ourselves there.

Before we could manage it, though, I recognized the impulse as coming from a previous life, and in the present lifetime it wasn't what I'd set up to do or where I needed to live. The desire slowly left me, so that when the unplanned opportunity to return to San Diego arose four years later, I was ready to embrace the idea as the right place to be—*now*.

During my thirty previous years in California, I'd always longed for the beautiful woods I'd left behind in Michigan but I'm no longer troubled by that echo of the past. I can appreciate them, of course, but without such emotional pain. That's because during our four-year "visit" to Michigan, I had my father's help, along with my Cosmic CoAuthors, to put the clues together regarding my prior life there: to be led to the right books, to hear the Grandfathers speaking to me while we walked through the woods, and to dream and hear and sense the full story. My father and Cosmic CoAuthors helped me see his past-life connections to each member of my family, particularly my mother. Even his challenge with alcohol and his own love for Michigan's natural environment were explained.

Shortly after we'd moved into our forest home, I was prompted to read a novel called *The Red Heart*, which explained that you don't need to be in a red man's (or woman's) body to have a red man's heart (perspective, frequency, affinities). That insight unleashed the whole picture in my mind: my father had a red heart, and so do I. Although it certainly wasn't the first time our paths had crossed, we'd met during a tribal lifetime which must have taken place in Michigan.

Families are complicated because, like mine, they may have multiple lifetime connections. But during my four-year interlude in Michigan, this particular life-theme dominated my past-life awareness. Michigan is a place still rich with Native American tribal energy, both present and past. Or at least it seems that way to me!

**Test Your New Analytical Powers**

What do you think? Here's a quick look at my family members. Can you discern red hearts from white hearts? Can you see their past lives affecting their present? Because I'm the youngest by six years, I've had the long view of their life choices as we've scattered to live in separate states. I could be wrong in my guesses, but take a look at these brief profiles. I'll give you my assessments below.

* ✳ My father spent his high school years in a house on the tree-lined residential streets of my small Michigan hometown;

his parents were also city people. He worked a white collar job like his father, but after his time as a WWII pilot, he bought a hundred and sixteen acres of Michigan hills and woods on which to raise his growing family. He taught himself and then taught us all how to fish and hunt and grow vegetables. He dredged a one-acre pond from natural springs in the old pasture (our front yard), stocked it with fish, and we enjoyed swimming, fishing, skating, and paddling a canoe in it. These were the things he loved.

✳ My mother had grown up in a larger city and adapted to the country life reluctantly. But she started writing a regular column for the tiny local newspaper and soon became fascinated by the old photographs mouldering in the paper's archives. They depicted the town in its infancy, when settlers and manufacturers took over from the local tribes. Her columns on the subject were published in what became a very popular local history book, which is the one Joseph and I republished (*The Real McCoy: The Story of a Creek and Its Town*). I was eight or nine when she was doing her research and she kept dragging me into museums where the Indian artifacts gave me the heebie-jeebies. The book is beautifully written, but I wish she'd given the tribal history more space; she focused her admiration instead on the steady flow of white people into Southwestern Michigan's "Land of the Four Flags," taken over sequentially by French, British, Spanish, and American military forces.

✳ My oldest, Colorado-based brother is a former valedictorian, an intellectual computer geek poet who also writes plays, acts, directs, and produces murder mysteries in Colorado's "old west" communities. He performs on moving trains, in businesses, and wherever his troupe is hired. I hear he loves to play the bad guy, and especially the cowboy. He also writes poetry and performs solo as the Cowboy Poet, and has taught himself scary tricks he performs with a genuine bullwhip and a courageous volunteer. His favorite outfit as a little boy was a cowboy suit and a six-shooter, and by golly, he still wears that costume when he performs!

✳ My Wisconsin-based brother, the former pilot, is also an inventor and professional musician who writes ballads and stories, performing in concerts, restaurants, and nursing homes, alone and with his band. He generally affects everyone who talks to him or hears his songs with his gentle, humanitarian, sensitive, and loving nature. Recruited in his twenties by Mormons who came to his door, he was immediately "promoted" within the church to a status position as a healer, traveling to visit people in hospitals and such. He's now broadened his views, but still counts among his circle many women friends who are always ready with a hot meal and caring concern for him.

✳ My older sister, whose birth fell between the other two, wound up in a Southern California coastal city where she became one of the first women to earn an ocean-going yacht captain's license. She captained vessels for private employers, learned every form of surfing (board, wind, etc.), and now lives on a river in the Pacific Northwest where she is an author, artist, wilderness travel advisor, and cofounder of a professional tracking society—animals and particularly bears being her specialty. She's spent time as a tour guide on the Columbia River talking about Lewis & Clark, as crew on a naturalist cruise line in Alaska, and as a grizzly-bear-viewing guide at an Alaskan resort. That's the subject of her published book, *Lonesome for Bears*. I've seen a video of one of her bear presentations and wasn't too surprised to "see" a tribal elder superimposing himself over her features when she spoke. He's one of her spirit guides, he tells me, and has sent me an out-of-place alligator lizard a few times to get my attention when he needed to convey a message to her because she'd stopped paying attention to him. She and her husband now split their time between Washington wilderness and Baja surf.

Of course each one of us is much more complicated and has lived many past-life stories within our present lives. But I've plucked out these details that seem to link us in one particular era. I've known each one of them in several lifetimes (surely as writers and performers?) but the red heart/white heart tendencies seem vivid to me when I look through the lens of our original family home in Michigan:

✳ Father – tribal red heart

✳ Mother – white heart: soldier or settler

✳ Colorado Brother – white heart: wild west adventurer, gunslinger or cowboy

✳ Wisconsin Brother – white heart: Quaker or Mormon, possibly with more than one wife in one of his lives.

✳ Washington Sister – tribal red heart: wilderness guide

I'll go so far as to say my sister might be working out some kind of karma with the Lewis and Clark expedition, or at least trying to mitigate their influence on history and perception. Not only does she live on the Columbia River near the end of their pioneering, cross-country journey, but she's often mentioned that bears were given a bad name as fearsome creatures by Meriwether Lewis and she'd like to put that right. No, I don't think she *was* Lewis! She thinks like a red heart—and many red hearts were affected drastically by white perceptions during that time period, so there's plenty of karma to go around. She was also very close to my father.

Me? Red heart.

Weeks after I'd finished reading *The Red Heart,* a special dream showed me that my father and mother had crossed paths in unfortunate, conflicting roles during that era of white settlement, with tragic results. It was as if he'd felt in the present life that he needed to make amends to his former white enemy, who had been so many other things to him in so many earlier lives. Could that have been what caused them to "fall in love" as early as high school? During the dream, I felt his horror and regret over this tragic encounter in a previous life.

And now, while editing this chapter, another amazing, "chance" discovery! I was googling tribal name spellings and I immediately landed on a passage from an obscure history book about Grand Rapids, Michigan, written in 1891. It describes a scene that fits perfectly with that dream! (My mother the historian would be proud; or did she have something to do with my discovery of this document?)

The description is from a period in Michigan history when Chief Pontiac had gathered and roused thousands of tribal warriors in an attempt to defeat the British, who'd begun taking over Michigan from the previous French settlers. Pontiac was right: British ways were much less amenable to tribal interests than the French traders had been.

"During the Pontiac war the English garrisons of both Mackinaw [sic] and St. Joseph were massacred. At Mackinaw the soldiers were induced to attend an Indian game of ball near the fort, and when thrown off their guard they were attacked and nearly all murdered. A few escaped, after some of the most remarkable adventures in the whole history of barbarous captivities. It is estimated that about seventy white persons were killed in the Mackinaw massacre. The place was deserted for more than a year, but was finally reoccupied by a detachment of British troops sent for the protection of the English traders in the Northwest." (Baxter, Albert, *History of the City of Grand Rapids*, New York and Grand Rapids, 1891.)

My mother was always fascinated by and drawn to this area of northern Michigan. In my dream, I was shown a few white men surrounded by Native men in much the way this passage describes, as if in a game. I saw the red man my father was strike down the man who my mother had been, much to my father's deep and instant regret. I now believe she/he may have been among those killed, and now I wonder if I was there. I don't know why this helped me understand both of my parents better. You would never have guessed such a past—they loved each other deeply. But the explanation shown to me in the dream-vision gave me much peace.

✹ *Does location affect which past lives you're reliving at any given time?* You bet! Even if you're only passing through on vacation.

Apparently, my family reincarnated together in Michigan because we each had significant reasons to address lives we'd spent there previously, and for purposes of achieving our present-life goals. We all scattered once that initial connection had been made. (Reliving our westward migrations?) I'm the only one who tried Michigan a second time, and my conclusion was that it no longer feels like home.

"Home" now means to me the place you find support for your true life-goals and vocations. In some ways, home is wherever my polarity (Joseph) is, but it's also wherever I feel relative to the surrounding frequency or atmosphere, which is created by the combined energies of the people who live there.

**Letting Go**

After Joseph and I had been in Michigan for about two years, after I'd put all this together, explaining so much that had troubled me about my family, one day Joseph was using techniques of Energy Medicine to balance my acupuncture meridians. As he moved that energy, it came to me that it was time to let my father go. I didn't realize I'd been holding on.

But I found myself crying, and crying, and I heard, as if the Tribal Elders were speaking to me, that he was no longer my father but a free Spirit, and that I must learn to see and feel and hear him in the trees and in the wind and in the birds and in the grasses. I felt the relationship shift in the most healing way.

His presence has not been so close or frequent since then—only those beautiful drifts of loving thought that we normally share with departed loved ones. But before this shift set us both free, he'd been able to answer questions I'd posed during our Soul to Soul conversation, initiated so many years before in the Family Psychodrama!

From his new vantage point in the higher worlds, and with Cosmic assistance, he was able to help me see the past-life connections, answering my plaintive questions at last—for both of us. I can even see that his difficult relationship with alcohol may have been exacerbated by the Native American past, as even the 1891 history text describes the trouble Michigan's tribes suffered when traders brought the wrong kind of "spirit" into their lives.

Whenever or wherever we meet again, our father-daughter

relationship will be a thing of distant memory, as it should be if we're both moving forward in our creative evolution. The same will be true with my mother, as our karmic resolutions have carried on, past the veil of so-called "death!"

I've always considered my father one of the best influences in my life, and our close history goes back through many lives. But at the time of the Family Psychodrama, I'd become so distressed about his present-life choices that it was interfering in my own well-being. So that first psychic conversation accomplished a great deal for both of us. Yet in hindsight, which can be such a trickster, I might think that day's experience a fluke of my active imagination if I hadn't seen similar results among others.

**Finding Your Own Peace**

A decade after my own Family Psychodrama, Joseph and I watched an equally magnificent healing take place in a class we were teaching. A middle-aged woman we'll call Susie needed to resolve some issues with her own father. We suggested she try the Family Psychodrama method.

Like Joseph years before, the student Susie chose to portray her father probably thought he'd be acting, not channeling, and we did not interfere. Susie also asked another student known for her sensitive nature to sit by her side for moral support. None of our students had experience with psychodrama, but Susie proceeded without question and with complete confidence.

As you know, healing like mine, my father's, and Susie's takes a mutual desire for healing, a high-frequency connection, and spiritual preparation—interdimensional conference calls are tricky! But as Susie began to tell her side of the story, the frequency in the hushed room rose tangibly. Soon all our eyes were leaking tears! We could see and feel tremendous love when her father stepped into this un-coached young man's consciousness and began to speak to Susie of things only she and her father would know. She told us afterwards that even the young man's spontaneous physical gestures were things her father would have done, so meaningful to her in her healing quest.

Susie's father had been deceased for a number of years—or at least his body had been—and she'd felt unable to express things she'd needed to clarify. Her psychodrama was beautiful, stunning, and unforgettable.

But the proof of the pudding came with her results. This woman, who had been institutionalized in the past for mental stress (as had her father), suddenly found more balance and creativity in her life. Passionate about the subject, she stepped forward when we moved back to California to initiate and lead a series of creative workshops in Michigan, with a particular focus on past-life healing.

We also felt and knew that her father received help as well, stepping up his schooling in the higher worlds.

Whether at Mrs. Norman's healing center or in my own classes, every student or teacher in the room is helped by participating in such precious experiences. You couldn't be exposed to that kind of interdimensional healing energy without being positively affected!

And that's yet another reason to pursue your quest for healing: you'll help so many people beyond yourself.

Each time you clear away the psychic blockages and restrictions you've created in past lives, you clear your Infinite channel a little bit more—or a lot more. Infinite Intelligence pours more freely into all that you say and do, making you a greater part of the in-breathing and out-breathing of the higher effulgences of life. By your healing, you also step up the intensity of your individual spark, and that, in turn, spills over to light the lives of your fellow humans.

Nowhere is this more welcome than within the bonds of your own family!

∞ ✹ ∞

## Heal Your Family

Don't wait for a classroom! You can conduct your own healing Family Psychodrama right now.

1. If you cannot find anyone suitable to serve as a surrogate for the family member in question (who may be in this world or beyond it), write a letter to that individual, pouring your heart into it. If they're still in this world, you do not have to share it with them unless you choose to do so. Consider first (and carefully) whether this will be a benefit or a detriment to the other person. Chances are, you are the only one consciously ready for this step. But save your letter. Things might change later on.

    If it's a troubled relationship, we often tell people that such connections are like two people sitting on a seesaw or teeter-totter, as they called it where I grew up. You are both keeping that oscillation going, up and down, up and down. If one of you gets off the teeter-totter, the oscillation ends. The other individual can't keep it going without your participation!

    If you can be the wiser one and climb off the teeter-totter, healing will inevitably ensue and your partner never needs to know the details. Not in this dimension! In the higher worlds, they will deeply benefit from your actions. Don't be surprised to see rapid change appearing in this world as a result of this karmic resolution!

2. If you have secured the aid of a trusted friend whom you can

envision as this family member, then proceed with a request to your Cosmic CoAuthors to assist in a psychodrama. You don't need to record this event unless you wish to. If all goes well, you will never forget its healing impact.

3. Even better, enlist a circle or group of like-minded friends who will share in this experience with you. Choose carefully. Perhaps you can institute a series of these psychodramas among your spiritual group or class, where you all support each other's healing objectives. I believe that the energies of love and compassion projected to the participants by observers aid in raising the frequency of the entire endeavor, resulting in greater success for all.

4. *Psychic channeling is not required for this exercise.* Your chosen surrogate may simply act out the role, and you and your loved one will still derive ample benefits! I've seen many family psychodramas conducted successfully in this way, some quite elaborate and others very simple. In fact, it is the usual way.

5. The procedure is simple: Follow your heart. Make sure that it is a two-way conversation if you're working with a surrogate. Keep the contact reasonably short. If they do show up to participate, be sure to send any discarnate loved ones back to school in the higher worlds, with love, as you close your contact.

6. Do not use this psychodrama like a séance, as an excuse to contact someone who has gone over. They need to be undisturbed in their studies! The Family Psychodrama is to help *you* resolve issues seriously affecting your ability to let go and move forward.

# 22

## Surfing the Cosmic Cycles

*Timing is everything. But on* this planet in these bodies, we often don't know the right questions to ask at the right time. That's an issue for our Superconscious Selves to determine, with the help of whatever higher spiritual agencies you've teamed up with.

If information from your past lives is to be useful to you, it must come to you in the right cycle of time. Otherwise, if you're completely out of phase with that particular past lifetime, it may mean little or nothing to you. It's useless. That doesn't mean it's not true. Hold on to it, set it aside, forget it, and perhaps one day it may mean something when the right cycles come into play.

In my experience, if past-life information is truly coming to you from the highest, you won't be receiving it—whether from dreams, flashbacks, journaling, analysis, psychodrama, regressions, readings, massage, chakra clearing, or whatever—until and unless you can put it to good use.

What does that mean, "put it to good use"?

To accomplish permanent change in the psychic structures of your Mental Consciousness using this faster method (versus the "slow transformation" of long, evolutionary change), a minimum of five things must occur, as you first learned in Chapter 10. To review, they are:

1. Recognition and validation of the past;

2. Acceptance and belief

3. Remorse and/or a different perspective on the situation;

4. Change in your energy and/or life habits in your present life; and, at this stage in your evolutionary development,

5. Assistance from Advanced Beings who can project perfectly-tuned, healing energy to cancel or rectify the fourth-dimensional, destructive vortical patterns of energy-information in your psychic anatomy.

In other words, your responsibility doesn't end when someone tells you about a past-life or you discover the details on your own. You've only begun your quest for healing! Now comes the hard part.

I've carved this up into arbitrary "steps," but of course life and growth aren't always so neat. The first two steps may happen simultaneously as you set out to prove and test the validity of the information. You'll come to recognize and believe it to have been your experience, but to heal, you'll need to accept responsibility in the depths of your soul for all that it means to you. Even if you seem to have been a "victim" of some event, you may still find it difficult to accept. But we're after soul-deep change here, so without that, you'll be no further along on your progressive path.

As soon as you've recognized some truth of your past and accepted it as real, many trauma-inducing past-life incidents are going to cause you some kind of regret or remorse, say, over a decision you made that you now wish you hadn't. In fact, nearly all of our past contains information that to us, now, with our present perspective on life, takes on a different coloration. We'd take a different turn in the road, if we could. But we can't live in the past to change it. We can only change our present, with hopes for improving our future. Future-life therapy. So that's the fourth step, making personal changes in attitude and behavior that are fueled by your knowledge of the past. When you look back from your new elevation of consciousness—assuming you've been tooling along improving your ideas and discarding old ones—you'll reap the wisdom of your experience in a new, more complete way. Putting that wisdom to work now in your present lifetime, you begin to build a better future. That's what you'll be drawing from in all your future lifetimes.

This is the real gem and purpose of understanding your continuity of life from life to life: after a few of these experiences, you'll begin to live your life with a new awareness that won't require details of your past lives to prove beneficial. With the self-proven knowledge that you're going to be living your life continuously, from life to life, you'll have many reasons for living differently, in a more constructive and balanced way. The motivations will be strong, so the change in habits will be easier to make.

And that constructive motivation and purpose will help you to achieve the last, fifth step: Rectification or cancellation.

To speed your evolutionary growth, this is where you benefit from higher-world assistance to make rapid, permanent, electronic changes in your psychic anatomy. It's as if you push the button in your own consciousness by your positive intent, attitude, and striving, but your Spiritual Mentors complete the operations that rebuild your engine. To reiterate a point made earlier, at this stage in our evolution, we're not sufficiently developed to create the precisely counterbalanced energies necessary to cancel out, or rectify, the complex, fourth-dimensional energy configurations in our psychic anatomy. Even putting it all into one sentence is difficult! We may one day acquire this ability, if we continue to develop our Superconscious by our constructive distillations of experience. But for now, we need a strong, overshadowing Force configured correctly, and applied at exactly the right conjunction of elements, in order to positively influence our psychic anatomy in what we on Earth generally term "healing." Our other alternative is to make change the slow way, living our current and future lives from this new perspective, until the structures in our psychic anatomy are gradually changed.

If you'd like to know more about this interdimensional process, read Ernest Norman's *Tempus Interludium*, Volume 2, a chapter called, "Further Discussion on Canceling Out Past Negations."

In the book you're reading, we're barely scratching the surface of this topic. But hopefully it will inspire you to further your education about the interdimensional nature of your true Self. As you build your understanding, continuous healing of your past selves will start to unfold naturally. You'll need to apply yourself diligently in your quest, but as people are so fond of echoing, if you take the first steps, all manner of assistance will then come to your aid. It's a truth worth repeating! Your steady growth will unfold as quickly as you are able to discard your old ideas and habits. The process will follow you right up into the higher worlds and beyond.

Joseph wrote a song about it once: "I used to think I knew everything…then I changed my mind." Pretty simple, right?

**Cyclic Learning**

If spiritual growth were only a matter of our efforts at self-improvement, we'd all be perfected beings by now, wouldn't we? Because you and I are the motivated type! Obviously there's another factor at work.

We can't learn about the Infinite all at once. (Then it wouldn't be infinite, would it?) And everything in this world transpires in cyclic patterns. Remember this diagram?

Since everything *of* us and *around* us is being fueled by the energy intelligence of non-physical dimensions, where energy travels in these spiral patterns, our life here reflects that circling motion. As we've already discussed, you'll find this radiating pattern expressed throughout nature, from snails to galaxies.

We learn by spiraling up the rungs one at a time, but each time we circle around, we contact the same points on the cycle or circle again, yet from a (hopefully) higher elevation of consciousness.

So when my gladiator exploits came to light the first time, then the second, then the third—each time I was spiraling up those circular rungs of consciousness, tapping into the old cycle once again as I crossed that point on the circle. But each time with a slightly different perspective, because I was climbing out of my past into a more positive association with this aspect of the Infinite (because even the worst of what we know is a part of the Infinite experience of life).

That's one way to look at our association with cycles of past-life experience.

Another way is to look at the overall society in which we live.

**Planetary Cycles**

We can see historically that civilizations have risen and fallen, which might make you think of a sinusoidal wave pattern, such as the way energy travels in a third-dimensional world.

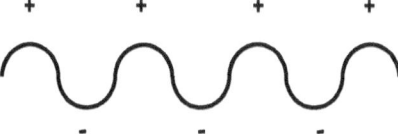

But you can also view it as particular elements of expression coming around again—with all of us reincarnating and passing through these elements with a new or different state of consciousness, because nothing remains static in our universe. It's either progressing or regressing, and that includes us. Of course, not everyone is *progressing* through these rungs of experience, in terms of developing a more useful mind. Some are lagging behind, some are speeding forward, a few are falling backward.

If you picture the vortex again, you can imagine that some are standing on a higher rung, some on a lower rung, but all together the group of us living on Earth, let us say, are contacting cycles of experience that resonate through the higher and lower rungs of the Infinite.

As a society, we are connecting to a set of circumstances, a pattern of expression, simultaneously at any given point in time, and although we all are connected to one another and to this expression through harmonic resonance, we all may respond differently.

You don't condone war, for instance, but perhaps the society around you does. Right now, our planetary civilization is passing through a time when war erupts. All around you, people are making choices about how they will align themselves to that war situation. They are choosing which rung of experience they will be standing on as they pass through the cycle of war. Their prior experience of war and whatever they've learned or not learned from it will inevitably color their choices.

Still too abstract? Let's try another example, from my experience with group past-life therapy.

**Group Cycles**

Perhaps you've heard or experienced that women who live together for any length of time soon begin to express coinciding menstrual cycles? It was much like that with the students of Ernest Norman's books who gathered at Mrs. Norman's learning center in the 1970s through the early 1990s, only it wasn't menstrual cycles but cycles of shared history that the group began to "relive" in the present.

At any given time, some historical era would seem to emerge from the depths of the psychic anatomies of the individuals present, replaying its energy in the external, present lives of the students.

At first—unidentified—unusual blocks or quirks would begin to hinder the activities underway, whether it was a music rehearsal or a building project. Most organizations or businesses or social groups would soldier on in this situation, pushing their way through with blood, sweat, and tears to the conclusion of whatever goal they'd been working on.

This group was highly unusual, however. We were all students of interdimensional science, and the fact of past lives affecting present-life circumstances had become a part of our personal storehouses of knowledge, thanks to the books we were studying.

With this mutual, growing awareness that something was afoot, it didn't take long for the kind of analytical sleuthing I used in ferreting out my gladiator past to yield a consensus, as we compared notes and flashbacks and dreams and insights. Once the past-life epoch infiltrating our minds and actions was identified (a pivotal time in Egypt, say, or South America), it didn't take much work to identify one's own role in the past. We were often wrong about details, however, because of peer pressure to find one's part. Nevertheless we would still benefit because we'd identified the nature of the past and, in a general sense, the type of activity we'd engaged in. That was often enough for healing, and if necessary, we could sort out individual identities at some future time when egos weren't involved.

On the other hand, often we knew exactly what we'd been up to in the past, and it wasn't pretty. Those were the juicy opportunities we'd been working toward, individually and as a group. We surely arranged to take part in this pioneering past-life therapy group long before we were born! I believe our purpose was to record our experience for the benefit of future generations.

During these years of intensive practice and study, we managed to fill several books with personal testimonials about our past-life recalls and detailed descriptions of our healing experiences, which Mrs. Norman compiled and published. (See Resources.)

Was this simply a rarefied opportunity, set up by our Cosmic CoAuthors, for one particular group of souls who'd gathered to pool their learning and thus write books for others to learn from? I don't know. But I'm extremely fortunate and grateful to have experienced it.

Once I learned this mental habit of identifying what past-life cycle is in play, my life became a lot easier to navigate. When trouble arises, as it always does, I look for immediate solutions, look to my present life for answers, and then look deeper if it stubbornly refuses to be corrected. *What am I reliving?* I'll ask myself if times are desperate.

Without the intensity of that group therapy experience, which I haven't been part of since 1995, these incidents now rise and fall through my personal life in a slower rhythm. I assume this means my progress has been slowed to a pace I can keep up with on my own. But the practice is still a good one and has "saved my life" more than once—or at the very least, saved my sanity! *Ah, of course I feel X! That's energy flowing to me from Y lifetime!* And with that thought, the impact of X simply fades from importance.

Very often, it's enough to merely identify the cyclic replay of the past in your life, and that puts all things in their proper perspective. The blocks and emotions recede with this objectification, and your life goes on a little more smoothly. You don't always need to know the details of who, what, when, or how. Using only your Conscious Mind awareness, you're still able to move yourself out of phase with the past. That's an essential skill for anyone on a creative, evolutionary path!

"What goes around, comes around." It's not only a saying. It's an interdimensional energy principle!

**Cosmic Cycles**

Summer, Autumn, Winter, Spring. The Seven Ages of Man (and woman!). Birth, death, rebirth, death, rebirth. All are cycles, large and small.

If you observe nature, you'll understand that this is how the Infinite expresses itself. If you can dispense with linear time and think instead of cycles—a quantity of effort expressed, a passage from beginning to end to beginning again—you will more closely align yourself with that Infinite Consciousness, achieving more harmony and less resistance, and ultimately peace of mind in this knowledge that all things pass through cycles, never ceasing, including you and me.

As I write the concluding chapters of this book, we've passed through the year 2012 and headed well into the year 2013, as our calendars record the cycles of this time-and-space world. Much has been made of the changing of this particular annual cycle:

Have we entered a new time, a Shift, a massive developmental cycle for all of the Earth's people?

Are we speeding ahead on a new evolutionary track?

Is it an invisible, individual shift?

Or will we witness and perhaps suffer through major environmental shifts and changes, only to come out thriving on the other end of it, those of us who match the external with internal changes?

Certainly the very act of asking such questions has brought about a shift in consciousness for large groups of people, and that can't be a bad thing. Group consciousness affects, not only the cyclic replay of particular historical pasts, but it also affects the energy that surrounds us individually, and globally.

As we say in the practice of Energy Medicine: energy first, physical follows. So it is with the emanations of thought from humans who live together: they create an energy atmosphere. In that atmosphere, things thrive or decay, depending on the nature of that energy. So a shift in thinking toward a positive goal is always helpful!

Many wonderful books are being written about this global consciousness and even about the science of global, physical changes we're beginning to witness, with speculation about what connects to what, what causes what, and what doesn't. But this book is about you and your personal, evolutionary growth. So I'm going to address what you need to know about any situation forthcoming, be it positive or negative.

1. If the planet is destroyed by solar activity or galactic activity or human activity, your experience will depend on your individual state of consciousness. By now, you should understand that it is your personal, spiritual development that will determine where and how you associate yourself.

2. If life on this planet is no longer tenable, you will find a planet to which you are relative to carry on with your personal, evolutionary development (preferably *after* a beautiful, between-life sojourn of study in higher worlds).

3. If, on the other hand, life on this planet becomes a paradise of cosmic awareness and higher-frequency living, you will only be able to reincarnate here if you have kept up with these changes in your personal realm of consciousness and maintain a compatible frequency with this new, positive development.

4. Or, if indeed the planet's populations descend too far into destructive patterns of life, feeding off one another

in increasingly despicable ways and fostering a more violent and self-centered necessity for brute survival, *and you are no longer compatible with these destructive ways* (hopefully!), then you will, again, find another planet of a higher development to continue your personal evolutionary experience.

5. If you die during the course of any of these changes, you will not be terminated at all, but will carry on as described above, depending on your state of consciousness and development and karmic necessities.

6. If you "survive" any cataclysm such as solar outburst, plasma storm, ice age, fire, or brimstone (whatever that is), then you will still need to apply all that you've learned about energy and consciousness to maintain your progressive course of creative evolution. In other words, each day will still bring its evolutionary challenges and opportunities.

The point is that worrying about aspects of evolutionary transformation that affect galactic and solar and planetary bodies will only bring about the same effects as worrying about whether or not you remembered to turn off the lights back home. Worry is a very unconstructive state of mind, and worse, it causes a stress reaction to ripple through your energy systems and hence your body, and it sends nothing but sludge back to your psychic anatomy, which will pour out at some future time when you really don't need it.

For my own benefit, I think I should plaster that paragraph on my forehead.

It's one thing to do what we can to improve the little bit of the planetary environment that we can influence. That's certainly a positive endeavor. And if we have the opportunity to influence a larger portion of the environment or the states of mind of our fellow citizens, even better. But bottom line is always going to be your own mind and body. They are our primary tools here. Don't clutter them up with concern over issues that are best taken up by the Advanced Minds who play major roles in the unfoldment of vast evolutionary plans that involve universes beyond universes. I'm pretty sure we'll have plenty of opportunities to work on that scale, if we keep up with our little evolutionary plan of personal growth! So we can put off such concerns until then.

Oh, of course, I've got my emergency backpack in the closet and an exit plan in case of wildfires (biggest danger where I live). I carry an extra pair of flat shoes any time I go out in high heels. I take my jacket along just in case and I've got an extended tow-insurance card in my wallet. I am fascinated by stories of survival, a subject I've toyed with in a novel I'm writing. And I have just finished reading a wonderful book by my favorite visionary geologist, Dr. Robert Schoch, speculating on solar activity as the cause of those sine-wave ups and downs in the planet's ancient and current history. (I recommend it, *Forgotten Civilization*.)

I fully expect that our planet's higher-dimensional computer system (its own psychic anatomy) and its integrated, interconnected role in the universe will one day mandate big changes down here at the third-dimensional level; such is evolutionary growth.

But I am not losing sleep over any of this. I'm doing what I can to ensure that, living or dead, my life will resonate at a frequency clearer and higher than it was yesterday, day after day, cycle after cycle.

As Dr. Schoch explains, ice ages have come and gone and come back again. Just as we do. We'll always find our place in the universe! We are eternal beings of Light-energy, indestructible.

∞ ✳ ∞

## Calm Your Panic

From Donna Eden's Energy Medicine comes another wonderful exercise called "Taking Down the Flame." Unfortunately, I have to use it often, or maybe I should say fortunately? Because it really works to sooth a panicked state of mind. I don't mean running around in hysterics, although it works for that, too. I mean a subtle, inner state of agitation I feel when something either good or bad is about to happen.

It's akin to a manic feeling when it's something good, and akin to panic when it's something bad. You'll feel it in your stomach, most likely. Do you feel a bit trembly? Or faintly nauseous or unsettled? Have trouble eating? (That's my biggest clue.) For instance, when the day comes that I release this book from my hands for publication, I will be experiencing that state of excitement, I'm sure, and I will be using this exercise to keep my energies humming along more peacefully, and to keep me from stumbling, dropping things, whining or screeching, pulling out in front of other cars, and otherwise screwing things up dangerously.

This exercise, by the way, comes from a rhythmic classification of life used in Eastern medicine called the Chinese Five Rhythms, each named after five seasonal cycles and states of matter: Summer/Air, Equinoxes/Earth, Autumn/Metal, Winter/Water, Spring/Wood. This exercise helps to balance the often hyperactive Summer Rhythm. I am classified as primarily an Earth/Water person, but we all have all five rhythms to balance, so it's when my Summer rhythm goes haywire that I need to "take down the flame."

1. Stand upright with hands on your thighs. Breathe. Now touch the fingers and thumbs of your hands together in front of you.

2. Still holding them together, bring your hands up over your head as you inhale deeply. Now touch down at the crown of your head with the point made by your thumbs as you exhale with a sound like "Haaaaaaaa."

3. Lift your thumbs with another deep inhale, then repeat the exhale and "Haaaaaa" sound as you touch with your thumbs the point between your eyebrows known as the center of your third eye or sixth chakra.

4. Lift again on an inhale and, skipping the throat, touch down with a "Haaa" for each of these points: center of your chest between the breasts (heart or fourth chakra); belly button.

5. At the belly button, as you "Haaa" exhale, leave your thumbs touching and fold your hands down flat against your abdomen, releasing all the fingers from touching each other except index fingers and thumbs. This makes a kind of heart or diamond shape.

6. Holding that pose, inhale again, then release and run your hands down your legs with the exhaled "Haaa." Hang for a moment. Breathe and exhale a "Haaa."

7. Run your hands back up your legs as you inhale and straighten, exhaling one last "Haaaaaaaaaa ....." Feel better? Repeat as necessary. You'll find this exercise in *Energy Medicine, Energy Medicine for Women*, and *The Little Book of Energy Medicine*.

# 23

## The Power in You

*Here's the simplest summation of* all you've learned thus far:

At any given moment of your life, you are faced with three streams of energy-information flowing from:

1. Your present-life sensory input

2. Your prior experience including past lives

3. Infinite Intelligence through your Superconscious Self

As these three streams connect in your psychic anatomy and pour that augmented and conjoined data back onto the screen of your Conscious Mind, you will choose how you shape your present, and thereby your future lives. This is your raw material, and you will decide how to use it, whether you realize you're making choices or not. The energy-intelligence you make a part of yourself does not lie, and does not die.

So this is your opportunity to speed your evolution by practicing Future Life Therapy: (a) using your knowledge of the past to unblock creativity and stop destructive habits and conditions in your life, and (b) using your knowledge of how your future is designed to motivate better choices in the present.

A recent discussion about that most feared condition on Earth, cancer, reminded me that the confusion about this energy state in which we live is causing harm all over the planet. Ignorance is not bliss! Fortunately, you are no longer ignorant of this truth.

As for cancer, now that I've brought it up, let's consider a cell in light of the list that opens this chapter. It receives its basic design and Intelligence—via your body's circuitry—from your psychic anatomy. External influences may impact its physical structure, but its basic design and function are determined by information flowing out from higher dimensions.

A cancerous cell is one that has experienced some disruption in this two-way, interdimensional flow of information. In other words, either something in the psychic anatomy has gone awry and begun outputting damaged information, or something in the physical body has disrupted the cell's receptivity and response to a normally creative, intelligent, higher-dimensional inflow from and through the psychic anatomy.

After reading the previous chapters, you know that such glitches come around cyclically and can originate far back in prior lifetimes. They can also be amended and corrected with the proper *multi-dimensional* therapy.

The cancer might be residue from a prior bodily injury, such as a sword or bullet wound. This might have been either experienced or inflicted for, as you know, either way the energy of destructive information is recorded in one's psychic anatomy. This cancer cell could have begun as any one of a countless number of things that affected one's own or one's victim's body, present or past.

An old saying, "If you point your finger at someone, three fingers are pointing back at you," isn't far from the truth. The psychic-energetic impact on a perpetrator seems to be stronger than for a victim. (For this reason, most of my early past-life therapy studies focused on destructive actions I'd taken in the past, rather than any states of "victimhood" I might have experienced. It's a much more helpful approach if you're interested in speeding your evolution.)

How and when a cancer cell will be healed is a complex and individual story.

Will it be through a past-life flashback and healing projection from the higher Minds residing in higher worlds—long prepared for—which will correct the destructive information at the level of the psychic anatomy, which will then translate down into visible healing of the physical cell?

Or will there be an external catalyst, say a doctor who was also present for the original, past-life damage, who now becomes a partner in the individual's healing attempt as they both resolve this karmic connection?

Will this healing take a long time, a short time, or lifetimes of repetition before it's accomplished?

With your new tools of introspection, you may realize that a cancerous cell does not infect other cells, or spread its malaise by physical proximity. The "spread" of cancer we observe is much more likely the spread of malformed energy-information flowing into or out of the higher-dimensional psychic anatomy, and therefore must be corrected at that level first, before healing is observed in the physical body. Therefore, consciousness and perception, our way of contacting our higher-dimensional Selves, will ultimately be involved in this healing.

Attacking or making war on the cell—killing it—will not prevent or cure the spread of the malady in and of itself. But the process of going through some form of "treatment" will certainly affect the individual's state of mind, for better or worse, and also add more energy-information to the psychic anatomy, for better or worse.

It's a simple situation of a broken, interdimensional energy circuit, and yet one complicated by all the factors unique to the patient: personal history, state of interdimensional awareness, present mental perspective and attitude, overall physical endurance for any treatment undertaken, and perhaps most importantly, their pre-determined plan for their present lifetime.

Is dying from a difficult disease one of the challenges they've set up? Or is it their objective to "beat this disease" and come out of the experience with new perspectives on life? And so on.

If friend, family, or your own body is one day confronted by a challenge such as this, I do hope that you will take a deep breath and view all from a compassionate, interdimensional perspective. The true power over any such situation still remains with the individual undergoing the experience. Whatever the outcome, it will be one more lesson in their ongoing education, all to the benefit and growth of their eternal Self.

I suppose we've saved this discussion for the last chapter because it encompasses some of the most difficult challenges we face in life: death of our own bodies, or those of our loved ones. Our emotional attachments are an essential part of our life on Earth. They lead us in and out of our greatest tests. You might even say that we come into a life on Earth for the specific purpose of undertaking these growth experiences, and eventually, we shape ourselves into loving, compassionate, wise Beings by these very experiences.

Keep in mind that what you experience here always begins first in a higher dimension, not the other way around. Life or "time" as we experience it flows from the top down, from higher dimension to lower, but information travels both ways, from dimension to dimension.

Hence current leading-edge experiments regarding whether or not the future can affect the past (as Dr. Schoch discusses in *Forgotten Civilization*) are bringing contemporary researchers very close to the knowledge of interdimensional exchange that you've now learned! As Joseph puts it, these experiments about the future potentially affecting the past have led to some very "trippy" results. But if you look at them through your interdimensional lens, they're not so surprising after all.

The connecting link—whether you're observing the spread of cancer, or, as one researcher did, the results of students studying *after* they've taken a test and thereby influencing their scores—is the higher-dimensional system of vortical energies spinning just beyond our current instruments' detection, governing and guiding all that we experience on Earth in our third-dimensional state of awareness. We help to shape aspects of this fourth-dimensional information in some small way through our feedback loop, but at any given moment, we entirely depend upon the Infinite Whole of this information system for our very existence.

Personally, I think the veil between dimensions is beginning to drop rapidly away with each new development at the fringes of our scientific exploration. I'm so grateful to be already initiated into this understanding. I hope you are too.

**An Experiment**

In keeping with our scientific adventurousness, Joseph and I once conducted an experiment of our own, back at the dawn of the twenty-first century. We wanted to see how past-life information would affect people who had not previously studied the interdimensional, scientific principles of reincarnation—at least not in their present lifetimes. They hadn't read the same books we'd been studying, although many were at least interested enough in metaphysical topics to be open to the experiment.

We thought we were doing this for a book we planned to write called *The Power in You*. Our volunteers were business associates, friends, or family of friends who agreed to participate, and I recall that at our CoAuthors' suggestion, we charged them a token fee for the reading so that they'd be encouraged to take it more seriously (human nature being what it is).

We tried to keep up with our subjects through email exchanges after they received the readings, to see how the information might have benefitted them. Dear souls, they diligently tried to answer our questions and questionnaires over the course of the next couple of years, some more successfully than others. We did note positive changes in their lives and a lot of "aha" moments, but we were also reminded that once a thing has been truly and fully healed, it vanishes from Conscious Mind awareness and the individual moves on to the next challenge in their cycles of life. That's how it should be, and so we eventually left them alone.

Meanwhile, as we also moved into new projects, we felt a reluctance to publish these readings after all. Joseph in particular was leery that people might come to us asking for past-life readings and he was unwilling to become anyone's guru. I had to agree.

The next time we did a group of past-life readings was for a workshop we gave while we were living in Michigan, after our students had done a reasonable amount of reading and studying about interdimensional energy principles.

Interestingly, the results of both groups were similar! So these two experimental projects together underlined something we'd known before:

> **A reading alone won't change anyone, and neither will dreams, flashbacks, insights, analysis, or the study of universal energy principles.**
> **It's how the information is applied (or not) that makes the difference.**
> **That's the true Power in You!**

As Ernest Norman puts it in *The Infinite Concept of Cosmic Creation:*

> ...we should never at any time lose sight of the fact that it is the birthright of every individual to go through various dimensions or reincarnations to learn of himself through experience and what experience means to him. We do not have the power or the jurisdiction to go to him in weaknesses and frustrations and to give him some sort of a material message that might divert

*him from a truly realistic approach to a certain problem. In a psychological sense, we could completely change the whole tenor of his existence by giving him a message. The inner contact with the self is of utmost importance because there we find the solution of everything without going to anyone else.*

It's time to discuss how you're going to develop and exercise that massive inner potential you carry!

"The inner contact with the self is of utmost importance because there we find the solution of everything without going to anyone else." How wonderful is that? Personal liberation from any kind of spiritual dependence.

*Inter-dependence* is another thing altogether. You've learned a little from earlier chapters about the infinite design of your consciousness, how it is linked and relinked throughout the Intelligent Universe. With this knowledge, there are no limitations placed upon you. You can learn how to access higher frequency worlds and individuals who can shine a Light back from their higher elevation to help guide you through the long, winding road of life.

As you do this, you will be developing your own Superconscious Self, which will eventually become a beacon for others, far into your future development. Everyone has this ability. We merely need to learn how it functions, and apply that knowledge.

How to do this? Life experience, study, and practice!

# Survival Skills for the 21st Century

Throughout this book, we've pointed up survival tools to help you speed your evolution in the current era on Earth. Here's a list:

* Your personal journal

* Books and other research materials about the new, inter-dimensional, universally connected science of life

* Your five senses

* Your willingness to let go of old ideas and replace them with new ones

* Your sincere desire to improve yourself

* Your sensitivity to inner communication—and your discernment of the frequency of this communication; i.e., *What is the source of this information? Is it wise? Does it help or hinder? Can I trust it? Who are my astral companions?*

* Catalysts—such as doctors, teachers, energy healers, friends, neighbors, loved ones, and so on. Anyone might become a sudden catalyst to help you trigger healing you've already developed during your time between lives. But be aware that others can also become a hindrance! Meet these individuals on the high road; if any drop down to the low road for a time, for their learning purposes, don't follow. And if you outgrow the beneficial aspects of this connection, move on.

* Your own daily healing and prevention skills—such as practical, self-healing skills in energy medicine, energy psychology, nutrition, massage therapy, therapeutic touch, and so on. Self-healing tools can help you apply information

you receive inwardly, thus freeing you from dependence on external "experts" who might not be so expert for *your* situation. Add these as soon as possible to your *Survival Skills for the 21st Century*.

✵ Polarities and partners—not your "soul mate" or catalyst for healing, necessarily, but individuals who share similar goals and who will support you energetically and emotionally in your quest. The same caution applies here: If their path veers off in a direction you don't want or need to go, let yourselves part. It won't benefit either of you to hang on or hold one another back. Your paths may converge again in the future—or not.

✵ Your practice of Future-Life Therapy—using what you learn about your past to heal your present and improve your future.

✵ To Be Determined—this should cover anything you might encounter on Earth, because you never know what's going to heal you next!

✵ Your Cosmic CoAuthors

Hm, when I typed that last line, it felt like a sign-off instead of a list item. It could be both!

And for days now I've stared at this page and nothing more has come to me. It's all up to you now. So I, too, will sign off—and see you in the higher classrooms!

With much love,
Your sister in the quest

# Epilogue

*Nothing remains static for long* in the Universe—it's either progressing or regressing. That includes you and me, both our ideas and our physical states. During the writing of this book, I've mentioned a few personal dilemmas, and with all this help from my Cosmic CoAuthors flowing through, I've received a few insights. I hate to leave loose ends lying, so here's the latest:

**About weight lifting vs. dancing:** Recently I went out of my way to purchase ballroom practice shoes—solid, stout, protective—before a dance session on a Saturday. We danced, we practiced—no problems. Two hours later while we were grocery shopping, my thong-style sandal slid sideways from under my foot and sent my big toe one way and my other toes the other, causing an injury that's kept me off my toes for two weeks. Karma had other ideas!

There's an old saying, "What you fear will come upon you," and it's based on the solid energy principles of attraction and repulsion. The energies of my past pouring into my present are inevitable, but it's what I do with them that matters, and how much reinforcement I give the past without realizing what I'm doing. The sandals, of course, provided a Roman tune-back, but I hadn't thought of that. The past that I was trying to avoid, and by so doing gave it strength, came upon me anyway!

So I'm not giving up either strength-training or partner dancing, but I've bought new sandals and I'm keeping my training routines as feminine as possible. Giving up something would be strengthening fear, which won't help me. Being fearless, however, might be a trait I trained for in the past. You can't escape or avoid your past, but you can mitigate its impact in your present life, changing your ideas, your choices, and your energetic bias. I've discovered that given my past-life associations, I'm prone to minor injuries no matter which activities I choose to pursue. More important is my state of mind. If I keep pushing back up to the positive bias, the inevitable discharge of past negative energy (a tweaked knee, a strained toe ligament) will have a relatively minor, diffused impact on my present life.

**About my siblings:** Courtesy demanded that I show my siblings Chapter 21 before I published it, since I'd never shared my theories and perspectives about our family with them. Over the years, they've all tolerated their little sister's belief in reincarnation, so apparently it didn't surprise them much.

*Older Sister* (the tracker): "Hey, does that mean I can put you in one of my books?"

*Colorado Brother* (the churchgoer): "I had to laugh when reading your description of me as a cowboy, since at that moment I was holding a bowie knife on which I'd been filing down some protruding brass buttons. Touché." Then he said: "Did I mention that I once wrote a murder mystery [for his theater troupe] about a religious group that believed in UFO's and reincarnation? I never used it, however—though I later transferred the story line to a speakeasy in the twenties and used that. No Lianne-like characters in either one, however."

*Wisconsin Brother*: "Did I ever tell you about the life in which I drowned?" He vividly remembers his last glimpse of daylight from the porthole as the ship went down, his body trapped by some broken piece of the vessel. But in the present life while snorkeling, he got trapped on the bottom of a lake by a pier's crossbar, which sank down onto him when group of people walked out on the floating structure. This time he didn't panic, he said, and calmly wiggled back and forth until the sandy bottom gave him clearance to reach the surface just as his breath ran out. Whew. He believes at that moment he worked out the fear from his prior-life drowning, and tested it later during the failure of a business jet he was piloting—his calm saved the day and his passengers' lives. Then he said: "You're already in the novel I'm working on." Not me exactly, but a personality he created "because I know you." And he sings about me to audiences in one of his original songs.

The moral of this story? If you choose to incarnate among a group of artists, you should plan on a certain amount of exploitation. At least they gave my chapter three thumbs up.

**About my mother and father and Native American karma:** While writing that chapter, and after discovering the nineteenth century history book that validated my dream, I began to wonder if I'd also been on the scene. Two new bits of information have resurfaced in my mind.

When I was three years old, my family made a trip to the area where the famous Mackinac (pronounced "Mackinaw") Bridge was still under construction, and we toured around other parts of northern Michigan. I don't recall much, but I've been told that I became so sick, the family had to head home early. I thought it was the black bears that frightened me, but perhaps it was something else?

In 2007, Joseph and I made plans with friends to visit Mackinac Island (famous setting for the film *Somewhere in Time*) and to carry on for a short stay in the Upper Peninsula. A week before, we both contracted some kind of horrible, mysterious, intestinal ailment so severe that we were eventually tested by the local government for lake-water bacterial infections, which thankfully came up negative. We had to cancel the trip because the recovery took weeks. We never discovered what caused this illness.

Does this answer my question? I don't know yet. And so the never-ending journey continues, and yours as well!

Even though my Cosmic CoAuthors and I have touched on a large number of topics in this book, it's only the beginning. We've barely scratched the surface of the interdimensional principles that guide your life and mine.

We urge you to use your new attunement, all your inner resources, and as many quality outer resources as you can locate in the future, none more valuable than your own skills of observation.

Watch for these energy principles manifesting within and around you in your future days. Validate them for yourself. You'll soon find it to be second nature to think in terms of Infinite Intelligence flowing into and throughout all that you see and experience, interdimensionally linking you to a vast Universe teeming with intelligent life. Your own potential lies far and away from your present status in this universal life, and it is entirely up to you how long it takes you to achieve each new step along this spiralling pathway into the stars.

As my mentors have often said, "No limitations!" Allow nothing to stop you in this interdimensional, personal quest for self-emancipation from the rigors of life in a restricted, third-dimensional world of matter. Free your mind first! The rest will follow.

You will soon find yourself spending your time between lives and during your sleep hours in sparkling, higher-dimensional schools of learning, where you can achieve new heights of understanding to bring back with you into your future lives, thus making them more productive, rewarding, and constructive of better and clearer states of mind and body, until that point where you no longer require these earth-world incarnations to achieve your learning objectives.

Meanwhile, don't be surprised if you travel the galaxies to reside on other worlds in future lives, other planetary bodies where life unfolds in perhaps a more logical, integrated, and uplifting way, where the spiritual/scientific understanding of the general population surpasses that of Earth in her present state of confusion.

If you keep up with your studies and personal aspirations for expanded consciousness, you will not need to wait until this present world of your incarnation catches up to your speedy progress.

The Universe awaits! Let no one stop you on this journey toward a more humanitarian Cosmic Consciousness!

# Appendix A

## How This Book Was Written

*When I'm writing, I consciously* and purposely cultivate the assistance of my Cosmic CoAuthors. This form of psychic transceiving is slightly different from the ongoing openness we all strive to maintain in order to receive inspirational guidance throughout our lives.

It's an arrangement we agreed upon, my CoAuthors and I, prior to my present incarnation. I serve as an amanuensis for them (a nice older word for stenographer) in order to create certain collaborative works. Joseph also uses this skill in his creative work as an author and composer, and I'm sure many others do as well. We thought some of you might like to know how this process works, or at least how it works for me.

While writing this particular book, I have used both methods of communication with my Cosmic CoAuthors, writing in my own voice mostly but always with an ear to their advice, and occasionally taking dictation from them and jotting the words directly.

Other books of mine have featured their words as dictated to me mentally while I spoke them aloud and recorded them. This was true of my novel, *The Liberator: A Psychic-Spiritual History of the Orion Empire*, and an earlier work, *Biography of an Archangel: The Accomplishments of Uriel*, and other works still unpublished. The choice depends on the purpose and effect desired.

In the case of this volume, my personal experiences were needed and who better to tell those stories than me?

## Q&A: Psychic Transceiving

*Do your Cosmic CoAuthors have individual names?*
Yes, if you mean former Earth names. They probably also have spiritual names, but I wouldn't necessarily recognize those.

*Do they announce themselves by name?*
Almost never.

*Do they make a big show of being present?*
Sometimes.

*Do they often work in groups?*
Yes.

*Do you know how many of them are connecting with your consciousness at a given time?*
Not really; size doesn't matter? (They often crack jokes.)

*How do you recognize them, if not by name?*
That's a really good and important question. By their energy frequency, which I've learned to sense, as you might identify a radio station by its frequency. And by their Intelligence, which so far surpasses my own. Even by their vocabulary, or their ability to convince me to use words for which I must run to find a definition later on, to be sure that, yes, it's exactly the precise shade of meaning required. (That's happened so often, I think now they do it to amuse and delight me. And to prove their presence was not my imagination.) They have countless ways of letting me know that I am not working alone. They'll sometimes flash their (psychic) Lights on a written or printed page while I'm working, usually blue, white, or gold.

*How does it happen that you know of them?*

My first introduction was through reading of their work and contacting their frequency via Ernest Norman's books, which are also psychically transceived. Later on, I realized I've known them for many lifetimes, which is why I was drawn to one of their twentieth-century, interdimensional spokespersons.

*How did you learn how to work with them?*

Lifetimes of practice and preparation for the present era in which I can openly declare my collaboration. Plus more practice and study in the present lifetime to improve my skill sets so as to be more useful and to improve the final products of our collaborations. This is a never-ending process.

In other words, if you want to be a concert pianist, you've got to train your hands and then you will serve as a better conduit for the higher energies infused into your performances. In *Cosmic Dancer,* Amy studies ballet in the higher worlds *and* in an ordinary dance studio on Earth. You have to keep your instrument tuned and trained!

But Amy was also creating, between lifetimes, connections with Those who would be providing a surcharge of higher frequencies every time she performed on Earth, for the spiritual healing and benefit of her audiences. Surely you've experienced such performances by individuals who've trained multi-dimensionally? That's what gives them their quality of extraordinariness, the difference between the technically proficient and the other-worldly, whether in the arts, sports, healing, or any other endeavor that benefits others.

*Why do they work with you?*

I know, I know! But as already pointed out, on this planet we are desperately in need of restoring knowledge of the interdimensional nature of life. So they work with *anyone* who is open to their influence, anyone who is able to tune their minds to that higher-frequency oscillation of their radiant thoughts. And though I said that I trained long and hard for this over the course of many lifetimes, this may be true for some of you, as well.

And even if you haven't, you can begin right this minute to forge this vital connection with higher spiritual mentors. They are speaking to you through this text, interweaving their thoughts and projections of healing energy in and around my words. That should give you another sense of their energy-signature or frequency.

*So what about all the channelers and channeled material now flowing into the planet's communications media?*

Yes, indeed, there's a lot of information flying about, now that most of us are not being burned at the stake for it. Some of it is excellent, some is mediocre, some comes from subastral planes and causes havoc, some comes from the highest reservoirs of Intelligence. You have to learn to discern for yourself which deserves your attention, and which should be discarded as useless or even harmful.

A good test is this: Does it provide useful, applicable information that improves my life? Is it more than pretty words? Is it benefitting me? Or is it making me a slave to the source of it? Is it addictive? Or liberating?

We each must decide for ourselves, in every instance. Even among variable material from the same source. Even among my own work.

*Can anyone learn to do this?*

With training and discernment, plus positive motivation, absolutely.

∞ ✵ ∞

# Appendix B

## Resources

*This is by no means* a comprehensive list of all the material available on the subject of reincarnation, or the energetic nature of life, or the new science beginning to emerge in all disciplines. It's a highly selective list of items I've either referred to in this book, or have found particularly useful, eye-opening, and enjoyable during my own studies.

I've tried to separate fiction from nonfiction, but discovered that when you're dealing with reincarnation, the line isn't so clear, as with my own book, *The Liberator,* or Joan Grant's Far Memory books. And after watching a lot of bad movies I found on someone's list of "reincarnation films," I've spared you those and listed a few I've found helpful or enjoyable. (Write to me if I missed your favorites!)

I frequently find "reincarnation stories" in ordinary news and feature stories. Now that you've developed your interdimensional analytical skills, you'll probably see them everywhere, too, as you read between the lines. I sometimes link those to my Pinterest page:
http://pinterest.com/liannedowney/
or perhaps mention them on my *Soul Pursuits* blog:
www.liannedowney.com
You'll also find me reviewing books for my "Reincarnation Resources" shelf on Goodreads:
http://www.goodreads.com/author/show/4067117.Lianne_Downey

I'm confident your Cosmic CoAuthors will lead you to many fascinating resources of your own, precisely at the moment you need them.

## Survival Skills for the 21st Century

∞ *The Voice of Venus* by Ernest L. Norman (first of his Pulse of Creation series, followed by *The Voice of Eros, The Voice of Hermes, The Voice of Orion, The Voice of Muse, Unarius, Elysium*)—A beautiful, inspiring introduction to interdimensional concepts. Provides a psychic tour of higher-world teaching centers, introducing members of a universal brotherhood of Advanced Minds working for the benefit of humanity. If you liked the notion of night school, you'll love these books (or if you want to know my Cosmic CoAuthors better).

∞ *The Infinite Concept of Cosmic Creation* by Ernest L. Norman— In simple, non-mathematical terms, presents a detailed, interdimensional science of life, including the personal ramifications of the human continuity of consciousness (reincarnation). New developments in all scientific disciplines continue to prove the science in this book, which nevertheless remains the best overview and all-round advanced education in interdimensional cosmology and personal, creative evolution. Fifteen additional books by Ernest L. Norman expand on these principles and concepts.

∞ *Energy Medicine* by Donna Eden with David Feinstein, Ph.D.— The most complete introduction to Eden Energy Medicine. It's followed by *Energy Medicine for Women* by Donna Eden with David Feinstein, Ph.D., and *The Little Book of Energy Medicine* by Donna Eden with Dondi Dahlin, a new and highly accessible manual of essentials for daily self-care. Video instruction is also available.

∞ *The EFT Manual* by Gary Craig—The fastest way to learn a self-help, energy psychology tapping method. You can also learn online for free at http://www.emofree.com/eft/eft-tutorial.html

- *The Promise of Energy Psychology: Revolutionary Tools for Dramatic Personal Change* by David Feinstein, Donna Eden, and Gary Craig—A comprehensive book for self-help energy psychology.

- *The Case for Energy Psychology* by David Feinstein, Ph.D.— http://www.innersource.net/ep/images/stories/downloads/PN_article.pdf

- *Radiant Circuits/Freeing the Spirit class* with Donna Eden (mentioned in the text) is an Intermediate/Advanced course available on DVD from Innersource: http://www.innersource.net/innersource/

- *Lights Out: Sleep, Sugar, and Survival* by T. S. Wiley—Controversial author, but her thoughts and advice regarding sleep and light exposure have enhanced my life and sleep significantly.

- The website of Dr. Magda Havas, Ph.D. offers updated information about EMF fields and human health. Here's a link to information about compact fluorescent bulbs, etc. http://www.magdahavas.com/category/electrosmog-exposure/lighting/

- *Dirty Electricity: Electrification and the Diseases of Civilization* by Dr. Samuel Milham, M.D., M.P.H—A must-read book by a public health expert.

- *The Biology of Belief* by Bruce Lipton—Introduces the new science of epigenetics.

- *The Unquiet Dead: A Psychologist Treats Spirit Possession* by Dr. Edith Fiore—More on astral obsession.

- *Touch for Health: A Practical Guide to Natural Health with Acupressure*

*Touch and Massage* by John Thie and Matthew Thie

∞ *Life Colors* and *Love Colors,* both by Pamala Oslie—Learn about visible, auric "life colors" and how to view them from these books. This understanding can really improve your relationships with others and yourself! Highly recommended; read *Life Colors* first.

∞ *Principles and Practice of Past-Life Therapy* and *The Last Inca Atahualpa: An Eyewitness Account of the Conquest of Peru in 1535* by Ruth Norman and Charles Spaegel—Close-up view of group past-life therapy, taken from class transcripts and testimonials.

**Fiction & Nonfiction**

∞ *Cosmic Dancer: An Interdimensional Fantasy* by Lianne Downey—. In waking life, she's struggling with ballet, boyfriends, and an alcoholic mother. In her dreams, she's back in the place she came from—or rather, all the places she's come from, life after life, and especially, all the people she has known. Again and again.

∞ *The Liberator: A Psychic-Spiritual History of the Orion Empire* by Lianne Downey—A novel about our long ago, extraterrestrial past; a psychic reading for the planet's entire population transceived from my Cosmic CoAuthors. The story tells of a dramatic, worlds-shattering confrontation between forces of Light and forces of Dark.

∞ The Deverry Series by Katherine Kerr—The first four books are best, beginning with *Daggerspell;* later books drag on but still depict the sequential incarnations of characters who show appropriate change and development, so that by the last of the fifteen books, you're satisfied. An epic achievement!

∞ *Green Darkness* by Anya Seton—Was prompted to buy a 50-cent, plain-black-cover copy at a used book sale and had no idea it was a reincarnation mystery! Stayed up all night reading.

∞ *The Celestial Bar* and *In the Shadow of the Sphere* by Thomas Youngholm—Great stories from a dear friend who writes about reincarnation and spirituality with humor and insight.

∞ *The Red Heart* by James Alexander Thom—Historical fiction that feels real to me. If you have an affinity with Native American culture, look into Thom's other books as well.

∞ *Reincarnation* by Susanne Weyn—A rather hurried tale for young adults, but great for youthful readers to sample the idea of being born again and again. Her characters travel through their incarnations doing the slow version of transformation in this love story.

∞ *Cloud Atlas* by David Mitchell—Complex, "literary fiction" in which (according to the author) one main character reincarnates through five of the six stories. He undergoes wildly varied experiences and changes slightly throughout, which could have served to depict the natural, slow transformation of an evolving soul, but the author says his intention was to pick up and put down his character in new settings to show "fixed human nature," with a recurring theme of "predacity." A difficult book for me to read, since I heartily disagree with that premise, but it reached many people because of the author's literary status and the book's translation to film (which was even more confusing).

∞ *Captain Stormfield's Visit to Heaven* by Mark Twain—Hilarious truth! Find his short version, *Extract from Captain Stormfield's*

*Visit to Heaven* singularly or in modern anthologies, or as a free ebook from The Gutenberg Project, http://www.gutenberg.org/ebooks/1044. A longer version was printed in *Report from Paradise* (Harper & Brothers Publishers), now out of print.

∞ The *Far Memory* books of Joan Grant—Vivid recalls in story form.

∞ *Proof of Heaven* by Eben Alexander, M.D.—The best near-death experience because his status as a neurosurgeon and the unlikely circumstances of his illness make his tale hard to refute. And he's validated some of the scenes in my "fictional" *Cosmic Dancer!*

∞ *The True Life of Jesus of Nazareth: The Confessions of St. Paul* by Alexander Smyth—Amazing psychic history transceived through its visionary author in 1899 (much to his startled surprise). You'll find a republished edition through online searches, and you might even find yourself in this story.

∞ A helpful discussion of in-phase, out-of-phase wave cancellation, as found in electric guitar pick-ups: http://music.stackexchange.com/questions/1354/in-phase-out-of-phase-pickups

∞ *The Search for a Soul: Taylor Caldwell's Psychic Lives* by Jess Stearn

∞ *Life Before Life* and *Reliving Past Lives: The Evidence Under Hypnosis* by Helen Wambach, Ph.D.

∞ *Forgotten Civilization: The Role of Solar Outbursts in Our Past and Future* by Robert M. Schoch, Ph.D.—Fascinating theory, with easy-to-grasp overviews of the new science in several disciplines.

## Films

∞ *Groundhog Day*—Excellent and enjoyable example of what true healing requires. Highly recommended! Bill Murray is perfect in this movie. Wonderful script writing by Harold Ramis and company.

∞ *Sleepless in Seattle*—Fascinated by the concept of multiple polarities? I didn't realize or remember that this film was about reincarnation until watching recently and with a modern sound system, heard the verbal reference to it (out of the mouths of babes). Everything in this wonderful movie supports the concept of reincarnation and multiple polarities. Tom Hanks' character has three, possibly four in this story—can you identify them?

∞ *Racing Dawn*—A rather strange Indie film starring Melissa Leo and David Strathairn that nevertheless depicts reincarnation, spirit possession, and other aspects of past-life continuities. Slightly creepy; watch with a friend.

∞ *The Search for Bridey Murphy*—True to its 1956 production date, everyone in this film smokes, drinks, and exhibits a level of education that makes you grateful you live in the twenty-first century (so maybe it has its merits). Still, it's a really good primer on why hypnosis isn't the best way to learn about past lives. Because the case was so famous in the twentieth century, I felt obligated to watch and list this film. Feel free to skip it! Unless you're tempted to try hypnosis. [As this book goes to press, I see Danny Boyle has directed a new, scary-looking film called *Trance* that's all about hypnosis. Yikes.]

∞ *Dead Again*—Of course you've all heard about this popular reincarnation thriller directed by Kenneth Branagh. (Why are so many past-life tales focused on the dark side?) Well-acted and directed.

∞ *Cloud Atlas*—Fortunately, you'll find character charts online to help make sense of the casting choices and sequential incarnations in the film version of David Mitchell's book.

∞ *Salmon Fishing in the Yemen* with Ewan McGregor and Emily Blunt—Never ignore your inner vision!

**Also Mentioned in the Text**

∞ *The Story of Suntrakker: How One Man's Commitment Inspired a Team of Volunteers to Make His Dream Come True* by Bruce Rogow—A truly inspiring story from a man who proved the "no limitations" motto by putting his time and money where his dreams were, thus motivating several generations of students and dreamers alike.

∞ *History of the City of Grand Rapids* by Albert Baxter, published 1891

∞ *French Women Don't Get Fat: The Secret of Eating for Pleasure* by Mireille Guiliano

∞ Songs: "Determinate" by Lemonade Mouth; video at http://www.youtube.com/watch?v=iO6TjZzcRGQ and "Jillian (I'd Give My Heart)" by Within Temptation; video at http://www.youtube.com/watch?v=wjkGCjV1woU